Close Encounters:
A Relational View
of the Therapeutic
Process

CLOSE ENCOUNTERS: A RELATIONAL VIEW OF THE THERAPEUTIC PROCESS

Robert Winer, M.D.

JASON ARONSON INC.
Northvale, New Jersey
London

The author gratefully acknowledges permission to quote from the following sources:

From the book *Rockaby and Other Short Pieces* by Samuel Beckett, copyright © 1981 Grove Press. Used with permission of Grove/Atlantic Monthly Press.

From "Echoes of the Wolf Man: Reverberations of Psychic Reality" by Robert Winer, in *Telling Facts: History and Narration in Psychoanalysis*, ed. J. H. Smith and H. Morris, copyright © 1992. Used by permission of The Johns Hopkins University Press.

This book was set in 11 pt. Goudy by Lind Graphics of Upper Saddle River, New Jersey, and printed and bound by Haddon Craftsmen of Scranton, Pennsylvania.

Library of Congress Cataloging-in-Publication Data

Winer, Robert, 1940–
    Close Encounters : a relational view of the therapeutic process /
by Robert Winer.
        p. cm.
    Includes biliographical references and index.
    ISBN 0-87668-165-8
    1. Psychotherapist and patient. 2. Psychotherapy. I. Title.
RC480.8.W56 1994
616.89'14—dc20   93–5090

Manufactured in the United States of America. Jason Aronson Inc. offers books and cassettes. For information and catalog write to Jason Aronson Inc., 230 Livingston Street, Northvale, New Jersey 07647.

For Bonita

THE LIBRARY OF OBJECT RELATIONS

A SERIES OF BOOKS EDITED BY
DAVID E. SCHARFF AND JILL SAVEGE SCHARFF

Object relations theories of human interaction and development provide an expanding, increasingly useful body of theory for the understanding of individual development and pathology, for generating theories of human interaction, and for offering new avenues of treatment. They apply across the realms of human experience from the internal world of the individual to the human community, and from the clinical situation to everyday life. They inform clinical technique in every format from individual psychoanalysis and psychotherapy, through group therapy, to couple and family therapy.

The Library of Object Relations aims to introduce works that approach psychodynamic theory and therapy from an object relations point of view. It includes works from established and new writers who employ diverse aspects of British and American object relations theory in helping individuals, families, couples, and groups. It features books that stress integration of psychoanalytic approaches with marital and family therapy, as well as those centered on individual psychotherapy and psychoanalysis.

Refinding the Object and Reclaiming the Self
  David E. Scharff

Scharff Notes: A Primer of Object Relations Therapy
  Jill Savege Scharff and David E. Scharff

Object Relations Couple Therapy
  David E. Scharff and Jill Savege Scharff

Object Relations Family Therapy
  David E. Scharff and Jill Savege Scharff

Projective and Introjective Identification and the Use of the Therapist's Self
  Jill Savege Scharff

Foundations of Object Relations Family Therapy
  Jill Savege Scharff, Editor

From Inner Sources: New Directions in Object Relations Psychotherapy
  N. Gregory Hamilton, Editor

Betwixt and Between: The Understanding and Treatment of the
Borderline Marriage
  Charles McCormack

Repairing Intimacy: An Object Relations Approach to
Couples Therapy
  Judith Siegel

Family and Couple Therapy
  John Zinner

Close Encounters: A Relational View of the Therapeutic Process
  Robert Winer

The Autonomous Self: The Work of John D. Sutherland
  Jill Savege Scharff, Editor

Crisis at Adolescence: Object Relations Therapy with the Family
  Sally Box, Beta Copley, Jeanne Magagna, and
  Errica Moustaki Smilansky, Editors

Personal Relations Therapy: The Collected Papers of H. J. S. Guntrip
  Jeremy Hazell, Editor

Psychoanalytic Group Therapy
  Karl Konig and Wulf-Volker Lindner

Psychoanalytic Therapy
  Karl Konig

From Instinct to Self: Selected Papers of W. R. D. Fairbairn
  David E. Scharff and Ellinor Fairbairn Birtles, Editors

Treating Developmental Trauma
  Jill Savege Scharff and David E. Scharff

Object Relations Individual Therapy
  David E. Scharff and Jill Savege Scharff

How to Survive as a Psychotherapist
  Nina Coltart

Contents

Part 3

BOUNDARIES OF TREATMENT

Part 4

THE THERAPIST AND CHANGE

Acknowledgments

Perhaps first books are like first babies: both burdens (because we can't leave them alone) and labors of love (because they come from the heart). I have many to thank for their midwifery:

The writers who have helped me to clarify my thinking about the analytic process – particularly Roy Schafer, Harold Searles, Hans Loewald, and Thomas Ogden.

The colleagues at the Washington School of Psychiatry who have with great vitality supported my professional development over the past two decades – the faculty of our Family Therapy Program, and especially Justin Frank, Joyce Lowenstein, Charles Privitera, David Scharff, Jill Scharff, Kent Ravenscroft, Roger Shapiro, and John Zinner.

The friends and colleagues who read various drafts of these chapters and offered helpful critiques – Bonita Winer, David and Jill Scharff, Jonathan Winer, Steven Schulman, Kathryn Camicia, and Maggie Scarf.

Those who encouraged and prodded me, each in his or her own way, and against the resistance alluded to in the final chapter, to get the book done—Bonita, Jill, and, in the interpretive way that analysis works, my second analyst.

My personal editor, Sara Blackburn, who helped me clarify my speaking while faithfully remaining within my own voice.

My publisher, Jason Aronson, M. D., and his editorial staff, who provided support and encouragement.

The patients I have worked with over the years, who have struggled with me to get the best from me that I could give them, and who have worked hard to make use of my efforts to be of use to them. I am sorry for the surprise or embarrassment they may experience should they chance to come across themselves in these pages. I have tried to tell the story of our work together in a way that might be useful to others.

My wife, Bonita, and my children Gabriel, Jessamine, and Isabelle, who have both lovingly supported and endured my efforts to put this book together.

1

Close Encounter

This book is about the therapeutic relationship and the underlying interpersonal aspect of that engagement, but it doesn't advocate a particular approach to treatment. Its point, in a nutshell, is that psychotherapy and psychoanalysis, in the customary ways in which they are practiced, are even more complexly interpersonal than we ordinarily realize. This issue will be approached from a variety of vantage points. The title, *Close Encounters*, is meant to evoke both the intimacy and the estranged otherworldliness of the meeting of therapist and patient.

This might all get a bit less fuzzy if I offer you two accounts of the opening of a psychotherapy.

TWO VIEWS OF A PATIENT-THERAPIST ENCOUNTER

In his first session with his new psychiatrist, a business executive in his forties explained that he was seeking treatment because his depression was getting the better of him. It was becoming so difficult for him to get

1

out of bed in the morning that on some days he never made it in to work. He took his listener through an accounting of the three times earlier in his adult life when he had been overwhelmed by the darkness—on one occasion he had even thought about killing himself. He had sought treatment that last time, and the therapist had been a great help to him, he said. The listener could hear the high regard this man felt for his former therapist, the affection and longing in his voice. The therapist had died a few years earlier after a long illness, and so now he had to turn somewhere else for help.

After talking a bit about his successful career and his devoted marriage, he finally turned to the matter that was breaking his heart. His teenage daughter had been in psychiatric hospitals for more than a year now and she wasn't getting better. She had made a number of suicide attempts and had succeeded in mutilating herself, both in the hospital and at home. Nothing seemed to be helping. The listener sensed that beyond his ordinary deep caring, and even given how terrible his story was, this man seemed to be unusually identified with his daughter, in a way almost merged with her. The man shifted to talking about how his wife's mother had died a few years back in a freak accident; the question of who had been to blame had never been answered, he added. The listener made a mental note of this and imagined that his patient might be feeling responsible for his daughter's sickness.

The listener was to understand that this was a deeply religious man, given to turning to meditation and prayer as a way of coping with his fears and sorrows. The listener sensed that there was to be no questioning of the church's authority. The patient then spoke of his father, a distant, detached man he'd never been able to please. His father hadn't had much success in life. Some years ago, as his father approached death, the patient had realized that they would never have the chance to sort things out with each other, and this had prompted one of his periods of depression. He'd had dreams then of being unprepared for an exam and of being out in public with only his underwear on. And he'd thought then of driving his car into a bridge abutment—he had a lot of life insurance, he said. The listener thought about Willy Loman, remembered how Arthur Miller's salesman protagonist had planned to kill himself so that his family could benefit from his insurance. The patient then spoke of a situation at work where he'd unseated a former mentor and taken his place. The mentor had accused him of screwing him over and the patient had felt hurt by his mentor's reaction, considering it unjustified. Finally, the patient returned to talking about his daughter, her fights with the authorities in the hospital, her rage toward the staff. He then hesitated and said that when hope is deferred, the heart gets sick.

Reflecting on the hour, the listener thought that it had been a stunningly assured self-presentation. His patient had been quite careful to define the terms of their encounter: the therapist was to view him as a highly moral, committed man, as a devoted father and husband, as a competent and successful worker, as a respectful patient. It wasn't clear what role was to be allowed for the therapist beyond listener, but there was some implication that the therapist might be permitted the status of assistant coach, allowed to wander the sidelines and yell periodic encouragement to the player on the field. The therapist also thought that his patient had placed his religious commitment squarely in the space between them. Any ideas the therapist might offer would have to negotiate that obstacle. Some weeks later, the therapist would decide that working with this patient was like trying to trap a bead of mercury. It wasn't just the slipperiness; it was also the shininess, and the way the bead stayed all massed together as it slithered around the surface.

One accounting of this first hour might run as follows. The patient's presenting problem is his depression, which, while also chronic, seems to have been exacerbated by the course of his daughter's difficulties. We might expect to find both depression and difficulty with boundaries in his relationship with his parents, perhaps especially with his mother. (In fact, we would later learn that he thought his mother was quite enmeshed with him—one example being the occasion when, as a 5-year-old he had asked her about nursing and she had responded by encouraging and then allowing him to suck on her breast. There were no younger siblings and so she couldn't have been nursing at the time.) We also get a sense that this man longs for closeness with an older man and also has intensely competitive, albeit well-disguised, needs to defeat all men. We imagine that we may come to discover intense ambition to outdo his father and guilt over his considerable success in this area.

The patient seems relentlessly loyal, earnest, and controlling. The therapist is impressed by the degree of his reaction formation, the imperative need to keep all aggression concealed. The patient presents himself as excessively nice and unfailingly good, and he must be paying quite a price for this. (A month later the patient will recall a story his first therapist told him. It was about a young man who was exceedingly diligent, and determined to please his parents. He had worked hard at college, at medical school, and in residency, sending home copies of all the good grades. And then, that accomplished, he had showed up on his father's doorstep and killed himself with a shotgun.)

In terms of initial transference manifestations, the therapist senses that the patient is managing his anxiety about encountering this stranger by offering a tightly controlled package. There were to be no surprises in the hour, no emotional moments in which his guard might be dropped. While it's not unusual for men to handle first hours this way, the degree of this patient's control seemed exceptional. To an unusual degree, the therapist felt deprived of the ordinary opportunity to be in a helping role. The patient seemed determined to be self-reliant. Any dependency needs, he made clear, would be managed by turning to his faith, not to another person. There must be a lot behind his mistrust, perhaps parents who could not tolerate his self-reliance. The therapist sensed that any activity beyond admiration and curiosity might be experienced as intrusive. There also seemed to be a puzzle in this, for the man's account of his first therapy sounded quite engaged and useful. Perhaps he hadn't gotten past the therapist's death. That, at least, would be a hopeful construction.

Diagnostically, the therapist's first impression might be that the patient had a personality disorder with obsessive-compulsive and narcissistic features, complicated by a moderately severe recurrent depression. Based upon his earlier experience in treatment, it would be reasonable to expect that the more striking depressive symptoms would be relieved rather quickly, and that the work would focus on the underlying personality issues. Should the depression persist, medication would be a consideration.

The case report, thus far, is framed in a one-person psychology. The understanding is generated by an ordinarily intelligent and responsive listener who is open, in a customary way, to the patient's experience of himself and his world. Let us now complicate the picture by considering the larger context of the treatment.

This patient was being referred to the therapist by a colleague he had taught approximately 10 years earlier. It was the second referral he had received from her, both in the past year. The first had been a couple—she had known the husband professionally and their marriage was in crisis. The effort at treatment had been a disaster. The wife had taken an immediate dislike to the therapist. By the third hour she had exhaustively critiqued his failings, professional and personal, and by the sixth hour she had fired him. That was all only moderately embarrassing, but he sensed that a second failure would be just too humbling for him in the eyes of the former student, who had rather looked up to him. Since she was now involved in the treatment of this current patient's family, she would certainly hear about any difficulties in the therapy. On the other hand, the patient seemed inclined to be accepting of a therapist's reasonable efforts, although it was unclear that he would let himself really be touched by them, and so the therapist did not feel especially vulnerable in relation to the referral. At another level, whenever a colleague refers an untreatable case one wonders what it implies about your colleague's opinion of you—who you are in the patient–practitioner fit that the colleague had in mind. So the therapist found it heartening that this second referral seemed like an ordinarily treatable patient. The treatment might be burdened, however, at least to a subtle degree, by his need to prove himself to his former student, to justify her high regard for him. And at moments, this vector might intersect with the father's need to be highly regarded by his ill daughter.

The referring therapist was not the only person looking over this therapist's shoulder. The patient's health insurance did not ordinarily provide coverage for outpatient treatment, and his personal finances had been severely depleted by the partial costs he'd had to absorb in connection with his daughter's hospitalizations. Officially, the insurance company would support outpatient treatment only to prevent a possible hospitalization. In that case, however, they would pay 100 percent of the practitioner's fee. In the current instance the patient had determined, before coming for help, that the insurance company would, under this rubric, cover the treatment. It was unclear to the therapist just why the insurance company was willing to do this. The patient was not so depressed that hospitalization was at issue. It later seemed to him that the company considered the father's difficulties to be interfering with the daughter's treatment, a rather sophisticated perception on its part, and that the company recognized that his being in treatment might reduce its ultimate expense with her. She had already cost them a few hundred thousand dollars.

As a condition of supporting the father's therapy, which was to proceed on a twice-a-week basis, the insurance company wanted monthly reports about the treatment in the form of phone-call discussions with one of their staff. They would only authorize payment for eight sessions at a time. And so the therapist understood that each month he would have to provide enough encouragement to the insurance company to get them to support the treatment, but indicate enough difficulty to justify its need. Being a psychoanalyst, he was not accustomed to seeing monthly spurts of progress, and he was not sure how realistic the insurance company was in its expectations. It was his first experience with this sort of surveillance. He felt a pressure to make something happen, and also felt a bit helpless in relation to this pressure, a state of affairs that mirrored his patient's response to his own superego pressures. Having to achieve to satisfy another, and resenting it, would be a dimension of both parties' experience.

The referring therapist and the insurance company representative would not be the only people looking in on the treatment, of course. Others would be there, even though they would be more entirely of the therapist's creation. The need to succeed has its rhythms and seasons in every practitioner's life, and particular treatments will intersect that curve at different points. This patient arrived at a time in the therapist's career when he was feeling less pressure to make things happen, more inclined to be drawn by the flow. He understood that this state of mind might be useful to this particular patient, who seemed in general too full of agendas, too determined to be productive.

When he encountered a new patient, the therapist was accustomed to feeling that he was, at least at that moment, the less vulnerable of the two parties. This was not the case here, and he felt a bit unnerved by the realization. As he listened to his new client patiently filling him in, he wondered why this man had come for help. Beyond his not exposing himself to scrutiny, he wasn't even exposing his illness. Given the therapist's capacity for passivity, and the fact that his patient wasn't making any great overt demands of him, he felt able to just settle in for the ride. The description of his patient's depression felt familiar enough—the therapist knew about depression—and although the talk about past suicidal feelings seemed a bit unreal, perhaps it was simply a way of communicating that there was more than met the eye.

One further matter: the therapist believed he had known his patient's former psychiatrist. He thought he had met him once when he was first starting to practice and was looking for someone to share space with. The man he remembered was really sleazy. It was hard to believe that he had stayed in practice over the years. What did it mean that this patient had found him so useful? It seemed unthinkable. In fact, it indeed was unthinkable—he later realized he had gotten it wrong, that it was a different man with a somewhat similar name, a man he didn't know at all. But what did his confusion mean? A defensive contempt for the patient, pairing him up with a charlatan? An unconscious sense that the patient's polished demeanor concealed corruption? Certainly there was something slick about this patient that the therapist found off-putting. The referring doctor had told him that this man had significant marital problems and that he was seductive with his daughter; all this was being denied or minimized. The therapist felt a bit conned. And yet he had also felt the power of his patient's adoration of his former therapist, the man who had died. Perhaps listening to this had been hard to take. His own experience with therapists and analysts had involved this kind of pain and longing. So perhaps it was envy. That, and a feeling that by comparison he'd never measure up.

The patient told him that in the early morning hours when he couldn't sleep he kept a journal; he offered to bring it in. The therapist felt put off by the offer, assuming that it would be sentimental blather designed to fill up the rest of the space between them. His feelings about the journal ran parallel with his sense about the patient's use of religion. The therapist had never been a religious man—since adolescence he had been in synagogues only for weddings, funerals, and bar mitzvahs, and few enough of those. He felt inferior to this man now and, perhaps for that reason, a bit irritated with his religiosity. He also felt a bit pushed aside, as though the patient were telling him again that there were some matters he'd be excluded from. The therapist had treated devoutly religious patients before without having these reactions, and so he assumed that there was a good deal about this that had to do with the patient's defensive use of religion, but he also didn't want to glibly use that reflection to explain his discomfort away. Such facileness would be being too much like his patient—or at least like the version of the patient that he had constructed in his mind.

As he thought about it, he realized that exclusion seemed a pervasive issue between the two of them. The patient's idealized relationships with both his daughter and his wife were not to be challenged. At a deeper level the patient seemed exclusively engaged with his own mind. Any interested outsider, it seemed, could only be experienced as an interloper. The therapist's own vulnerability was such that he could easily feel upset in the face of exclusion. But there were still only the two of them in the room, and the patient said he had come for help, so there wasn't a crisis at hand.

Finally, there was the matter of the daughter. The therapist imagined himself quite identified with her, resenting the father's intrusive interest. The referring practitioner had told him that on one occasion the hospital staff had found him in bed with her, reading her a book, and another time they'd discovered that he had sent her flowers. Neither of these actions on his part was stunningly inappropriate, just enough over the line to be disconcerting. They gave the therapist the creeps. He thought about charismatic ministers who seduced their parishioners. He wasn't usually squeamish about such matters—what was different here? Was it too much like his relationship with his mother, whose erotic intrusions had always been subtle, easily rationalized, invisible to outsiders? Was that why he felt so identified with this girl?

This second accounting, which gives more prominence to the therapist's psychology, leads to a muddier view. We now have the therapist's motivations in the picture, and it's often unclear where his responses are mainly ordinary reactions to the patient that any therapist might well have, or where they are idiosyncratic to him. We have a more complex field in which both parties are thinking and reacting, and where the flow of influence is Byzantine. Each will influence the other with his ideas, his moods, his transferences, his countertransferences, his character style. Their shared gravitational field will draw certain issues in and spin others off. Both participants are wrestling with themselves and acting upon each other in ways that are both within and beyond their ken. Their experience is integrated by their common understanding of the task: the treatment of the emotional difficulties of the person who has come for help. That shared understanding of task gives their venture meaning, lifts it from the ordinary obscurity of conventional intercourse, and provides it with direction.

I believe that therapy works both through its content and its process. The content is the understandings mutually reached of why the patient thinks, feels, and behaves as he does. The process is the joined struggle toward grasping these meanings. Both the struggle and the understandings contribute to learning and growth. The contention of this book is that this process is what therapy is about. Our efforts to make therapy comprehensible by reducing it to a one-person field convey a picture that is limited and misleading, the sort of court portrait that presents only the subject's nobler — and less revealing — features. Our motives for making this simplification are worth reviewing, however, and it is this history to which I now turn.

THE PROCESS OF PSYCHOTHERAPY

The therapist, like the artist, must invent himself. The radiologist encounters the patient as densities on film. He scans the contours, following a praxis laid out by the generations of radiologists who have preceded him. Having looked into his patient, or having seen through her, and having come to understand what he has seen, his work is done. For the therapist, this understanding would be only the first sighting.

The guidelines, rules, and procedures offered to the therapist provide a little focus and a little structure for his undertaking. But not much. In this regard, therapy most resembles chess. The initial lines of play are well established (although not infallibly so), but once you get beyond the first ten or fifteen moves, you're in a situation you've never seen before. As a beginner, you're first taught the endgame, which in its simplest forms can be made entirely predictable — and thus entirely learnable. While endgame play teaches the beginner the way the pieces move — this being the main virtue of teaching it — you soon discover that you'll never use this knowledge to end a game. The other player will have resigned long before the board reaches this point of simplification. The teaching of psychotherapy offers comparable illusions, most notably the career oasis of the successfully completed case, which turns out to be, for the most part, a mirage.

At a meeting of the faculty that teaches the technique and clinical case curriculum at my psychoanalytic institute, we were each asked to summarize in a few words the purpose of the course we were giving. At that time I was conducting a continuous case seminar in which we followed a single treatment over the course of the year. I said that my purpose was to undo the effects of all my students' earlier courses on psychoanalytic technique. No one seemed much surprised by this, for we all understood that technique courses furnish students with armor and weaponry, the better to feel clothed and equipped as they step onto the psychoanalytic battlefield to confront the enemy, the psychoanalytic patient. We also knew that students use technique to manage their anxiety and that it becomes a body of learning that is wedged between themselves and their patients, an obstacle to empathic communication. It seems to me that the purpose of continuous case courses, and of supervision, is to help the student to discover and come to know the two people in the room, the patient and her analyst.[1] I hope to help the student to worry less about getting it right and more about being there. In their most egregious form, early training cases constitute treatment by proxy, with the student dutifully delivering his supervisor's insights to his patient. In this circumstance both people disappear, the therapist reduced to ghostly messenger and the patient to the creature of the supervisor's speculations.

It was not, of course, the radiologist that Freud had in mind when he was searching for a medical metaphor for our new profession. He opted for the practitioner most in the middle of the fray: the surgeon.

---

[1] I have introduced an element of distraction into my text by giving the therapist and patient genders, often male and female respectively. I refer to the therapist as male because I am often speaking of myself, or of a part of myself that I believe I share with other therapists, and I don't want to obscure that. My sometimes referring to the patient as female makes it clearer of whom the pronoun speaks. More generic constructions usually seem awkward and impersonal. Because this gendering practice can lead to the sensibility that women suffer and men help them, I have sometimes made the patient male. (The timing of that choice might be a matter for sophisticated political analysis.) I have also complicated matters by variously referring to the practitioner as "analyst" and "therapist." The ideas that I am writing about apply to both psychoanalysis and psychotherapy, although at times there will be differences of nuance. I use "analyst" where the example cited comes from an analysis, or where I am writing in response to an idea that is specifically central to the analytic literature.

While every metaphor carries a host of meanings, some of which will be intended and others not, I'd like to think that one dimension of the appeal of the surgeon as metaphor to Freud was that the surgeon's work is hands-on. The surgeon knows that he will cut flesh, spill blood, have his patient's heart in his hands. This sense of engagement is missing in much of the writing about psychoanalysis that followed Freud; it was as though the warrior surgeon had been replaced by the detached diagnostician—perhaps more aptly, the player-combatant replaced by the coach. We took our distance.

Freud, in fact, had been thinking about a different dimension of the surgeon's work. He wrote, "I cannot advise my colleagues too urgently to model themselves during psycho-analytic treatment on the surgeon, who puts aside all his feelings, even his human sympathy, and concentrates his mental forces on the single aim of performing the operation as skillfully as possible" (1912, p. 115). While Freud was writing this with concern for the analyst too ambitious for his patient's recovery (he went on to cite the motto of a French surgeon: "I dressed his wounds, God cured him"), he was also recognizing that it would be impossible to cut into flesh without in some measure making the patient inanimate.

The act of *interpretation* then became for the analyst the equivalent of the surgeon's wielding his scalpel. Interpreting was the *procedure* the analyst would apply to his patient's verbal productions, and around the act of interpretation we mapped out a technique, first a modest set of rules in Freud's technical papers written between 1911 and 1915, and later whole volumes of emendations and refinements. As we reread those original papers now, we sense Freud's concern that in the hands of unscrupulous or self-indulgent or even just incautious practitioners, the remedy might create greater illness. The transference could be incendiary. Freud himself had been touched by the flame, and some of his colleagues had been badly burned.

Listening to the work of our current generations of student analysts, we might say that our effort to establish a host of procedures to ensure antisepsis has had a consequence the opposite of the one Freud feared: our novitiates are frightened mice in the corner, afraid that if they move they'll be pounced on. It is commonplace to listen to reports of hours in which the student analyst cannot, at least at a manifest level, be found. The student appropriates those aspects of technique that support emotional distancing and intellectualization, his greatest fear being that his superiors will judge him to be overinvolved, acting out, a victim of his own countertransference. The humane goal of creating a procedure within which the analyst can work, a context in which the analyst can be not only protected from being overwhelmed by his own feelings and the provocations of his patient but also helped to be of use to him, is lost sight of as technique is idealized, becoming an end in itself, that nefarious operation that can succeed even though the patient dies.

The practice of making the patient manageable by making her inanimate continues in our current texts. The patient is a concatenation of (depending on your dialect) id, ego, and superego derivatives, resistances, transferences, part-objects, selfobjects, exciting objects, affect states, life and death instincts, and the like. The self is one more aspect of the patient's "thingness."

A female therapist who felt overwhelmed by a male patient's near-psychotic infatuation with her decided to stop the treatment. Over his protests she reassured him that in two months he'd understand that it was for the best. Two months later, to the hour, this 30-year-old man, apparently in good health, suffered a heart attack and was hospitalized on a coronary care ward. I spoke with the physician on call and took the liberty of explaining the outlines of the situation to him. After a long pause, a light seemed to dawn in the mind of this young, overworked medical resident and he exclaimed to me, "You mean I should treat him with empathy!"

What startled me was that this physician seemed to have been selecting from among various options that I guess included empathy, avoidance, and heaven knows what else. This episode has stayed with me over the years because it is a caricature of our own practice, in which the use of empathy can be presented as a therapeutic strategy, part of what we call our armamentarium. But empathy must be the matrix for therapy, as language is for writing.

We speak of empathy to disguise our art as a science. We refer to empathy and transference and interpretation as we attempt to operationalize what happens in our close encounters. The trick we've used to accomplish this has been to conceptualize our theory of technique as a "one-person" system. This theory, which has evolved over the past century, proposes a set of principles that governs the interaction of a personality (the patient) and an instrumentality (the therapist). Personal treatment of the therapist is encouraged or required to make him a better functioning instrument, less prone to distort the treatment process through the unfortunate emergence of difficulties in his own personality. The therapist establishes a treatment situation by setting up a framework, and within that frame he uses a set of technical procedures (unobtrusive listening, free-floating attention, focus on transference, integration of past and present, interpretation of resistance, reconstruction, and the like) to help the patient clarify the deeper sources of her difficulties. The therapist's capacity to understand the patient, with all that that entails, is the ultimate means through which the patient finds relief. In this model the therapist's psychology is essentially irrelevant. And this is the approach to treatment that still constitutes the mainstream of our teaching, even though most experienced therapists feel that it does not grasp the heart of the therapeutic situation.

What would seem to be called for is a two-person theory. Klauber (1981), for example, comments that "the most neglected feature of the psychoanalytic relationship still seems to me to be that it is a relationship: a very peculiar relationship, but a definite one" (p. 200). The contemporary psychoanalytic literature shows that many writers are wrestling with aspects of this issue. On the other hand, these contributions have not coalesced into an alternative view of the treatment process. What should a two-person clinical theory include? To begin with, an accounting of that "very peculiar relationship," what its nature is, and the particular and distinctive ways in which each party is both a personality and an instrument. This accounting must be located within a sensible set of ideas about the nature of the mind, of human adaptation and development, and of human relatedness. It should provide the therapist with an approach to treatment and a rationale for that approach. And it might offer some insight into the most difficult question: how people change.

When we consider treatment as a two-person process, the field becomes immensely more complex. Every treatment becomes unique in a way that greatly exceeds the uniqueness of individuals. Those of us who have had more than one analysis readily appreciate this—not only are the analysts different, but *we* also are different, although not only different, in each treatment. We discover that our personhood is both more and less stable than we thought. Furthermore, to write about our work from a two-person point of view requires far greater personal exposure than the traditional one-person perspective demands. For this reason, we tend to write about the patients of others— of Freud's, especially—or about cases we have supervised, and this is why we present our own work in such highly compacted and schematized forms that truly nobody is home.

On those relatively rare occasions when male analysts do share with us their own experience, the conflicts that they are willing to discuss tend to be in the area of male relationships. We may hear about rivalry, authority, defiance, ambivalence toward father, and the like. Yet I do not recall ever reading about a male analyst's lustful feelings toward a female patient, and I cannot imagine, short of being on my deathbed, writing about that myself.[2] Analysts have been far more willing to discuss their boredom and irritation with patients than their passions for them, whether love or hatred. We may hear about affection. We will never hear about carnality. It is understandable that the exposure seems unbearable, but this is part of what has made it so difficult to develop a shared understanding of what we do.

One consequence of the absence of an adequate shared clinical theory is that each of us writes his own book, shares his own

---

[2]It is my impression that female analysts are less likely to reveal their own conflictual responses at all.

experience, invents his own version of the wheel. In the chapters that follow, my intention is in the main descriptive, not prescriptive. I describe my understanding of how psychotherapy and psychoanalysis operate—how the parties are engaged and how their work unfolds. I maintain that we conceal from ourselves the ways in which our practice is less a procedure, and more a close encounter.

PART 1

THE RELATIONSHIP

2

Expanding One-Person Theory

Within the mainstream of psychoanalytic clinical theory, currents of innovation have introduced relational concepts without either changing the theory's essential one-person orientation or, in the main, suggesting significant modifications in its technique. (What constitutes significant revision of technique is a matter for dispute, of course, and the theorists I cite may disagree with me here.) In what follows, three important areas of innovation are outlined briefly to provide a sense of how mainstream clinical theory is evolving. The next chapter explores approaches that leave this main current to focus on relational considerations.

That our present models don't do justice to the clinical situation is a matter of wide agreement. Four decades ago Anna Freud (1954) recognized one dimension of the problem when she said, "With due respect for the necessary strictest handling and interpretation of the transference, I still feel that somewhere we should leave room for the realization that the analyst and patient are also two real people, of equal adult status, in a real personal relationship to each other" (p. 373). This only begins to hint at what's been omitted. The inhibition seems mainly a consequence of the fear of being viewed by one's colleagues as perverted. The surface of the perversion would be that one is not being faithful to the psychoanalytic commitment to an interpretive praxis, that one is covertly engaging in influence, manipulation, and seduction. As soon as the idea is introduced that the effect of treatment is in part achieved through elements of the process itself (the impact of being cared for by a devoted mentor, of committing oneself to sustained work at an interpersonal task, of negotiating the interpersonal exchanges through which the parties reach toward meaning, and of identifying with the therapist both in his role and in his personhood, to name a few), suspicions are raised that a therapist holding such an understanding of the process will want to maneuver the treatment in Machiavellian fashion toward those goals. The suspected deeper perversion is that the therapist is seeking to meet his own dependent and erotic needs through his work. After all, we establish rigid taboos only against those forces that really lure us. The temptation, in Boris's (1973) words, to "[stroll] about the other's mind as if it were one's own flat" (p. 198) can be irresistible.

The operation of these institutional forces, in their realized political dimension, has inhibited the discussion of treatment. With remarkable consistency, authors bend over backward to qualify any explorations in these areas with assertions of their loyalty to good practice. It's our own McCarthyism. Nonetheless, the need to explore these issues has led to certain forays into the field, and it is these that I take up now.

ALLIANCE

The first area is the recognition that the patient will only be able to open herself up if she experiences herself as being in a relationship with a helpful other. Until the patient can experience her therapist as empathically in tune with her, they will not be able to develop an alliance, a sense of joint participation in a task.

Some years ago, after dinner at a friend's house, a therapist agreed to try out a computer program called, I believe, "Doctor." He typed his thoughts into the keyboard and the program offered encouraging responses. The program was nondirective and also did not make interpretations; it seemed like a parody of the approach of the then-popular Carl Rogers school. While he began by entering his thoughts in a good-humored spirit, he soon found himself becoming annoyed, then furious, and finally feeling persecuted and impotent. In retaliation he became provocative, trying to wring a pained response out of the machine. The following excerpt is from the middle of the session. While the content, out of context, will be beyond comprehension, the reader might get a sense of the "patient's" increasing frustration and his wish to get a rise from the therapist.

PT: I love you!
DR: Do you wish to love me?
PT: Very much so!
DR: Earlier you said your mother has two breasts.
PT: So do you!
DR: We were discussing you, not me.
PT: You! It is you that I love! No one else! Not even me!
DR: You are sure.
PT: Positive!
DR: But your sister has two breasts.

The computer—for the adversary was now the iron monolith, no longer the ephemeral software—was relentlessly unflappable, although it did later accuse its patient of bad faith. In the face of the computer's absolute lack of empathy at earlier points in the session, the patient by now has turned both barrels on the machine, trying to create a short circuit. I believe that this would be the fate of treatment if a therapist did indeed act only like a surgeon, or like a mirror.

I draw two lessons from this. First, being in a relationship in which one is not treated empathically but is expected to expose oneself nonetheless is pretty unbearable, and being treated with a *facsimile* of empathy is truly intolerable. Second, one must feel that the other is capable of being impacted, of knowing he's been hit. Without that, one is driven to become increasingly provocative. If a therapist were truly able to become as invulnerable as the program was, in the name of therapeutic neutrality, I believe his patients would be driven mad.

I choose this extreme example to illustrate how necessary it was that the clinical dimension of our work be addressed by the concept of the therapeutic (Zetzel 1965) or the working (Greenson 1967) alliance. These authors, and others after them, identified a second layer of the analytic relationship, a sense shared by patient and analyst that they were two human beings engaged in a piece of work together. Only with this foundation in place could interpretive work on the transference proceed. In the main, this involved an assertion that the patient's ego was split into a mature collaborating part that stayed outside the fray and an experiencing part that set into motion a transference regression. The analyst's ego remained in one piece, so to speak, in this formulation. His work ego both acknowledged the spirit of a joint venture and conducted the interpretive work. The relational dimension introduced here was the acknowledgement that in one sense patient and analyst had to join as equal partners in the project.

This formulation has become another staple in the standard technique curriculum, even though we are uneasy with it on theoretical grounds. The practical utility of the concept is that it encourages the student to be less gratuitously impersonal; it counterbalances those aspects of clinical theory that are naively exploited to support a posture of estranging anonymity. Where the concept runs into difficulty is in work with relatively disturbed individuals.

With the reasonably healthy patient who has had the benefit of some helpful parenting along the way, the therapeutic alliance is not a problem. It comes naturally. The patient expects that the therapist will try to be helpful and she is straightforwardly inclined to join in the venture. Ironically, the concept actually derives from work with patients who are not inclined to trust us, with whom a therapeutic alliance can be fostered only through a great deal of hard work, if at all. The hard work that is required involves clarifying the transference distortions that lead such patients to believe that we are untrustworthy—helping them to move past their conviction that by a stroke of bad luck they've landed with therapists exactly like their mothers. Paradoxically, for these patients the treatment alliance is the *product* of interpretive work, not its precursor.

When we look more closely we realize that this is actually the case with all our patients, that even the healthier patients' voluntary dropping of their guards is, at least in some degree, a subtle act of compliance, more an appearance of wholehearted cooperation than an actuality. Paul Myerson (1991) observes that even patients well suited to psychoanalytic work—by which he means that the patients are capable of lifting repression in interpretively organized treatment—may fail if their anxieties about lifting repression are not addressed. To be effective, he advises, the analyst must help the patient to experience the analytic relationship as a continuation of the helpful dialogues of childhood. The thought occurs to us that the patient truly able to form an unfettered therapeutic alliance is a fiction, and if he existed he would not need treatment.

The concept is thus problematic insofar as the alliance is required as a precondition for therapeutic work. Its utility, however, has been that it draws our attention to the fact that therapy and analysis only work, ultimately, as a mutual undertaking, and in that regard psychoanalysis and surgery are very *different* enterprises. It would make more sense to think about gradations of alliance, recognizing that for even the most paranoid patient his willingness to stay in the room with his therapist bespeaks some rudimentary idea—however faint—that something may be gained. It also makes sense to recognize that the alliance ultimately cannot be separated from transference because all human relating is based on transference. It is impossible for anyone to have a truly novel relationship—which also means that the therapist, in his effort to treat, is always in some sense engaging in an enactment of his own transferences.

MISALLIANCE

The second area of innovation is the systematic recognition that therapists are as capable as patients are of making the enterprise more difficult. Langs (1976) has argued that therapy occurs in a bipersonal field, with each of the participants able to pose problems for the other. At times, Langs points out, the main activity in the field will be the patient's efforts to call attention to the therapist's errant conduct, most tellingly to the therapist's use of the patient to meet his own needs. Langs has offered us a rich systematic understanding of the various forms this misconduct may take, the various means by which patients will respond to it, the various ways in which therapists can act to set the treatment back on the rails, and the patients' varied reactions to these corrective efforts. This theorizing moves well beyond the concept of the therapeutic alliance to express the mutuality of the therapeutic endeavor: both parties are working to help and hinder each other within the greater goal of promoting the patient's mental health.

For Langs, however, model technique is still framed in a one-person clinical theory (as presented, for example, in his two-volume exegesis on technique [1973–1974]). The occurrence and resolution of therapeutic misalliances is not, properly, the way therapy works in Langs's view. In an expertly conducted treatment, he asserts, the therapist would not muddle things up. Langs is delineating, from his point of view, the psychopathology of the treatment process. His implicit assumption is that it could be got right. This seems a parallel to the taken-for-granted idea that, apart from genetic considerations, personal psychopathology is a result of miscarriages in the processes of maturation and development, and thus, in any given instance, potentially avoidable or at least not generically expectable. Harold Searles (1965), in contrast, sees the working through of misalliances as central to the treatment process.

TRANSFERENCE AND ACTUALITY

The third area in which the one-person theory has been expanded is in the understanding of transference manifestations in the analytic hour. Merton Gill (1982) has argued that transference reactions arise as responses to actual and significant aspects of the analyst's personality and behavior, including the ways in which the analyst sets up the treatment situation, and that the analyst must pay attention to this actuality along with the developmental aspects of the patient's perceptions.

This is in contrast to the idea that transferences are created entirely by the projection of schema in the patient's mind onto the analyst as a blank screen (one variant of which is that the projections are hung on an adventitious speck of the analyst's persona). It also goes beyond the idea that the analyst is provoked by the patient to behave in ways that replicate aspects of others in the patient's past experience, or replicate aspects of the patient herself, thus making the transference response more vividly palpable. In Gill's view the patient is always responding to the therapist's actuality and then elaborating that actuality in ways that are idiosyncratic for her. The therapist's job is to become aware of his contribution to the response, draw his patient's attention to the fact that she is in fact responding to him, and then explore the particular ways in which the patient gave meaning to the situation, which will elaborate her psychology. An example from Gill's (1979) writing should make this clearer:

> The patient describes her trouble with a subordinate who needs constant direction. The analyst suggests that she wants him to direct her too. She agrees and wonders whether her complaint about the subordinate is valid in itself or only a disguised way of expressing her wish for direction. The analyst says this is an evasion of directly confronting his interpretation. She responds with a memory of how she refused to carry out a request of a superior because she felt she was being treated like a lackey. She is implying she feels he is treating her like a lackey. [p. 12]

The analyst in this example is apparently persistently confronting, and we can imagine that this might be his style. The patient's first comment might reflect an identification with his aggressiveness, based on imagining that her analyst experiences her as helpless, or may be a complaint that her analyst is floundering and needs direction, which the analyst conceals behind a determined aggressiveness, to mention two possibilities. In any event, although the patient is talking about her work situation, she is implicating her treatment, and has, we imagine, various ideas about her analyst's behavior that reflect aspects both of the analyst's actuality and of her idiosyncratic construction of him. The analyst's job is to decide where the actuality lies and explore the idiosyncratic elaboration.

In this instance, the analyst moves to a particular interpretation, that the patient is looking for him to direct her. It is unclear whether the patient actually agrees with this or is merely being compliant. She continues, however, to wonder about the situation outside the treatment, and her analyst accuses her of evading his interpretation. She now complains that she feels treated like a lackey. Again, it is for the analyst to decide to what extent her response expresses an ordinary reaction to his being overzealous, and to what extent it reflects her propensity to experience herself as an angry lackey. The latter aspect he will interpret. That the analyst is a person, with a particular style of analyzing, with his own defensiveness, is taken for granted. His work is to be aware of that, and of its impact on his patient, and to work with what she makes of him and does with it.[1]

In this expansion of theory, the analyst is now present not only as a working collaborator and as a professional capable of malpractice but also as an individual whose unique personal characteristics constantly contribute to the process by evoking responses in the patient that then become part of the subject matter of the treatment. In this view, the analyst enters the analytic situation in two quite separate ways: as a particular person without privileged status, and as the practitioner. Although this contribution could be made part of a two-person clinical theory, I am choosing not to view it that way, admittedly a bit arbitrarily, because it is mainly offered as an elabora-

---

[1]Looking at this vignette afresh, Gill (personal communication, 1993) reflects that he would now be interested in the immediate interaction between himself and the patient. His confrontation of the patient in the text seems unnecessarily harsh and misleading to him; he thinks that her implied feeling that she was being treated as a lackey is related to the spirit of his previous response.

tion of our understanding of transference, and the analyst's task as analyst remains simply to analyze the (now conceptually expanded) transference. The analyst has a more complex field to attend to, but his form of participation, broadly conceived, remains the same. Gill's work has, of course, generated considerable debate. It challenges the notion of analytic anonymity and replaces it with an intense focus on the analyst's specificity.

Because the psychoanalytic model is based on bringing to light the patient's ways of constructing the world, which are understood to be rooted in his early experience, the wish embodied in traditional one-person theory is that our model technique could create an arena for the uncontaminated expression of that structure. In this view, the patient would present himself with his transferences and the analyst, as a neutral observer, would identify them. Insofar as the analyst's particularity enters the field, the patient is deprived of a blank canvas for his self-illustration. "Contamination" of the field is indeed the word often used by writers to bemoan this limitation in technique. Gill's argument, and the argument of this text, is that this view of the analytic process is simply wrong: analysis could never work this way because it operates through an interpersonal process, two persons working with each other toward a goal. Less ostensibly active behavior on the analyst's part does not allow him to recede into the background. With a silent analyst, the patient typically scans more actively for cues and gives those cues greater meaning. The fact that the napkin on the pillow was carelessly laid becomes a cue to the analyst's state of mind, an indication that the patient will elaborate both on the basis of his reading of his analyst and on the basis of his transferences. There is no contamination-free field. There is, inescapably, contagion everywhere.

If the analyst needs to believe that he can create an aseptic field, the danger is that the patient will feel compelled to support the analyst's conceit, and will be even less likely than usual to tell him about the observations she's made that are preoccupying her. This, of course, is always a problem. I've had days when I was certainly preoccupied or anxious or depressed for reasons that had nothing to do with my practice and have managed to go through those days without ever hearing a word about it from my patients. Standing back from it now, I don't believe that it didn't register on many of them. Sometimes one picks up the perception in a disguised reference, and it can then be brought into the dialogue. It seems plausible, at least, that in those treatments where the analyst needs to deny his personal impact on the process, patient and analyst will collude to keep a great deal more from view than would otherwise be necessary. Since all the patient's perceptions are also founded on transference—the transference having found its point of attachment at the present reality—paradoxically the effort at keeping a clean field obscures the transference.

Gill's emphasis on the analyst's particularity is consistent with what I consider to be the fundamental transformation in one-person clinical theory. We all now recognize that every action of the therapist will be experienced by the patient as having meaning and that the patient will be fundamentally right in this regard, no matter how she ultimately skews that meaning in response to her transferences. Every act of the therapist—whether to speak or remain silent; whether to question, clarify, or interpret—has an effect on the patient, stimulates transference (how could it be otherwise?), and generates meaning. That the clock reaches the fiftieth minute so that the session ends is not a subjective event, but everything that happens within that fifty minutes, no matter how appropriate, relevant, and skillful, will properly be experienced by both parties subjectively.

There is no privileged act that exists outside subjectivity. We take this for granted now. We know that our patients attach meanings to everything we do and that we ourselves are at every moment making choices that will have consequences. In this sense the original conception of the process has changed: we are not surgeons or mirrors or reflexively operating instrumentalities. It is this fact of mutual subjectivity that we missed from the computer—even though it jerked its knee precisely in response to being tapped—which made that experience so infuriating.

3

The Relational Dimension

Over the past half-century a variety of theoretical models of the mind have been generated that in one way or another introduce relational considerations. For the most part these models have had the aim of providing a richer understanding of the human condition, but all have also had implications for clinical practice. Some of the models were intended to revise technique, although I think it is fair to say that none of them has tried to devise a comprehensive clinical theory. Each model focuses on what its creators take to be weaknesses or misconceptions in mainstream theory and offers its own emendations. All the models I will be discussing remain committed to the broad psychoanalytic view of human beings as creatures in conflict, burdened by their past, and operating in ways that exceed their awareness.

This chapter examines four models that have had substantial impact on the practice of psychoanalysis—the ideas of Melanie Klein, Donald Winnicott, Harry Stack Sullivan, and Heinz Kohut—and considers them in relation to the ideas being developed in this text (thus hardly doing justice to their complexity and subtlety). Each model holds a view of the way in which humans are disordered that bears implications for clinical practice, both for what the subject matter of analysis should be and for the way it should be conducted. Insofar as they bring in relational dimensions, they tug at the foundations of our existing clinical theory. Schafer (1983) has characterized models of this sort as narratives, each to be taken as a story that places its heroine in a particular predicament from which her analyst must in a particular way rescue her. Let me present some of these tales.

MELANIE KLEIN

Schafer (1983) observes that Klein and her followers give "an account of the child or adult as being in some stage of recovering from a rageful infantile psychosis at the breast" (p. 217). The tale begins with demonic possession: the newborn infant is overwhelmed by the death instinct, and for the sake of psychic survival it projects a part of the death instinct into the breast, which is now experienced as persecutory. Through projective and introjective mechanisms (Klein 1946, 1952) the infant attempts to contend with this war of its own making, and in the process an internal phantasy[1] world is established (or, some would argue, an inborn phantasy world surfaces [Ogden 1986]). The infant's experiences with its caretakers will be important, over time, insofar as they support or disconfirm the beliefs that are embodied in these phantasies (Klein 1959).

In subsequent elaborations of Kleinian thought, we are told that the caretakers' responses will not simply be manifestations of their own established personalities, but that they will reflect the caretakers' success or failure at managing aspects of experience (especially feelings) evoked in them by their infants through the mechanism of projective identification. The infant thus creates a trial at which her parents will,

---

[1]In this book I follow the practice of using "phantasy" to refer to unconscious imaginings, which might be revealed to the therapist through displacements or derivatives, and "fantasy" to indicate conscious daydreams.

in varying degrees and ways, succeed and fail. In the main, however, the battleground is internal, between hating and loving, and growing up requires that the infant gradually develop the capacity to love in spite of hating and to hate in spite of loving (Klein 1935, 1940).

Because the concept of projective identification is central to my own understanding of interpersonal influence, I will briefly describe its evolution. Klein (1946) created the term to describe the way in which the infant, while in a state of mind in which splitting is the predominant way of organizing experience, disowns disturbing aspects of the self or "bad" internal objects and experiences those aspects as though they are in the mother. This serves both to rid temporarily the infant of an intolerable experience, and to locate that which is disowned in another where it can be controlled. For Klein, this was an intrapsychic event, the elaboration of a phantasy. Phantasy, for Klein, was the mental structure through which experience was organized. In its imagination, the infant located the bad experience in the mother. Bion made Klein's concept interpersonal. He observed (1959b) that the analyst is affected by the projective operations of his patient: "The analyst feels he is being manipulated so as to be playing a part, no matter how difficult to recognize, in somebody else's phantasy" (p. 149) unless, Bion continues, the analyst is so taken over by the situation that he loses insight into the fact that the patient is evoking what he is feeling and experiences the projected bad object as actually a part of himself. The analyst will experience the patient's projective identification; he may or may not, in the process, lose his own bearings. Bion believed that projective identification was a central aspect of communication between infant and mother (1959a), and that the mother's failure to be open to the infant's projections could be a basis for later illness. The concept has been substantially expanded by subsequent writers, by Ogden (1982, 1986), notably in relation to work with individual patients and, following the seminal work of Dicks (1967), by Berkowitz, E. Shapiro, R. Shapiro, and Zinner (Scharff 1989) in relation to the treatment of couples and families. Scharff (1992) offers a more detailed history of the evolution of the concept.

Leaving to one side Klein's discovery of play as a way of psychoanalytically engaging children, which may actually be her greatest contribution of all to our practice, I would like to focus on two ways in which the Kleinian contribution has influenced technique. First, Kleinians firmly place the patient at the center of the field: she is the source of intentionality and the cause of her own distress, and the work of analysis will be to make manifest her phantasies as revealed in the transference. In this spirit Kleinians keep the autonomous individual in the foreground, much as Freud did, and advocate the relentless maintenance of an interpretive stance, arguing that anything less is joining with the patient in evasion and enactment. Hanna Segal (1973) observes that at a time when many practitioners, struggling with patients with great and early pathology, feel "the analyst has to provide an environmental factor to make up for the deficiency experienced in infancy" (p. 118), the Kleinians see such action as the abandonment of analytic neutrality and subversion of the work.

The other Kleinian impact on technique that bears attention here is a change that was brought to the understanding of the analyst's role. Putting the mechanism of projective identification at the center of the analytic interchange means recognizing that the analyst is continually being worked on by his patient, maneuvered and manipulated to feel, to think, and to act in particular ways that at least in the short run serve the patient's needs. This puts the analyst's efforts to comprehend his countertransferences, understood here as the analyst's response to his patient's transferences, at the heart of his work (best described by Racker 1968). In this view of technique, the analyst is more than an empathic listener, sitting, so to speak, beside the patient; he is the feast of vampires, witches, and ghosts, always at risk of being invaded by the patient. The analyst has moved beyond listening to a particular kind of experiencing that exceeds what we usually mean when we speak of empathy. His task, within this technique, is to permit invasion and resist capture. Here is a clear expression and illustration of the process:

If the patient is to sort out what is external and what is internal, how far his view of the world is coloured by omnipotent phantasy, he can only do so if the analyst remains unaltered in his basic function by the patient's projections. This was expressed succinctly by a schizophrenic patient of mine. The patient was frequently late, and once when he came nearly at the end of his session he put great pressure on me to overstep the time, and in view of the precariousness of the situation I was very tempted to do so. But having interpreted to him the situation he had put me into, I terminated the session. The next day he expressed that it brought him tremendous relief and said "in my world you are the one person who knows the time. If you didn't know what time it was, then all would be lost." [Segal 1973, p. 119]

Segal is arguing here that her crucial act was to resist her patient's projection. It seems to me, however, that the conception could be broadened in this way: the patient was setting a test for Segal, testing her capacity to hold the situation, trying both to subvert her and to evoke a containing response, and Segal took in both sides of the projective identification and then responded in a therapeutically useful way by ending the hour on time. In this view Segal did not resist taking in the projection. She felt the tension of conflicting pressures, worked it through within herself, and responded in a constructive way.

In another case, describing her work with a patient who was obstinately silent, Segal traced a succession of meanings of the silence as the work evolved. The silence was first understood as a communication of what it felt like to be cut off, then as what it felt like to have a lifeless internal object, and eventually as an aggressive projection of feelings of failure and inadequacy. Initially Segal frequently interrupted the silences "to interpret a fair amount, as it was quite clear [the patient] could not speak until I established contact with her by understanding her projective identification" (p. 122). Later Segal was able to be silent for long stretches. At one point, while bitterly complaining about her analyst's much longer silences but also understanding the need for them, the patient reflected on the earlier activity and said, "but I suppose then you had no choice."

Segal seems to be arguing that in fact, earlier, she had had no reasonable alternative to actively breaking through the silences, and that may be correct. But I would like at least to raise an alternative possibility: that Segal had earlier been taken over by the patient's projective identification in such a way that she *had felt that she had no choice*, and that the patient was recognizing her earlier impact on Segal in the quoted statement. In this view, Segal had had to work her way clear of her patient's usurpation of her will, through an act of understanding that was perhaps in part intuitive and in part conscious, to be able to reach a point at which she could constructively be silent. Her regaining her own capacity for choice unblocked the treatment. In all fairness, I find this view of the process more appealing because it expresses my own sense of how treatment works, and I will later offer an illustration from my work in which the crux of the matter was my being able to find my way to silence.

In summary, leaving aside the Kleinian shift in emphasis regarding the *content* of interpretation—work on primitive phantasy, especially early oedipal constructions—the Kleinians have shifted technique in work with adults in two major directions. On the one hand they emphatically put the focus on the individual, countering the trend toward seeing the patient as victim rather than protagonist, and on the other side they bring in a relational dimension to the structure of the treatment process through their focus on working with projective identification.

DONALD WINNICOTT

Winnicott's narrative centers on the baby and its mother; the story is well told by both Greenberg and Mitchell (1983) and by Ogden (1986). Beginning in the late stages of pregnancy, the mother enters a frame of mind that we might describe as a state of devotion to her baby, "primary maternal preoccupation." In the first weeks of her infant's life she "brings the world to the child," which is Winnicott's way of saying that she is so finely attuned to her baby's needs that if he were capable of subjective experience he would experience the illusion that need does not exist. This is, of course, a paradoxical statement, because the purpose of the illusion is to protect the child from premature subjectivity. Within this "holding environment" provided by the mother, the pair exist in a state approaching seamless oneness (Winnicott 1960a). Over time, as the mother resonates with her baby's wants and needs, he becomes attuned to his functions and desires, begins to experience them as his own, and thus evolves a nascent sense of selfhood. At the same time, the mother's inevitable small failures and lapses in responsiveness also promote her infant's development of a sense of separateness.

In some measure, however, the mother's inevitable inability to responsively "go on being" with her baby will lead him to experience her as "impinging." Play now stops as he becomes preoccupied with the need to meet her needs. He manufactures a "false self" based on compliance with what he takes to be her needs and his "true self" goes into hiding (Winnicott 1960b). The false self will become the face presented to the outside world, the instrument through which relationships will be managed. Put another way, Thomas Ogden (1986) points out that, for Winnicott, to the extent that the mother is able to allow the child freedom to play "in the presence of the absent mother [without her impingement]" (p. 182), he will come to internalize the mother-as-holding-environment and develop the capacity to be self-soothing. To the extent that she cannot grant her child this space because of her own needs, she interferes with this movement and promotes an addiction to herself as an omnipotent object, thereby disrupting the child's progress toward autonomy.

In this telling, maternal failure is the source of psychopathology. The analyst, in Winnicott's accounting, needs to make the missing maternal provision that will hold the situation while the patient gets her development back on track. For Winnicott what is mainly important here is what the analyst does not do: he does not impinge on the patient with his own needs; he does not stand in the way of his patient's need to regress; he works to counter the patient's making him into an omnipotent object ("I retain some outside quality by not being quite on the mark—or even by being wrong" [1965, p. 167]); he tries hard not to be bright or clever; he withstands the patient's attacks without retaliating; and he does not disrupt his patient's gradual transition toward separateness (her appropriating the right to be behind her own eyes, in Milner's sensitive phrasing [Hughes 1989, p. 177]). During the later stages of treatment, "the now independent ego of the patient begins to show and to assert its own individual characteristics, and the patient begins to take for granted a feeling of existing in his or her own right" (Winnicott 1965, p. 168). To this reader it sounds like treatment is about being born.

The controversial aspect of Winnicott's technique involves his work with those patients he referred to as needing a regression. Winnicott believed that such work was not necessary with most patients, although some commentators have asserted that his actual work belied this claim. In any event, this is how Winnicott (1965) described the treatment:

> If the hidden true self is to come into its own in such a case the patient will break down as part of the treatment, and the analyst will need to be able to play the part of mother to the patient's infant. This means giving ego-support in a big way. The analyst will need to remain orientated to external reality while in fact being identified with the patient, even merged in with the patient. The patient must become highly dependent, even absolutely dependent, and these words are true even when there is a healthy part of the personality that acts all along as an ally of the analyst and in fact tells the analyst how to behave. [p. 163]

Winnicott's work in England was in part a response to what he considered Melanie Klein's stark dismissal of the role of the environment. (Judith M. Hughes (1989) discloses a letter Winnicott wrote to his second analyst, Joan Riviere, in which he said, "My trouble when I start to speak to Melanie about her statement of early infancy is that

I feel as if I were talking about colour to the colour-blind" [p. 174]). Winnicott's revision of the course of development was matched by his revision of clinical technique. He was arguing for the analyst's taking a more explicitly maternal role, *in certain ways* with all patients, and more extensively with particular patients. As an example of what might be called for, he observed: "Regression to dependence is part and parcel of early infancy phenomena, and if the couch gets wetted, or if the patient soils, or dribbles, we know that this is inherent, not a complication. Interpretation is not what is needed, and indeed speech or even movement can ruin the process and can be excessively painful to the patient" (1954, p. 289). At moments Winnicott wrote as though the provision of a maternal holding environment was a *prerequisite* for interpretive work, which would, along traditional lines, unfold the transference. At other times, however, more obviously in his work with regressed patients but to some degree in all his work, he seemed to believe that the maternal facilitation of the patient's movement toward independence was the crux of the treatment. (Phillips [1988] observed that "the difference that language makes, like the difference the father makes, is never theoretically elaborated by Winnicott" [p. 139].)

It seems likely to me that Winnicott actually held both points of view and never definitively resolved the question in his own mind, which makes his perspective on technique difficult to discuss. Insofar as the maternal provision was essential, however, he was changing the conception of the analyst's role. This new conception was not built on the notion that we each bring particular maternal capabilities to our work. On the contrary, Winnicott had a model in mind for the "good enough" analyst that is daunting to contemplate: he calls upon us to have a capacity for objectivity and freedom from need and ambition that indeed few of us could live up to much of the time (while at the same time disingenuously asserting that in doing analysis he aims at simply keeping alive, keeping well, and keeping awake [1965, p. 166]). Recognizing his clinical theory, as he stated it, to be an oversimplification, we might, in a spirit of Winnicottian excess, say that it is the treatment designed for what he considers to be the universal illness:

false selfhood brought about by maternal impingement. The lost heroine is rescued by the mother capable of tolerance.

HARRY STACK SULLIVAN

Working on the opposite side of the Atlantic, Harry Stack Sullivan (1953) put forward a sensibility about the analytic process that was quite similar to Winnicott's. Their theories of personality were kindred in that both centered on the implications of the idea that the child developed in a social field, although Winnicott focused in a bit more explicitly on the mother and on the earliest stages of life, while Sullivan took a more expanded view both of the social field and of the crucial stages of development. In one important nuance of difference, where Winnicott stressed the disruption of the holding environment by the impingement of the mother's *needs*, which the infant had to mold himself around, Sullivan emphasized the mother's communication of *anxiety* to her infant, which mobilized him to develop various security operations designed to preclude the repetition of anxious experience. Both believed that the analytic situation inevitably recreated aspects of these earlier situations.

Sullivan's emphasis on the role of anxiety informed his own practice. He took great pains to manage the flow of anxiety in the session. A supervisor I worked with whom I know to have been directly involved with Sullivan was far more attuned than the dozen other supervisors I've had over the course of my career to the actual way I worded what I said to my patient. This practitioner was particularly sensitive to the matter of how I could get myself heard in a way that could have an effect without scaring the patient off or intensifying his defensiveness (perhaps another way of saying the same thing). This concern on the part of the supervisor went well beyond the normal attention to tact and timing. I learned here as never before that being heard can hardly be taken for granted, that in fact it is a relatively rare event, that patients are so busy managing us to keep us from (what they fear will be) our traumatizing them that they can hardly pay attention to what we are saying, and that they are in fact so vulnerable to being made more anxious that the vast majority of comments we might feel inclined to make are actually likely to fulfill their prophecy. It was not unusual for this supervisor and me to spend a good part of a session trying to think out *something* I might actually be able to get away with saying. On the other hand, Sullivan thought that at times he could only break through to his patients by making startling statements because, as Havens [1976] comments in his book on Sullivan, "we are a good deal more schizoid than admirers of the human race like to believe. . . . [and] as Chekhov illustrates so vividly, even startling statements may not be heard, so that the Sullivanian practitioner has a good deal more leeway than some would think" (p. 28).

In summary, Sullivan is concerned with the therapist's potential for making the patient anxious, and his need to attend to that process. I recall Sullivan writing somewhere about his attempt to raise the subject of masturbation with a young male patient. He described how he conspicuously got busy searching all over and under his desk for an imaginary missing object while mumbling to the patient that By God! they never had come around to that impossible subject. Along similar lines, the aforementioned supervisor suggested to me that I might get elaborately busy apologizing for my negligence in having *completely* forgotten to ask my patient about his masturbation fantasies when we first started meeting together, thus deflecting the moment from his embarrassment to my asserted incompetence. Indirectly, I thought, my supervisor was dramatizing the matter to manage *my* embarrassment with him.

Sullivan referred to his technique as *participant observation*, and in that phrase he captured his sense of both the intimacy and distance in the position from which the therapist worked.

HEINZ KOHUT

Heinz Kohut (1971, 1977) and his associates offer a third model in which parental malfeasance is the source of psychopathology, but the problem here is framed as something the parents have *failed* to do.

Kohut's conception thus stands in contrast to Winnicott's and Sullivan's models, in which the difficulty is certain forms of parental *presence*—respectively, and with great oversimplification, neediness, and anxiety. While this could certainly be thought of as a linguistic distinction of my own invention, I am using it because Kohut's self psychology model is, most particularly among the theories, a *deficit* model. The caretakers, for Kohut, are most notably *absent* in the particular regard that he has brought to our attention—that is, in terms of providing the required responsiveness to the child's narcissistic needs, and thus facilitating the development of a cohesive self.

For Kohut, what the analyst encounters in working with a patient with a disorder of self-organization is a particular form of transference in which the patient attempts to use the analyst as a "selfobject" (an object not clearly differentiated from the self) to perform functions that she is unable to perform for herself. In particular, her need to have her capabilities recognized and admired, and her need to idealize a parental figure will not have been adequately met during early development, leaving the child, and later the adult, unable to organize self-regard around either healthy ambitiousness or the valuing of honorable ideals. The patient will try to use—or struggle against using—her analyst to fulfill these needs. She will do this in an effort to heal herself, to fashion a self that will be sufficient.

The task for the analyst is, broadly, twofold. First and foremost, he must be able to develop an empathic stance beside his patient, from which he can comprehend and value the patient—value her profound and desperate efforts to cope with her lack of self-cohesion. He must be especially sensitive to her narcissistic vulnerabilities, and not be put off by her need to use him for mirroring and idealizing purposes. The wish to reject such uses, Kohut maintains, is a frequent countertransference problem. Second (and it makes no sense to talk of this unless the analyst is in an empathic position), the analyst interprets to the patient by paying attention to the ways in which the patient responds to his inevitable moments of empathic failure or absence.

In Kohut's original theory of the treatment process, the analyst's work at interpreting to the patient the actual and transferential dimensions of her reactions to his failures helps her to gradually gain mastery over her propensity toward narcissistic collapse. She accomplishes this both by reaching a reconstructed understanding of the form of the original parental failure, and by internalizing her analyst's selfobject functions, thus creating for the first time her own cohesive self. In subsequent writing by some of the self psychology theorists, it appears that neither reconstructive interpretation nor analysis of empathic failure may be at the heart of the curative process, but that simply being treated empathically may in itself be what is crucial for selfobject internalization. This begins to sound like the healing power of the prince's kiss.

What are the implications for the theory of technique? In Kohut's first formulation, the structure of treatment remained the same—the analysis of transference—with the modification that average expectable failures of empathy on the analyst's part would fuel the appearance of selfobject transference problems, thus providing the needed grist for the analytic mill. In fact, as I understand the first formulation, if the analyst were perfectly empathic the treatment would never proceed, because there would be no stimulus for internalization, in the same sense that for Winnicott the mother's incremental failures are needed if the child is to individuate. This creates a new conception of the role of the analyst: it is through his attention to the impact of his inevitable insensitivities that the work goes forward.

The formulation in which the empathic response itself is restorative is a more radical departure from the mainstream theory of technique. This is indeed a deficit model approach—the deficit now being absent psychic structure—in which the analyst's function is to supply a missing piece. To the extent that self psychologists think of their work as proceeding along this line (this being a charge regularly leveled against them, at times inappropriately), it seems fair to say that they see the analyst's function as parenting rather than as providing understanding, and this becomes a quite different form of treatment. They might reply that it is the empathic integration of patient and analyst in ordinary analytic technique that is actually most helpful to patients, but that we blind ourselves to the role of this nonhermeneutic aspect of the treatment. The great impact of the self psychology movement on all analysts has been to make them more sensitive to their patients, to challenge them to notice the subtle ways in which standard procedure—silence, interpretation of resistance, insistence on meaningfulness—can become traumatic and persecutory. While it is not true that the self psychologists invented tact, they have been of great service in reminding us that we are treating *people*.

Although it is hardly the final word on this confusion of goals, this example from his earlier writing of Kohut's (1971) thinking on the role of empathy is worth our attention:

> [E]mpathy, especially when it is surrounded by an attitude of wanting to cure *directly* through the giving of loving understanding, may indeed become basically overbearing and annoying; i.e., it may rest on the therapist's unresolved omnipotence fantasies. Provided, however, that the analyst has largely come to terms with his wish to cure directly through the magic of his loving understanding and is indeed not patronizing toward the patient (i.e., he recognizes empathy as a tool of observation and of appropriate communication), the mere fact that the patient dropped his defenses against the possibility of being empathically understood and responded to exposes him to the archaic fear of earliest disappointments [which in turn are worked with]. [p. 307]

In this reading, empathy is clearly in the service of a larger undertaking and not a technical approach in itself.

This brief excursion highlights the major ways in which four alternative models of the mind bear implications for technique, both for our understanding of the relationship between therapist and patient and for our theory of how therapy works. All four models introduce a relational dimension to the therapist's activity, although I have demonstrated that trends within the analytic mainstream have also opened up our conception of the treatment process. Many metaphors have been used to describe this evolution in theory, perhaps the most technically apt being the shift in science from mechanistic to relativistic models, but I would like to add yet another analogy: the movement in theater away from the use of the proscenium arch in favor of the open stage, through which the performers' relation to the audience changes from measured and formal distance to more immediate engagement.

The rattling in the background in this chapter has been the protest from our drive-theory progenitors that we are doing mazurkas on their caskets. Before proceeding further with my argument I should offer my thoughts as to what that controversy is about.

4

The Thinker and the Kiss

The story is told of a fellow from the Bronx who got stranded on a desert island. Realizing that he might be there for a long time, he built himself a little community. Eventually a ship that had strayed off course sighted him, and the crew came ashore. The islander took them on a tour and showed them the house he'd built for himself, his garden, the farm where he'd domesticated animals, and his two synagogues. The crew was startled by this last particular and asked him why he'd constructed two places of worship. Wasn't one enough? He proudly replied, "*That's* the one I wouldn't set foot in!"

We once told this story as a parable about the Americans and the Soviets to satirize their paranoid need for an enemy. Once these great nations had discovered that they could trust each other without the world coming to an end, the fable could find a new referent: psycho-analytic internecine warfare. The battle currently is most vigorously waged between the self psychologists and the mainstream post-Freudians in America, and also between the Kleinians and the Independent Group in London. But these battles have always been part of our professional life, with institutes cleaving, splinter groups breaking off, long-standing friendships ruined. Insofar as ideology is actually responsible for the division, the warring camps seem often to be, in one form or another, committed to an individualistic versus a communal view of human existence. With Robin's sculptures in mind, we might say that they're taken with *The Thinker*'s self-possession, or with the entwined lovers' *Kiss*.

I introduce this opposition of models because it underlies the conflict between the one-person and two-person views of the therapeutic process. The contending ideologies are the drive-discharge paradigm (which focuses on the vicissitudes of sexuality and aggression, both broadly defined) and the relational paradigm. In contemporary writing about ideologies, theorists tend to be crammed into one slot or the other, their own protests notwithstanding. The drive-discharge paradigm, including its further elaboration in ego psychology, is at the center of Freudian psychoanalysis. The drive concept, originally articulated by Freud in the context of nineteenth-century principles of physiology, leads to a focus on the internal workings of the mind and the conflicts between parts of the mind. While it is certainly understood that drive discharge occurs only in the context of human relations, the nuances of those actual relationships are, on the whole, of peripheral interest to theorists working within that system. Because the individual's thoughts, feelings, and actions are understood to be generated fundamentally from within, not fundamentally as a consequence of the actions of others, the drive-discharge paradigm is suited to a one-person model of treatment. In that model, the patient's transferences are evoked by his drive needs and propensities, which are both inborn and shaped by development, and the analyst is spectator to these unfoldings.

While there is not a single relational paradigm—the models of Winnicott, Sullivan, and Kohut described in the previous chapter, for example, are based on quite varying assumptions—they all share a common sensibility. The relational paradigms put much greater emphasis on the role of the important objects, the parents in particular, in shaping the individual's psychology. In this view, we are all much more social than otherwise. While the drive-discharge paradigm embodies a view of the individual's behavior that fits well with the one-person model of the therapeutic situation, the relational models are better suited to a two-person model of the treatment process, which emphasizes the mutual interactions of therapist and patient.

The one-person/two-person controversy has also been framed in terms of this question: Does the analyst have a major participation in the analytic situation? Gill (1988) points out that the answer to this question surprisingly does not always fall along the above paradigm lines—adherents of the drive-discharge paradigm do not uniformly assume that the analyst's participation is minor, nor do all relational theorists give the analyst a major role. His starkest example comes from Abrams and Shengold (1978), who sketched out the contemporary Freudian view and then said that

> clinical investigation and theory building over the past fifty years have tested and challenged much of this with the result that some analysts have developed substantially different views of the psychoanalytic situation . . . [In] the new model . . . the psychoanalytic situation is seen primarily as an *encounter* between two people, rather than as a setting whose purpose is the examination of the intrapsychic processes of one of them. [p. 402]

The question itself, however, needs to be refined further by clarifying the meaning of participation. Four aspects should be considered. First, we might understand the analyst to be a major participant in the sense that Gill does: because the analyst is *inescapably* involved in complex social interactions with his patient, his patient's transferences will always be determined by the analyst's behavior. The patient's perception of that behavior is shaped by both the actual event and the patient's predispositions. Second, the question of participation could refer to the issue of whether change is viewed as occurring through the experience of the analytic relationship— whether the relationship and analytic process constitute a new experience that has therapeutic value apart from the patient's achievement of insight. If one believes that this is a curative factor, then one must be granting the analyst a major participatory role. But granting him this role does not mean that his activity will necessarily go outside interpretation. Loewald's (1980) theory and practice would be one example of holding this view within an interpretive framework. Third, the question of participation might refer to the analyst's behavior during the sessions. In this sense, major participation would refer to activity other than listening, clarifying, and interpreting. Those modes of activity might be thought of as following behind the patient, whereas major participation would mean, in one way or another, taking the lead. Taking the lead might include support, direction, confrontation, suggestion, or various forms of manipulation. While *manipulation* in this context always seems to smack of criminal doings, we could find a variety of creative and useful manipulations in the work of Freud, Winnicott, and Sullivan, to name a few. The fourth aspect of participation might be that even the best analyzed therapist will inevitably lose his bearings in a deeply engaged treatment, under the pressure of the processes operating in the patient–therapist relationship, and have to work his way back to clarity; unlike the third form of participation, this would be understood as inevitable and involuntary.

I am arguing that it is in the nature of human experience and the therapeutic process that the therapist is inescapably a major participatory figure in the first, second, and fourth senses above. I share the belief with others that therapists are also far more participatory in the third sense than is generally acknowledged, more apt to take the lead, although whether this is a good or bad thing remains an open question. Holding a two-person view of the therapeutic process does not require being participatory in the third sense.

In exploring the drive-discharge and relational paradigms in greater detail, I will try to capture the appeal of each model. I will also be arguing that these two models, which simply appear to offer contrasting understandings of the human condition, are actually in a complex relationship with each other. Their views of man as fundamentally an individual and fundamentally connected are both half-truths. The conflict between being impelled toward separateness and connectedness, embodied in the two paradigms, actually begins early in infancy.

Accordingly, I will not be advocating that my two-person conception of the therapeutic process be embedded in the relational paradigm. On the contrary, my argument is that the paradigms constitute a false dichotomy, and that a sensibility that integrates them can only be made operational in a two-person view of the therapeutic process.

THE THINKER

The model of the mind based on drive theory has enormous appeal for us as therapists, despite its complications, because it locates the focus of initiative in the patient. In models that view the patient as having a deficit of one sort or another (and that is how most relational theories are characterized, not always fairly), the patient tends to be seen as passive and lacking, and the therapist's task is to create something that is missing for the patient. It is harder to build a highway than to remove a roadblock. In contrast, the therapist gains tremendous leverage when he treats the patient as fully accountable, responsible for the conduct of his life, for his perverse unconscious, for his fate. When the therapist begins to join the patient in blaming others, no matter with what finesse and subtlety, he loses that edge.

Roy Schafer (1976), in his elaboration of what he has chosen to call "action language" (the patient's necessary appropriation of her life), has drawn our attention to the ways in which we collude with our patient's constructions of themselves as passive vehicles. When, for example, we ask "What comes to mind?" rather than "What are you thinking?" we have slipped into a view in which the patient as cinema spectator replaces the patient as actor. Drive theory embodies our idealization of personal responsibility, even though we are not always able to stay faithful to our ideals.

A further appeal of the drive-conflict model is that it focuses on the patient as an individual. The thrust of Freud's psychology was to foster human individuation, our capacity to stand alone. Freud's mission was to tame the id with the rational mind, not simply because the id was hostile to reality, but more importantly because it interfered with growth. The Oedipus complex was problematic for the same reason—the lure of oedipal engagement threatened to keep the individual entangled in family passions, whether in his family of origin or in a new family inevitably structured to recreate the old. Ideally we humans would be without transferences, created in our own image and fashioning a new world free from incestuous object choice.

Freud's technique reflected these ambitions. Analysis was to explore *the individual* in depth; the emphasis, if you can allow me this distinction, was on knowing man's mind more than his life. The analyst was to stand apart from the patient as an observer. His persona would be a mannequin that the patient dressed with transferences; as costumer, the analyst would describe the fit. The patient's emotional life was to be given voice, the analyst's silenced. Although Freud acknowledged the importance of the analyst's empathy, his emphasis was on the analyst's thinking, which was to be used in the service of promoting the patient's *conscious* control so that he could *wittingly* forge his destiny.

Insofar as the patient is an individual, he can stand apart from his family. Freud regarded the family as always potentially dangerous, corrupting, undermining. And this remained so throughout the life cycle. Matters were hardly resolved for Freud, for example, at the end of the oedipal period with the renunciation of incestuous and parricidal intentions. In adolescence those incestuous longings were reawakened with new biological force, and only actual separation from the parents and the move into independent living made mastery possible.

Freud found families enough of an obstacle to treatment that for a period of time before the First World War he chose to take on only independent unmarried individuals as patients. While he believed it was in principle useful for patients living in families to "remain during the treatment in the conditions in which they have to struggle"

(1916–1917 [1915–1917], p. 461), he personally was happy to have no part of it. Nor did the oedipal struggle end when the individual left his family, for Freud argued that, after emancipation, it was the opposition between the new generation and the old that made the progress of civilization possible (1905 [1901], p. 227). The choice was between the new generation making its claims in acts of patricide or the leveling of civilization in incestuous merger.

That problem has tragically haunted the psychoanalytic movement. Freud tried to forestall an oedipal catastrophe by promoting asexual reproduction, cloning. During his lifetime we thus saw many disciples and few innovators. The new generation was not, in fact, allowed to oppose the old. Freud tended to treat his ideas and his movement as the product of spontaneous generation, not as a development in a historical tradition. As Galileo declared in defiance of the church that the earth moved, Freud saw himself declaring that man was impassioned in ways he had not, or had only, dreamed. The consequences of this form of stewardship are well known. As Stephen Mitchell (1988) put it, "Psychoanalysis was created by an individual intellect of towering genius. . . . the singularity of his achievement became the model followed by his successors, who tend to present their contributions not as partial replacements or solutions to particular features which Freud addressed, but as alternative, comprehensive systems" (p. 6). Disdaining generational transmission, Freud's intellectual family would live and die in acts of patricide. As Winnicott said to his old friend Masud Khan, "It is no use, Masud, asking me to read anything! If it bores me I shall fall asleep in the middle of the first page, and if it interests me I will start rewriting it by the end of that page" (Khan 1975, p. xvi).

THE KISS

These accents would not exist unless there were an underscoring that they were flowing against. Within us, within all of us, alongside the strivings for independent existence are other wishes, wishes for merger, fusion, loss of self in the other, an expanded unity, something that is not separate or differentiated, a longed-for existence within the other. If we are afraid of those desires we may disparage them, refer to them as pathological remnants of our earliest days, acceptable only for nursing mothers and during mutual orgasm. Of course those desires equally direct our lives; they are manifest in our needs for trust, intimacy, communion, ecstasy, and transcendence throughout the life cycle. Our lives are shaped every day by the dialectic between our strivings for individuality and for union.

The family is also shaped by this dialectic. It might be argued that our own profound ambivalence about our participation in our families—both our families of origin and our families of adulthood—is at the source of the dialectic tension within our work. And so we simultaneously try to help our patients to transcend their families and to become part of them.

Within the family there are two bonds, two forms of relatedness. One set is the bonds of primary identification, symbolized in the mother–infant union and shared across the family. In the state of primary identification, self and other are not distinctly differentiated. Family loyalty, in its deepest sense, is one expression of that bond, the bond of blood. Hans Loewald says that these bonds are felt "to be sacred, to belong to a state of innocence" (1979, p. 396). A friend said to me that before he'd had children he could not have imagined throwing himself in front of a moving car to save another person's life. I had no children yet and I couldn't appreciate that feeling until I did. In the moment in which I throw myself in front of that car it will not make psychological sense to think of me as an individual. This thought seems so heretical that I want to bring Loewald to my side; speaking to this issue, he challenged our assumptions about the individual psyche: "Some of these problems, in my opinion, raise the important but largely unexplored and for the present unanswerable question whether we are justified in simply equating, as we do, the psychic life with the intrapsychic" (1979, p. 399). Let me illustrate what I believe Loewald had in mind.

After a disturbing hour with a patient, I went out to run an errand. As I headed down my driveway, I imagined that she was walking across the opening and that I willfully drove into her, chopping off her legs. The next day she told me that she'd had a dream that night of a person in a wheelchair, a double amputee. We had not had occasion to speak of cars, amputations, or other violence during the previous hours. I experienced this as a remarkable unconscious communion.

Near the end of an analysis, another patient said to me that she thought she'd never really taken me on during the treatment. I was surprised by this—she'd certainly yelled at me at the top of her lungs, read me the riot act, and defiantly walked out on a session at various times in our years together. After telling her this, I felt three violent muscular spasms in my neck, an experience I'd never had before (or since). She said, in the same instant, "You've never felt me pick you up by the scruff of the neck!"

What do I make of these uncanny events? I think that we communicate, continuously, in complex and subtle ways with one another, that a profoundly rich dialogue goes on between us out of our awareness, even at the level, as in these examples, of very specific phantasies. I have no idea whether these particular images originated in me or in the patient, or were a joint creation. But as in these cases, such events take place even when the patient is on the couch, ostensibly in a situation where nonverbal communication is diminished. In a similar vein, I believe that two people probably discover as much about each other in a certain way during their first ten seconds together as they will come to learn over the next twenty-five years. This is not to diminish what is revealed in that quarter-century, but to emphasize how extraordinarily much is sensed unconsciously almost immediately. Given then the remarkable density of our interpersonal experience, it makes sense to me to say, as Loewald does, that we are less individual than we realize, that the sharp boundedness of intrapsychic life is an illusion.

The other set of bonds, that coexist with primary identification, are the object ties, the bonds within which separateness is acknowledged. We think, in particular, of the oedipal bonds in which we, as separate individuals, struggle with loving and hating, caring, complaining, and, in the maturation of those bonds, teaching and learning. It is in the working through of oedipal conflicts (an ongoing challenge throughout the life cycle, hardly limited to 6-year-olds) that the contesting needs for autonomy and connection are negotiated. It is at the oedipal intersection that the thinker is confronted by the kiss.

When I returned to my bedroom at night and found my son asleep on my side of the mattress, and lifted him up and carried him back to his room, I was asserting that I was father and husband, and that he was son, defining each of us in our separateness. I felt some mixture of amusement and irritation with him for trying to appropriate my space, but in squaring things up I acknowledged who each of us was. I also think of the times when I was reading to my daughter and found her so magically enchanting that it was hard to leave her bed. The moment of lifting myself off the pillow was splashed with sadness, but I was again acknowledging who each of us was. That, in another telling, is what the working through of the Oedipus complex is about: the discovery of personhood.

And the crucial realization of personhood comes at the end of adolescence, not when the child is 6 or 7. The oedipal-age boy tries to take over his father's prerogatives by imitating his father's action, as though by doing what his father does he becomes his father. This identification rejects the differentiation of the two. My son, in my bed, was imagining that he was me. In accepting oedipal defeat he does not acquire his own identity, he bends to my will. The real challenge comes in late adolescence when the young man begins to find his own voice. Authority is now not being handed as a mantle from father to son; the young man discovers his own authority as he challenges his father, differentiates from him, and fashions an identity. Oedipus does not find his authority at the crossroads when he murders the king whom he does not know to be his father, or when he marries the woman he does not know to be his mother. He finds his authority when he blinds himself after Jocasta's suicide, after the truth has been uncoiled, for his authority comes from taking possession of his life, acknowledging authorship. The working through of the object ties, most vividly in the unfolding of oedipal relations that continues over our lifetime, both brings us to a realization of our separate selves and connects us to those we love.

A tension exists between these two forms of relatedness. Oedipal intensities threaten to disrupt the linkages of primary union, forcing a premature separation. Symbiotic longings interfere with working through the oedipal drama, mastering the guilt of parricide, and achieving individuation.

In the broadest sense, the other side of the psychoanalytic story, what has come to be called the relational side, arose in response to a need to give voice to the issues that are rooted in nondifferentiation and primary union. I do not mean by this that relational theorists are interested only in symbiotic strivings, but I do mean that their interests originate in the quality of existence that is not differentiated. That the two sides to the story exist and are in political conflict, that our journals are dense with subtle and not so subtle polemics on the issue, that case discussions degenerate into futile arguments about whether a patient's difficulties are oedipal or preoedipal as though these were separable categories of experience, is not simply a consequence of the inevitability of institutional conflict, or of the workings of the Oedipus complex, or the death instinct, or primal splitting, or a legacy of Freud's leadership, although all those may be involved. More fundamentally I am suggesting that the division is at the heart of human existence where we are all in conflict, for we are both one, alone, and not one, united.

This division can be symbolized as masculine and feminine, as phallic and receptive, as presence and absence. Let me frame the dichotomy yet another way: Freud's close associates were all men, Klein's women; Freud gave place of pride to the penis, Klein to the breast; Freud's epochal event was the struggle between father and son, Klein's was between infant and mother; Freud's interpretive voice was authoritative, rapierlike, intrusive, Klein's was containing, all-knowing; the father's daughter could not leave him, the mother's turned against her (Whitehead 1975).

As this contrast suggests, dialectic conflict is at the heart of our scientific evolution. We have id versus superego, parent versus child, masculine versus feminine, nature versus nurture, preoedipal versus oedipal, activity versus passivity, drive versus defense, interpretation versus resistance, love versus hate, aggression versus sexuality, the life instinct versus the death instinct, support versus insight—the list could fill pages. Many of these antinomies have become the grounds for political struggles (or one could argue that it works the other way around, that politics leads to conflict of ideology!). And so we have had Freud versus Jung, Freud versus Adler, the Freudians versus the Kleinians, the Kleinians versus the Independent Group, Lacan versus the International, Kernberg versus Kohut, the Kohutians versus everyone. The unfolding of a science may always resemble a drunk staggering up a street, first listing this way, then that, looking for the next lamppost to grab hold of. But just as the drunk eventually gets home, our theory gradually acquires depth as we move between points of illumination, using blacks and whites to fashion more interesting shades of gray.

PARADOX

I would like to exemplify these paradigms in yet another way, by locating them in our warpages of character. To become an individual, I must be capable of relatedness, for otherwise my individuality is a shell and I live in schizoid refuge. To be related, I must be capable of standing alone, for otherwise relatedness melts into merger, as the tiger who can only chase Little Black Sambo around the tree is reduced to butter. These are the paradoxes of development. We have our internal worlds to contend with, our personal anthologies of drama, drama not as faded text but as living theater, our trials and our passions. The schizoid lives in the privacy of that world, adamantly denying the possibility of novel experience, viewing the outside world only as a projection of an internal slide show. But even the internal experience becomes less comforting, increasingly persecutory, and so the schizoid tries to exterminate that world, to create an *internal* splendid isolation that matches the outside. Because the unconscious is indestructible, this effort will of course fail, and the schizoid lives in a rubble of relentlessly destroyed garbage, a world consumed by his own discarding. (The obsessional, in contrast, treasures his internal construction, is endlessly perfecting his doll house, then freezing it in time.)

If the schizoid is the paradigmatic unrelated individual, the borderline could be taken as the opposite pole, the unindividuated relational. The borderline appropriates the other people in his universe as vehicles for enacting his internal object life; he lives his life, so to speak, in the space between himself and the others. This, of course, makes him exhausting to treat or to live with. Where the schizoid seems to be supremely an individual, the borderline seems less than a person, more a part of a field. I am using the schizoid and the borderline as icons here, to represent two extreme positions in relation to the dialectic I have been discussing. In fact our schizoid and borderline patients each contain aspects of the other, as we all do.

THE READER AND THE LISTENER

Finally, I would like to explore these issues from another vantage point by looking at the text of a short play by Samuel Beckett, *Ohio Impromptu*. The poetic appeal of this play, for me, is that it expresses an individual's struggle between separateness and joining in the course of refinding himself as a person. Beckett's work further extends my understanding that these processes are quintessentially entwined.

Ohio Impromptu was written for a Beckett symposium at Ohio State University in 1981. A Listener and a Reader, identical in appearance, sit at a pine board table, and the Reader reads to the Listener from the last pages of a book. At intervals the Listener knocks on the table, thus directing the Reader to repeat himself. This is, abridged, the story he reads, which we may take to be the story of their relationship:

In a last attempt to obtain relief he moved from where they
had been so long together to a single room on the far bank.
[p. 28]

The story is about a man who has suffered a loss—perhaps a
death? Or is it a loss that was self-inflicted? And is the person trying to
find relief from being so long together, or from being alone?

. . . Relief he had hoped would flow from unfamiliarity. Unfamiliar room. Unfamiliar scene. Out to where nothing ever
shared. Back to where nothing ever shared.
. . . Day after day he could be seen slowly pacing the islet. . . .
At the tip he would always pause to dwell on the receding
stream. How in joyous eddies its two arms conflowed and flowed
united on. Then turn and his slow steps retrace. [p. 29]

While hoping to find relief in negation, in the abolition of meaning
and connection, the man in the story is drawn each day to pace the islet,
to watch the two arms of the stream conflow and flow united on, to
remind himself of the connection he has lost. And all the time we hear
the repetition, day after day, his slow steps retraced, as repetition itself
creates meaning. We find ourselves by making ourselves familiar.
    A colleague, reading this, comments: "I've always been struck by
the isolation of the different camps within psychoanalytic theory and
practice. Major theorists often claim never to have read the works of
others. This lack of connection is replaced by the connection of
repetition—same colleagues, same conferences, same type of patients . . . I remember when I used to enjoy going to different restau-
rants and could not understand why some people—usually middle-
aged and over—always returned to the same restaurant and, worse yet,
ordered the same meal. Now I find myself going in that direction."

. . . In his dreams he had been warned against this change. Seen
the dear face and heard the unspoken words, Stay where we were
so long alone together, my shade will comfort you. . . .

. . . Could he not now turn back? Acknowledge his error and
return to where they were once so long alone together. Alone
together so much shared. No. What he had done alone could not
be undone. Nothing he had ever done alone could ever be
undone. By him alone. [pp. 30–31]

Could he find shelter in his dear friend's spectral presence?
Return to memory for comfort? He judges that that would be an
evasion, an attempt to undo his action, thus an obliteration of his self.
He chose to leave and he is defined by that commitment. The refusal
to repeat, to return, creates meaning. We find ourselves by making
ourselves unfamiliar. (This is what psychoanalysis teaches us, that we
find ourselves precisely by making ourselves both familiar and unfamiliar.) But we face our novelty with fear and trembling:

. . . In this extremity his old terror of night laid hold on him
again. . . . Now with redoubled force. . . . White nights now
against his portion. As when his heart was young. No sleep no
braving sleep till—(turns page)—dawn of day.

[One night a man appeared and said that he had been sent by the
dear name to comfort him and he read to him until dawn.] So
from time to time unheralded he would appear to read the sad
tale through again and the long night away. Then disappear
without a word. . . . With never a word exchanged they grew to
be as one. [pp. 31–33]

In telling and retelling his story, listening to himself, he came to
recognize himself, to discover his narrator, that is, to discover himself
as his narrator. (This is the person we hope to ultimately locate
through treatment, the self who is the teller of the story. Until that self
is found we remain a cast of characters, milling around backstage,
waiting to be brought together.)

[Finally one night the visitor said that he had received word from
the dear one that he was not to come again.] So the sad tale

a last time told they sat on as though turned to stone. Through the single window dawn shed no light. From the street no sound of reawakening. Or was it that buried in who knows what thoughts they paid no heed? To light of day. To sound of reawakening . . . [they sat] Buried in who knows what profounds of mind. Of mindlessness. Whither no light can reach. No sound. Sat on as though turned to stone. The sad tale a last time told. (Pause) Nothing is left to tell. [p. 34]

Reading and rereading *Ohio Impromptu*, I find in it a moving description of the struggle to mourn, to separate, to join, to become a person. A terrible loneliness has set in. While in his dreams the man regrets the move, he is determined to stand his ground, as though the only possibility for living requires that he bear being alone. At the same time, it is only through finding a connection with the other that he can come to survive his aloneness. At the end the Reader will leave, but the two will also join together, joined as one as though turned to stone, and perhaps the Reader will read this story to the Listener about the reader and the listener every night forever. It is the paradox of our work that we come together with our patients, that we enable them to love us and to accept our love for them, so that they can bear to be alone. The kiss created by the thinker; the thinker created by the kiss.

PART 2

VISIONS OF THERAPY

5

Therapy as Marriage

Over the course of the next four chapters, I will be examining several ways of thinking about the therapeutic process. Each of these accounts of treatment elaborates aspects of the two-person model. This chapter explores how the therapeutic situation in many important regards resembles marriage, which of course is the prototypic dyadic situation. While this model has obvious limitations, most notably the absence of a somatic or sexual integration of the treatment pair, in many ways the analogy captures crucial aspects of the structure of the psychotherapy relationship.

The customary analogue for therapy has been the parent–child relationship. Leo Stone (1961) and Hans Loewald (1960) have offered us especially eloquent versions of this model. Stone proposed that the analyst's functioning corresponds to that of the mother of the incipiently separating 2-year-old who is beginning to use language to mediate experience. The analyst, by creating a context in which his patient will be helped to put words to her experience, facilitates her efforts to integrate and differentiate her world. The use of the analytic couch is a key element in the process. Because the patient's opportunity for nonverbal expression is reduced, she must find words to communicate her experience to the analyst. Like the mother with her child, the analyst moves his patient toward self-expression. For Loewald, the analyst is in the position of the parent who both empathically appreciates the child's developmental situation and holds in his mind a view of the child's potentialities, mediating this vision to the child in the course of their interactions.

While both Stone and Loewald offer useful constructions of the analytic experience, many other applications of the parent–child model present real problems. Uses of the model generally tend to be unacknowledged, and are perhaps made manifest in a patriarchal writing voice, or in a parental treatment style. It is too comfortable for therapist and patient to view themselves as parent and child, even seductive we might say. We all long for a wise protective authority. The patient invests her therapist with that power and the therapist finds security in identifying with his patient's idealization of him. Or, in another sense, it is the ruse of the oedipal child who hides erotic claims on the parent behind babyish appeals – and even the ruse of the parent who conspires with the concealment to mask his own desires. In these ways, the parent–child version of the treatment relationship is an enactment of childhood wishes. I can already hear many perfectly responsible therapists protesting that they don't think this way. Perhaps not – but to a surprising degree, as you listen to case discussions and to accounts of supervisions, you hear therapists *acting* this way. We begin to sense some of the limitations of the parent–child model.

Consider, instead, the usefulness of courtship and marriage as a model for the therapeutic relationship. Both parties enter the relationship voluntarily, as equal partners. They take some time to size each other up before making the commitment, and yet the joining together, for all its intuitive resonance, must largely be an act of faith. Both are committed to working out the relationship, although narcissistic needs will at times supervene. Both parties are free to dissolve the partnership at any time, a most significant point of difference from the parent–child relationship. The association progresses through its seasons, and the relationship deepens as the two come to know each other. The deepening occurs as both partners process their transferences toward each other. They create something which is a product of their own conception and which yet is independent of them as individuals. If the compact is spared premature rupture, it will end with a loss—although this is a point at which the analogy fares less well, for the nature of the losses, and the responses to them, markedly differ in marriage and treatment. I would now like to take up a number of these aspects in more detail.

EQUALITY

Because the need for help rests predominantly on the patient's side, and the helping expertise on the therapist's, it is easy to obscure the fundamental equality of the relationship. The patient's dependency shadows the reality that she is hiring a therapist to work on her behalf—a not uncommon eventuality when a professional is hired for any purpose, although the voluntary nature of the fee situation is more likely to be denied when dependency is in the picture. Patients may threaten to leave treatment, but they never threaten to fire me. (In fact, putting the patient's threat to leave in those terms may have a salutary effect. Then again, Freud was not open to hearing that his adolescent patient, Dora, considered him hired help [Malcolm 1987].)

The parent–child psychotherapy model can easily be taken to imply that the therapist has greater authority, based on his parental status. Authority rightly derives from role and task (Shapiro and Carr 1991). The therapist, in his role, brings certain knowledge and an empathic capacity to the task of helping the patient to clarify her difficulties. He can never know for certain what his patient is thinking or feeling, although he may have strong hunches; an interpretation must always start off as a hypothesis. One can never be absolutely certain that a patient is resisting one's interpretation, because the possibility always remains that one has not yet fully understood the situation. Most therapists have memories of having been caught off guard in that respect. The patient, in her role, brings her own best understanding of herself to the task; her authority derives from her honest commitment to that end. The patient does not *only* free-associate in psychoanalysis; if all goes well, she also uses her capacity to think, to differentiate and synthesize. Nevertheless, we have all listened to authoritarian accounts of treatments that wreak havoc with these sensibilities.

Thus the fundamental equality of the relationship in adult psychotherapy rests in the fact that both parties have chosen to work together toward a common goal, the relief of the patient's suffering. Yet in discussions of treatment, when the need for a working alliance between the participants is raised, we are told that the alliance is developed through the initiatives of the therapist—in particular, through the therapist's facilitating his patient's identification with his way of working, with his work ego. In this view, the problem would then be the patient's failure to accept certain aspects of the parent-child relationship implicit in the treatment. It would be far more apt to perceive the problem as the patient's persistent refusal to acknowledge, in all the forms that the acknowledgement must take, the *equality*—and the *mutuality*—of the endeavor. This perception would then necessitate an exploration of all the covert purposes served by the patient's avoidance, what in other terms might be called a dissection of her character structure and defenses; and this inquiry might constitute, or at least be a developing theme in, the first three-quarters of the treatment, leaving only the termination remaining to be dealt with. This, in fact, is what happens in most treatments, although the task is not conceptualized this way—it tends to be thought of as the therapist making a child into an adult. But it is certainly common that toward the end of treatment the quality of the dialogue shifts, that the work is experienced more as a partnership, and it may be precisely this that signifies the approaching conclusion. At the end of *Portnoy's Complaint*, we hear the analyst announce: "Now vee may perhaps to begin. Yes?" (Roth 1969, p. 274). Certainly, if a couple came to see me and I was impressed by a marked power imbalance in their marriage, I would see my work as exploring the defensive purposes served by their form of engagement. I certainly would not formulate this as promoting the internalization of a marital alliance.

No matter what the circumstances, I think that the treatment is always carried, in some fundamental sense, by the mutual awareness that it is a joint proposition, and that the tilt created by the patient's dependency never completely undermines this knowledge. Without this recognition the patient's resentment, played out in a host of ways, would be so great as to make treatment impossible. We get a glimpse of this in certain situations—when treatment is forced, or when the patient is not expected to pay a customary fee, for example. In these arrangements, the therapist in fact becomes a coercive or infantalizingly beneficent parent, as the following case illustrates:

Appreciating a college student's limited finances, I told him that I could treat him on a low-fee basis by making him a patient in our psychoanalytic clinic. I was required to see one person through the clinic as part of my training, and I decided that this would be in our mutual interest. I did not discuss this with him in any detail, but treated it as a fait accompli. In making the offer, I was also responding unwittingly to his presentation of himself as a depleted, helpless child. I needed to locate all my own felt helplessness as a novitiate in him.

In the next session, now on the couch, his first words were "I'll let you fill me in," followed by a prolonged apparently unanxious silence. When his silence had made me sufficiently anxious, I suggested that he describe to me a concrete image. He generously offered a picture of white fluid flowing from a truck into his mouth! In this comic theatrical homosexual quasi-compliance, I saw him converting my milk of human kindness into concrete, which would surely congeal in his stomach. So much for well-intentioned mothers.

Years later in the treatment, I reopened the fee issue. I discovered that the trust fund his grandparents had set up for him was not being used for college and thus could be used for the analysis. Had I been open to knowing it, I might have discovered this a lot earlier. I did, nonetheless, feel cheated; perhaps that mirrored what he had been feeling. After considerable (this time!) exploration, we raised his fee substantially. We both felt some relief. The low fee had meant both my devaluing him and his colluding with his father to defraud me. Now he feared I would exploit his love. He was uncertain whether the fee he proposed was too large or still too small (it was nearly a full fee), but he felt proud of his initiative and then dreamed of outrunning an atomic explosion— escaping my retaliation. (Could I really bear for him to be grown up?) Certain insensitivities on my part, which he might well have ignored in the past, now led to his reporting bowel sicknesses and disrupted functioning. He thought that lying on my couch had led to his swallowing mucus and getting diarrhea. He revealed that in a passive eroticization he had asked for and received enemas from his mother after his brother's birth.

In the context of my working my way free from a treatment situation in which I had infantilized him, he could now experience the analysis as a safer place in which he could regress in the service of our work together. What had originally been a glib satire of analysis—his image of the concrete—could now yield to a rich and actually gut-wrenching exploration of his phantasies of how I was affecting his insides.

It is only in the context of experiencing treatment as a mutual undertaking that the patient can make use of it for growthful regressive purposes. This, to be sure, is also true of marriage!

ENGAGEMENT

Marrying is a manic act, a vanquishing of childhood. All the complexities of longing and hurt, the unresolved attachments to mother, to father, to family, are overthrown and life begins afresh. When we consider how much has to be dispensed with, this is a remarkable achievement, for a fair inquiry into our characters would give us much reason to pause about our prospects for transcending our pasts. And so marriage, at least for the young, and probably also for the not-so-young, needs to be founded in an act of denial. Falling in love, whatever else it might represent, is an act of great hopefulness, making the partner magical.

Entering therapy is also a manic gesture, more obviously so for the patient. Most of our clients come to us after a host of discouraging experiences with potentially helpful partners, from parents to lovers to friends, and yet the flame still flickers in their hearts that they will find in us the long-sought companion. In spite of their awareness of their ability to abuse relationships, even to shatter them, hope springs anew that this time they can do it right. Therapy is a rebirth, a new beginning. This is the phantasy that guides all relationship seeking: it can be done right this time, the past can be recreated, restaged, this time with a different ending—the past can be unmade. A sense of timelessness courses through this vision. To the degree that patients (and marital partners) are able to make this manic gesture their prospects seem improved. (Which is not to say that skeptics aren't sometimes transformed by treatment and marriage.) And the gesture may later stand as a bulwark against harder times.

We see the absence of this capacity in couples that live together but are unable to marry. For some, it is the inability to live in time. Burdened by the past, experiencing the present relationship only as a continuation of that past, they imagine marriage to be a commitment to an unbearable fate. For them, *not marrying* is an attempt to suspend time, a protest against the relentless oppression of their inner lives. For others, it is an inability to overthrow authority, a surrender to the external, now internal, parental objects. The husband in an unmarried couple is unable to challenge his chronic invalid father. His wife hides in the shadow of her profligate mother. They have lived for years like children together, both terrified of adulthood, deeply identified with their parents and also experiencing their parents in each other, the identification being a defense against the necessary rebellion.

It is also helpful if the therapist can take his patient on for treatment without reservation, and therapists are ordinarily able to do this. At times, this may require a suspension of disbelief comparable to that made by the patient. When confronted with great psychopathology, it would be all too easy to surrender to hopelessness, or, more likely, to benign indifference. Hearing that I am about to become someone's sixth therapist is usually enough to stop me dead in my tracks, but I find some way to recover. The state of mind I am talking about here should not, of course, be confused with optimism, for optimism on the therapist's part can sink any ship. I am thinking more about the enthusiasm that beginning therapists bring to their work, which surprisingly often works miracles for patients whom an outsider would view with despair.

JOINING

The great threat of marriage is the loss of individuality. We are terrified by our longing to merge with the other (Freud's lost object refound) — I remember a friend who, hedging his bets, always referred to his wife as his "first wife." We are terrified by the tempting invitation to play out all our inner dramas with an intimate partner, by incestuous desire, by the power of shared identifications. Love wrenches us from our privacy. But at the same moment, love separates us from our past, from childhood and family, as it constitutes a new beginning. As we experience that loss, we discover our individuality, we are no longer only our parents' children. This paradox of marriage, that it both creates and undermines our individuality, is what gives it the potential to promote our development as adults. Each intensity of interdependence evokes a regressive turn in which the old problems are experienced anew — once more a wife becomes a mother, or a projection of an injured child self. (See Frank's (1989) essay "Who Are You and What Have You Done with My Wife?") Each working-through of those intensities (intensities that surface in part with the seasonal changes of the life cycle) helps us to define ourselves more sharply, to recreate ourselves as persons with pasts, not as persons created by pasts.

Marriage, in this sense, is the adult working-through of an ongoing rapprochement crisis. Drawing the parallel to the toddler's movements toward and away from its mother, we might think of this as cycles of remarriage and divorce. Along these lines Cavell (1981), who has defined the genre of Hollywood remarriage films, observed that "the intimacy conditional on narcissism or incestuousness must be ruptured in order that an intimacy of difference or reciprocity supervene" (p. 103). Picking up on Freud's thought that first marriages often don't work out for women because they repeat with their husbands their bad relations with their mothers, Cavell counters, "The moral of the genre of remarriage might be formulated so as to include the observation that even good marriages have to be shed; in happy circumstances they are able to shed themselves, in their own favor" (p. 139). The quest, in truth, is not the one we thought we were setting off on, and we find ourselves only through losing ourselves, again and again.

We can replay the last two paragraphs, substituting therapy for marriage. I use this device to highlight the parallels:

The great threat of treatment is the loss of individuality. We are terrified by our longing to merge with the other (Freud's lost object refound)—for safety we might hedge our bets and call our therapists our "first therapists." It's not unusual for analytic trainees to imagine that after they complete their training analyses they'll have real analyses. We are terrified by the tempting invitation to play out all our inner dramas with an intimate partner, a therapist. We are frightened by incestuous desire, by the power of shared identifications. Therapy wrenches us from our privacy. But at the same moment, treatment separates us from our past, from childhood and family, as it constitutes a new beginning. As we experience that loss, we discover our individuality; we are no longer only our parents' children or our therapists' patients. This paradox of treatment, that it both creates and undermines our individuality, is what gives it the potential to promote our development as adults. Each intensity of interdependence evokes a regressive turn in which the old problems are experienced anew—once more the therapist becomes a sibling, a father, a projection of unbearable self. Each working-through of those intensities (intensities that surface in part with the seasonal changes of the therapeutic process) helps us to more sharply define ourselves, to recreate ourselves as persons with pasts, not as persons created by pasts, to turn ghosts into ancestors.

Therapy, in this sense, is the adult working-through of an ongoing rapprochement crisis, a process we might think of as cycles of engagement and retreat. Some first therapies fail because the patient is unable to recognize that her therapist is not only her parent. Patients repeat with their therapists their bad relations with their mothers. "The intimacy conditional on narcissism or incestuousness must be ruptured in order that an intimacy of difference or reciprocity supervene." And "the moral of the genre [of therapy] might be formulated so as to include the observation that even good [therapies] have to be shed; in happy circumstances they are able to shed themselves, in their own favor." The quest, in truth, is not the one we thought we were setting off on, and we find ourselves only through losing ourselves, again and again.

The process I have just described is an accounting of what happens when therapy is going well. We are well familiar, of course, with the patient who barricades herself in her person-hood.

A colleague described to me a patient who refused to let herself feel that she required him. Whenever he announced a planned vacation, she sandwiched his time off between two vacations of her own. His absence was to go unnoticed. On one occasion, however, he had to take leave on short notice. She caught her breath—and in that moment saw the image of herself she had been so determined not to acknowledge: a person in need. She left the session and never returned.

I treated a likable young man who enjoyed meeting with me but who was also determined that nothing fundamental in his life was to change. He had married a woman who seemed to be so impossibly self-righteous (she'd worn out a couple of therapists already) that hope never needed to be on the horizon. A 10-year-old sister had been given up to a foster family when he was a toddler, and I came to believe that he felt impelled to sit perfectly still lest he suffer a comparable fate.

One summer afternoon, after a lengthy detour, he allowed as how his mother had just been found to have an inoperable cancer—an event that I imagined might shake even *his* capacity for self-containment. As we spoke, a sudden storm blew up and within moments the world outside my windows had turned pitch black. Rains lashed the office. The winds were later judged to have been blowing at over 100 miles an hour. During this downdraft, as such meteorological events are called, three huge trees on my property were knocked over and it was a measure of the loudness of the storm that we did not hear them fall.

Through all this, my patient went on, unperturbed, telling me about his mother. I remarked on the storm and he shrugged the comment off. I wondered whether I might be exaggerating in my mind the violence of what was happening outside; perhaps I was unconsciously reacting to the prospect of his mother's death, imagining cancer striking my own family, feeling his repressed rage. As I mused about this, my wife knocked on the office door and ordered us into the main house, which was more strongly constructed. Our neighbor's house had already been caved in. I felt nonplused by my ability to join my patient's capacity for denial. It turned out that our street was entirely blockaded by fallen trees and my patient needed to have his wife retrieve him on an open road a few blocks away. Throughout the entire event, he seemed unshakable.

I worked with a young woman who for the first 3 years of the treatment, then taking place three times a week, sat with her back to me and spoke only on the rarest of occasions despite countless attempts on my part to engage (entreat, seduce, browbeat, cajole) her. From early in the treatment, I experienced seeing her as an act of self-sacrifice. Feeling inept, awkward, even silly, I survived the hours. At times I felt desperate to get a response from her, any response, and I was aware of my pathetic gratitude for any crumbs thrown my way. She seemed to deeply mistrust me, and I could find no way around that.

When her mother succumbed to a fulminant cancer, she remarked, with estranged dispassion, that her mother had died today. Customarily, however, I heard her news months, even seasons, after it had occurred—she'd had a boyfriend and they had broken up, she'd had an abortion, she'd moved in with a roommate—she would tell me late enough that I couldn't get my hands on it, couldn't wreck it, couldn't possibly tell her where she'd gone wrong. The telling, by this time, was of course serving another purpose—a veiled arch comment on the state of our own affairs.

I will have more to report to you about my work with her later in the text, but at the moment I would like to comment on one turning point in the treatment:

On a Valentine's Day, five years into our work together, she noticed, for the first time, that others at her apartment complex had had valentines awaiting them at the desk when they returned from work. She had allowed herself, for a remarkable moment, to defrost her ice citadel, to feel sadness, to entertain the possibility of being cared for by the sender of valentines, to imagine that she might want a valentine from me. Now brought to life in this way, she soon fell in love with her previously devalued father.

It is not only patients who cling to their individuality. Whether the analyst's emotional engagement with his patients is viewed as a useful dimension of the work or as an interference with the task is the watershed that divides the psychoanalytic literature on technique. In 1953, Eissler introduced the concept of the parameter, a noninterpretive action on the analyst's part required to advance the treatment. In the intervening four decades, this term has become a critical judgment invoked to blaspheme another's technique. (I remember a teacher commenting when I was in medical school that 90 percent of our psychological comments about our friends are hostile in intent. He was being generous. Ninety percent of our comments about parameters are hostile in intent.) *Parameter* is now a term used to signify that the therapist has toppled over the barrier designed to separate him from his patient. It indicates that losing his balance, he has breached his separate stance.

When our patients throw a punch, they need to hear the sound of leather striking leather. When therapy is reduced to shadowboxing, it is a caricature of treatment, shadow puppet play. None of this, however, should be taken to imply that the therapist actively seeks out engagement, or that his response should be deliberately enactive. The vectors of the process will create engagement enough, and his work is, ultimately, to recover his balance and sort it all out. In raising the issue, however, I am thinking of the determinedly bloodless accounts one so frequently encounters in the literature, when the analyst seems to be observing the patient with binoculars across a chasm. These treatments seem more like mannered performances than therapeutic encounters—a characterization that would also be apt for some marriages. Then again, we may simply be suffering at the hands of shy writers who are too embarrassed to let us in.

CHOICE

Parents and children are free to abuse each other, knowing that the other really has nowhere to turn. While that state of involuntary commitment may at times be a shared sensibility in the treatment (most poignantly, perhaps, for the patient who feels that this is his final chance and most chronically in sadomasochistic couplings), the reality remains that each hour can be made to be the last one, unilaterally, by each party. In the same sense that an imminent hanging does wonders to sharpen the senses (and recognizing that at the same time one might share what the prosecutor imagined to be Dmitri's hopeful sensibility in *The Brothers Karamazov* [1991]: many houses still remain to be passed before reaching the gallows), this reality hangs over the treatment and gives at least a little urgency to the proceedings. In contemporary marriage the possibility of divorce prompts the partners to try a bit harder, to try to make contact.

It is common practice for therapists to urge patients who have chosen to terminate unilaterally by mail or phone, or in the closing words of an hour, to come in for a final session. While this practice has certain advantages, the foremost being that the patient may be talked into changing his mind, it is worth recognizing that this gesture undercuts the patient's freedom to have the last word. The ending will now be on the therapist's terms. For therapy to be useful, the patient must be free to act destructively. To make matters worse, such hours tend to end in handshakes and assurances by the therapist of future availability, which may or may not have been solicited by the patient, but if solicited will mainly have been only a sop thrown in the therapist's direction.

A very troubled patient was gleefully enjoying tormenting me with tales of his misadventures. His evening routine had settled into stopping at every bar on his route back to his apartment, then imagining that a woman he was interested in was persecuting him by hanging around his building. His sadistic treatment of me and my helplessness to affect him closely paralleled what he had described of his fate at his mother's hands, but that recognition had taken us nowhere. I became even more alarmed when he told me that he'd taken to following the woman around town, and had put sugar in the gas tank of her car, a potentially homicidal act. I felt that I was a spectator watching a locomotive steaming down a hill out of control, helpless to stop the impending crash. Suddenly recognizing that this was my situation, I realized that I was in fact free to act, and I terminated the treatment. To be precise about it, I told him that I would only see him if he came in four times a week, not once a week—an offer I was certain he would refuse, although I had made it in good faith. Hospitalization didn't seem to be a realistic option, as I did not believe that a hospital would hold him against his will for very long. I heard some months later from him that after we had stopped he had settled down.

I am certainly open to the idea that I missed the boat with this man, that I might have found another way to work with him that would have been more productive. My point here, however, is that recognizing I felt paralyzed in the situation freed me to realize that I had a choice, and I was then in a position to make a decision about participating in the treatment. This was, in fact, a choice he had not felt free to make with his mother—he had put his adult life on hold for several years at one point, refusing to work or engage in social relationships, while he watched her slowly die of cancer. My action in ending our therapy may even have been of use to him, although it seems defensive to try to put too cheery a face on the matter.

Although the current propensity in our culture to readily opt for divorce as a solution to marital discord has its many dark sides, it may be that the practice has bought us to value marriage more, to take marital unhappiness less for granted. Maybe this is not simply putting a cheerful face on *that* subject.

CONCEPTION

Marriage might be thought of as a cultural evolutionary achievement, designed to promote the survival of the species by intermixing internal object pools. Partner selection is guided in large part by our need to recreate our internal object worlds in our actual lives. Our motives are twofold. First, patterns of relationship established in childhood are meaningful, and familiarity breeds content. Fairbairn (1952) has referred to this as our loyalty to our inner object relations, and it is exemplified by the woman whose situation I noted a little earlier:

> My patient who did not receive valentines had apparently had a truly torturous relationship with her mother. By the time she was 3, her mother had taken to calling her "my miserable rotten child." She has a memory of hiding under the bed at age 4 while her mother called the rag man to take her away. I was told that her mother hung a card on my patient's door that had a picture of a good girl on one side and that of a bad girl on the other. Except on rare occasions the bad girl was face up. In treatment, the patient was mainly my miserable rotten child— except for those times when she treated me as though I were hers. And I certainly had my moments of feeling perfectly enraged with her. In time I came to understand that she felt connected to me through this particular path of relatedness, that we were engaged in something deeply meaningful to her. This was especially apparent on those occasions when, in the course of our work, a warm front settled in—then

she'd become anxious, as though in unfamiliar and dangerous weather, and this state of mind would persist until she could resurrect our struggle. At which point she was back home.

Our second motive in externalizing the struggle is to grapple with the issues involved. It is an irony fundamental to human experience that we always want it both to come out the same and to come out differently. In the ordinary course of things, the marital partner will be a foil for the reenactment—both because of our expertise in casting and recruitment, and because of our plasticity— but will in some regards resist the scripting—because in fact the partner will internally have other fish to fry. The fit can be too good of course, and the partners may settle into a malignant stalemate, or it can be so bad that divorce becomes the likely outcome. But in most marriages it is precisely the partial fit that makes revision and growth possible. The partner takes in the spouse's projections and processes them in the context of an internal object world that is not only like but also unlike that of the spouse. Most fundamentally, difference is insured by the fact of differing genders, and similarity by the circumstance that both had mothers. The outcome is a measure of transformation. Marriage then becomes not only a developmental challenge but also a facilitator of development in waves of regression and restitution.

This is, to my way of thinking, also how psychotherapy works, and it is my strongest reason for choosing marriage as the analogue to treatment. Therapists are able to help patients not because they are wiser, more mature, or less conflicted, for they may, in a given instance, be none of these. They are able to help their patients because they are both like them and different from them, because psychic flexibility makes empathy and identification possible, and because they are trained to turn these factors to the advantage of treatment. In the course both of marriage and of psychotherapy respectively, at critical junctures the partners' projective systems coalesce into shared unconscious assumptions (Shapiro 1989) that regulate and stabilize their interaction, at the price of restricting growth. It is the therapist's training, facilitated by his own experience in treatment, that enables him to work his way free from this conspiracy. Therapy works in cycles of loyalty and mutiny.

> A middle-aged patient told me that she and her older brother had coped with the misery of their childhoods through a nightly experience in which he read to her and they then engaged in sex play, which included intercourse. This had ended at her brother's insistence when she was 7 because he had become afraid of impregnating her. She had never forgiven him for stopping.
>
> In psychoanalysis, my patient found the limitations of the therapeutic relationship intolerable. She peeked inside my car, watered my waiting-room plants, stole food from the kitchen adjacent to my waiting room, and contorted herself on the couch wishing that I would anally penetrate her. I found her relentlessly demanding. Two years into the treatment, to my astonishment, I discovered that I was not certain that this woman would not succeed in seducing me, despite my lack of conscious sexual attraction to her. She was, after all (indeed!), old enough to be my mother. I discovered that we shared a belief that the appeal of incest was irresistible. The dawning awareness that she would actually not be able to seduce me was followed by my realization that she was perfectly capable of destroying the treatment. This double recognition allowed me to move the treatment forward.

This example highlights for me the center of the therapeutic process. I had been captured by my patient's incestuous experience of relationships, and I had not been aware that this had happened. I had tolerated her continual invasions of my privacy because I had unconsciously believed that in some sense she was entitled to them. I had identified with her conflict, and it had rubbed against my own incestuous issues. While the process occurred out of my awareness, or at least out of the range of any focused awareness, I now imagine that I must have finally been able to feel an attraction to her—that is, to finally have stopped defending against feeling it—so that I could register the seduction and then take my measure of it. I could master the experience when I stopped blocking it. This resourceful woman was then able to make good use of the following four years of treatment, which included her employing it for growth through regressive experience. She became able to express her sexual longing and her conflicts about her desire in a way that she could learn from. Had I been able to keep enough distance from her not to feel her incestuous demand in the first place, I believe that I would have ultimately been of less use to her.

In the course of both marriage and treatment, the conflict resolutions of childhood are reworked. In that sense, both marriage and treatment offer developmental second chances. The seasons of marriage—pairing, developing a sexual/somatic bond, moving to threeness with the addition of children, identifying with the children through the various stages and conflicts of childhood, suffering the losses of the children's emancipation, rejoining at midlife, bearing the losses of aging—offer the chance to find new solutions to the oldest problems. This can also be said for the seasons of therapy. The developmental issues that Stone and Loewald raised can alternatively be thought about as childhood issues reworked in therapy *conceptualized as marriage*, in the ways that marriage ordinarily offers an arena for these reworkings.

PARTING

Parting is a quite different issue in marriage and in psychotherapy; the contrast may be instructive. Workable marriages have an aura of everlastingness. While the threat of loss through death appears on the horizon at midlife, that anxiety commingles with fear of personal death and becomes part of the growing awareness that everything will end, that loss is inescapable. Those thoughts will be on the minds of patient and therapist also, especially if they themselves have crested the rise, but there will also be an awareness that the objective of the work is separation, helping the patient to negotiate her life more effectively on her own, and this is not central to the meaning of marriage. In another sense, termination may resemble that marital situation in which one member of the couple is dying and this fact is acknowledged by both. The mutually felt pressure to make the most of the available time, the willingness to take greater risks knowing that the sun will set, may characterize both endeavors.

The irony of therapy is that every step forward, every deepening move, brings therapist and patient closer to separation. Joining and loss are thus simultaneous aspects of therapy's best moments. This has its special usefulness, because in a certain sense therapy is always about working through losses, and foremost among them are the losses of omnipotence and innocence. The nature of therapy's ending is such that the separation of parent and child at the end of adolescence constitutes a useful analogue, a conception that I will develop later in the text.

Practitioners might resist placing psychotherapy in the frame of marriage because it shifts the power structure of the relationship. We find it more comfortable as therapists to have the deck slope in our direction. It has been observed that analysts tend to fail to recognize transference material that unfolds along adolescent development lines. Conflicts related to adolescence are often misread as expressing earlier issues—an error easy to make, because the struggles of adolescence do recapitulate childhood conflicts. The truth is that analysts usually find it more comfortable to think of their patients as miscreant children who might be carried to their rooms than as strapping adolescents who are too big to manhandle. Considering therapy a form of marriage is likely to meet comparable resistance, because it deprives the therapist of one measure of his authority. Marriage is about mutuality and passion, touchy issues for the therapist.

6

Therapy as Narrative: Stories

During the past decade considerable interest has developed in the idea that new light can be shed on the psychoanalytic process by considering it as the unfolding of a narrative, constructed by the analyst and patient working together. Some writers have approached this as a question of meanings – they ask what sort of meanings can be developed in the therapeutic situation. This has led to quite complex arguments about the nature of experience and reality (e.g., Grünbaum 1990, Hanly 1990, and Sass and Woolfolk 1988). Hanly (1992) sums up the question being debated this way: "Is psychoanalysis an empirical science or is it a hermeneutic psychology?" (p. 293). His concerns are expressed in the final sentence of his summary: "If these experiments in theory testing are reliable they show that psychoanalysis is not limited to being a hermeneutic discipline but rather has legitimate claims to be a natural science" (p. 301). Limitation and legitimacy are at stake in this debate.

The controversy has generated considerable heat. Valenstein (1989), for example, in response to Spence (1982) and Schafer (1982), proposes that "reconstructive work in analysis is to be distinguished from the ingenious innovation between patient and analyst, but more led by the analyst, of a coherent material or historical narrative which may serve plausibility and even carry conviction, but which only incidentally, if at all, holds within it some element of historical truth" (p. 434). I believe that his argument is based on a false dichotomy between narrative truth and historical truth. In contrast, Leavy (1980) says: "It would . . . be naive to claim that our progress in analyzing is also a progress away from the fictive to the realistic narrative; all we can claim is a more inclusive and coherent story as the basis of our history" (p. 99). As we enter this discussion, we will take care to consider the question of the nature of psychic reality.

In my mind, the narrative model is embedded in two-person psychology; the narrative of the treatment is quintessentially coauthored. Furthermore, because (as I will be demonstrating) the nature of psychic reality is such that neither party can claim *certain* knowledge, all psychoanalytic meanings must be *negotiated*. The process of negotiation, from another perspective, is the creation of the narrative. Without a *collaborative* perspective, the therapist is in danger of treating what can at most be his hunches as things that he believes are known. Shapiro and Carr (1991) refer to this outcome as the development of pathological certainty. Played out between patient and therapist, this would be an adult version of a problem that has its roots in childhood—the parents' contribution to the child's development of a "false self" (Winnicott 1960b). With reference to the childhood situation, Shapiro and Carr (1991) comment:

> The creation of a false self, which hinges on *both* the parents' pathological certainty and the child's willingness (unconscious) to sacrifice his true self to his parents' needs, illuminates the existence of a third aspect of the parent–child relationship: the "parent–child unit." The parent–child unit transcends both

parent and child and describes the context within which their
relationship develops. [p. 15]

In psychotherapy we have the therapist–patient unit transcending
both parties and identifying the context in which therapy develops.
The therapist–patient unit executes the authorship function that
creates the joint narrative. This cannot be conceptualized within a
one-person framework.

To explore this further we must turn to the subject matter of our
craft: psychic reality.

PSYCHIC REALITY

Constructions and Motives

The material that we're working toward in therapy falls into two main
categories: constructions and motives. Constructions are the ways in
which we make sense of our worlds; they are what constitute psychic
reality. Our motives are our intentions. Constructions and motives
are intricately related: intentions exist only in relation to the ways we
organize the world. The wish for revenge doesn't arise from the
unconscious searching for a target; it surfaces because of perceptions
about felt injury. Neither constructions nor motivations are trans-
parent to the therapist. The kind of constructions we're interested in
are always based on highly complex integrations of real experience
and phantasy. No accounting of a childhood—or of an afternoon
outing, for that matter—can be taken at face value. And those
intentions of which we take special notice are usually so problematic
for the individual that they are hidden behind intricate countermea-
sures (recognizing that we are at war, we call them defenses).

I want to dwell on these two categories of experience because
certain discussions of treatment tend to highlight memory and stifle
desire. The past that we wish to retrieve in therapy is not simply an
itinerary of events, it is also a reckoning of purposes. In the transfer-

ence we not only want to know what our patients make of us, we also want to know what they want to do to us. Motives are harder to acknowledge than happenings – they usually arouse more embarrassment, more shame and guilt. One of the important contributions of the Kleinian group has been to keep motives in the foreground. Conversely, relational theorists are often accused of downplaying motivation, making the patient a passive victim. The idea that therapy can be thought about as a construction of a narrative might be taken to mean that patient and therapist will concoct a congenial fable to encapsulate experience. But the experienced reader knows that stories are foremost about desire. The core of our narratives is constructed memory, and it is that phenomenon which we must now take up.

Constructed Memory

In psychoanalysis I can only explore psychic reality; in that sense, the past only exists *as it is now constructed*. Transference is the precipitate of that past, the joining together of the critical elements in one's life, past to present, crystallized from the ocean of experience. And transference is the *coming to life* of that past in the way in which present experience is interpreted. Memories are not transcriptions of past experience, archives open to any interested reader, independent data that can be recalled in an analysis to confirm an interpretation – although we often treat them as such. While we are, in the course of our work, constantly in search of the past, we must remember that the memories we encounter are in fact always *interpretations* of events (and I include here childhood fantasies themselves as "events" that are immediately interpreted). These interpretations are organized by the patient for particular purposes. They are, moreover, continually being reshaped both by new encounters and by new agendas. A patient's father died when he was 11. How he remembered his father's dying changed as his need to use it for various explanatory purposes changed. As he no longer needed to use that event to justify certain ways of leading his life, for example, the memory itself changed, and he remembered his father's dying in a different way.

Thus memory is tendentious, and motives are always creations of the present. To carry this argument all the way, I now need to assert that remembering is itself often (and especially early in treatment) a symptomatic act, a turning away from present intensities. The "I" whom I remember is a former me, a curious character whom I observe with bemused detachment. In time I will approach the painful recognition that we are the same person, that that person is also the present me, and the past will then no longer be a refuge, it will lose its interest for me. (Of course for some patients the past has been so traumatic that it cannot even be remembered in this distanced way.) Hillman (1975) proposes, along these lines, that historicizing can be an intermediate step toward understanding: historicizing is "a means of *separating an act from actuality*," moving acts "from confession into fiction where they can be looked at in another light" (p. 164).

Working as an analyst, I can only know my patient in his present psychic reality, and that is where he will come to know me. As I listen to his recounting of his life, I will have this question in my mind: How do I understand his choosing to tell this to me now? As I develop ideas about his past experience, and even as I arrive at reconstructions about his early past, I need to keep in mind that I am making sense of his *current* interpretations of these ancient events, whether those interpretations are presented to me directly as ideas or are enacted with me in the transference. Transference enactments are themselves always interpretations, constructions the patient is privately making of what I must really be about. Sharpe (1987) makes the useful analogy that as analysts we are kin not to historians, but to historiographers — we are studying our patients' formulations of their lives, interpreting their interpretations.

This emphasis on subjectivity in one regard needs to be countered. Psychoanalysts, beginning with Freud, have been quite interested in the question of whether memories refer to events or phantasies. Reality traumas and disturbing phantasies indeed have different effects on development. It is harder for the child to encompass actual events within his sphere of omnipotence — the phantasy, on the other hand, was of his own construction — and he is thus more likely to experience unresolvable guilt. It is one of life's ironies that we generally feel guiltiest about those eventualities we had the least control over. The guilt, to be sure, is partly a defense against feeling helpless, which is even more unbearable. We are less helpless in relation to our phantasies. Wetzler (1985) points out the ways in which it makes a difference clinically which phenomenon one is reconstructing. To say that we are in any event working with the patient's interpretation does not erase the need to find out how and why the patient arrived at that understanding, how and why he reworked the trauma or phantasy. It may also be useful to the patient to discover facts that were concealed from him, for secrets often leave ghost trails that are scented but not understood, or leave omissions that must be filled with confabulation.

The Word and the Words

There are thus no facts in psychoanalysis that have independent standing outside the refraction of interpretation. We find this truth hard to keep in our grasp. As an example of this, in his otherwise excellent defense of a hermeneutic understanding of psychoanalysis, the aforementioned Sharpe, while discussing the formation of the narrative, lapses into "Either way he is now in possession of an accurate mental history" (1987, p. 340). "Accurate" implies that there are objective criteria outside the analysis against which insights are measured—a concept that implodes any hermeneutic argument.

Freud had a great deal of difficulty with this issue. In his case studies he worked constantly to arrive at reconstructions of actual events. His greatest tour de force was his reconstruction of the Wolf Man's purported primal-scene exposure (1918 [1914]). Based on the analysis of a dream, Freud concluded that the Wolf Man, at 1½ years of age, while lying in bedding on the floor and suffering from a malarial fever, observed in great detail his parents making love in bed, with his father entering his mother from behind. In his case report Freud took great pains to argue the plausibility of this as an actual event, unwilling to allow the option that this might have been a dream or phantasy. Countering such a position, Leavy (1980) claims that "it is irrelevant to psychoanalysis whether the recovered past is grounded in an objectively recognizable event or not. Paradoxical as it may seem, the only sure reality of the memory of the past is fantasy—the cluster of imaginings, wishful in nature, in which it exists" (p. 103).

Freud was writing up the treatment as a vehicle for defending his psychology against attacks by Jung and Adler, and Jung in particular was claiming that children's asserted sexual memories were adult fantasies displaced backward in time. Was Freud claiming factuality because he feared that his constructions of the child's psychic reality would be unconvincing? That Freud was also crisscrossing himself on this issue is reflected in the odd demurrer that appears in a footnote at the end of the case, allowing that perhaps for certain purposes it didn't matter after all whether we regarded the event "as a primal scene or as a primal phantasy" (p. 120). That he came to the point of arguing about the reality of his invention toward the end of that exposition is in its own way remarkable.

Hillman (1975), however, takes the argument a step further, and in the process sheds light on one of our deepest anxieties in the transactional trade. He imagines that our emphasis on the empirical is a way of managing our anxiety about the seductiveness of our isolation:

> Empiricism . . . is, psychologically, that fantasy which makes us safe from solipsism, its isolation, its paranoid potentialities. Therefore, since psychological material is essentially subjective and the therapeutic situation a reinforcement by mirroring or doubling (the closed vessel) of this isolated subjectivity, *the appeal to empiricism of therapy is a direct consequent of the solipsism of therapy.* The empirical disguise in case histories is an inevitable defense against the solipsistic power of the fictions with which therapy is engaged. [pp. 134–135]

If we resist the lure of the empiricist defense, we must acknowledge that psychoanalytic meaning is *created* in the patient–analyst dialogue. As Schafer observes, "Purported life-historical facts that are initially presented by analysands become *psychoanalytic* facts" (1983, p. 188) as they ricochet between the partners in the conversation. There is no Word, we have only the words. And Schafer continues:

> In this light, the history that the analyst comes to believe in with most justification is the history of the analysis itself. That history includes the varied tellings and contemporary reconstructions of the past. These tellings and reconstructions are both verbal and nonverbal, and both explicit and implicit, and they occur both within the bounds of the sessions and, through acting out, beyond these bounds. [p. 206]

An Illustration

Harold, a young therapist, came for treatment troubled by an imprint from his childhood. The memory was an image from a Sunday comic strip: Dick Tracy, strapped to the floor, anchored there by a woman tall as an Amazon with an entirely scarred face, Mrs. Pruneface, Tracy lying there, unable to move, a block of ice on each side of him, a weighted board supported at both ends by the ice, a spike driven through the middle of the board, the spike positioned over Tracy's heart, the ice melting, the spike descending, the spike beginning to impale Tracy. This memory had stayed with him over the years, bearing compelling meaning. Telling it, then shrugging it off, he referred to it fancifully as the story of his childhood. He wasn't far off the mark.

We came to learn that his father had read him this story when Harold was 3, shortly after the birth of his sister. His father had taken to bed that summer, ostensibly because of his heart condition. Yet, while his father did in fact have a progressive cardiac illness, the explanation for this brief infirmity seemed suspect because his father lived for another decade without relapse before suffering a fatal coronary. Harold thought that perhaps his father had been done in by his daughter's birth, which may have reawakened intensities of loss harkening back to his father's own situation as the oldest of many siblings. This hypothesis was supported for my patient by a development in his own life. When his own second child was born, a daughter who followed by three years a son (thus repeating his childhood situation), he became briefly psychotically depressed. During the psychosis, while gardening, he had a brief flash during which he wanted to chop off his daughter's head with a spade. Both his psychosis and his father's illness had occurred when an infant daughter was 4 months old. He later thought that he had, in part, been reenacting a trauma in his father's life, one with which he had identified.

Harold took the story to be an accounting of his father's heart condition (his father had angina during those years, spike piercing heart), caused by a woman both powerfully phallic (an Amazon with a spike) and castrated (scarred faceless). He thought that his anxiety about his father's terror had joined with his own helplessness and rage in the face of his sister's birth, that he had imagined an identification with his father as mother's victim. His father had read him the comics in bed each Sunday morning. Researching the matter, Harold discovered that the point in the story when Tracy was under the spike appeared in the papers a couple of months after his father's incapacitation. He conjectured that as a 3-year-old child he had taken the story as an explanation of the event.

Harold was unable to remember clearly how Tracy had escaped — he thought perhaps he had been rescued by his pal, Sam Catchem, and carried out by rope through an open window. This sounded suspiciously like a birth phantasy, the child rescued from the engorging mother by the father/partner, but it was not, in fact, the story that my patient unearthed when he refound the comics. Tracy had discovered that the floor was slightly tilted, and he had banged his bottom against the floorboards again and again until the ice had shifted enough to move the board. We wondered together whether he had repressed this detail of the story because of its implication of sex, replacing a phantasy of violent intercourse with a phallic mother in favor of a less threatening phantasy of pairing with father.

Psychic reality—we might say psychic history, the fictive elaboration of meaning—was, for Harold, composed of menacing mothers, at once terrifying and exciting, against whom all men, including sons and fathers, were helpless, pinioned butterflies. This was his experience of himself at 3, living in the wake of his sister's birth and his father's incapacity, as he now reconstructed it. He thought that matters hadn't changed much for him since. He was still frightened of assertive women, and fascinated by them. He'd taken to identifying with his father's illness, imagining that a coronary waited around the corner of his own life. Afraid to take initiative—he left this to the women around him—he lay on my couch, impassive, wondering whether I would be the dragon lady who gored him or the father who helplessly wished to be able to protect him. We might speculate that his father had, in some measure, evoked this construction of the world in him. It seemed remarkable to me that a father would read a story so drenched in sadism to a 3-year-old child. I guessed that the father must have been in a panic, trying to manage his own anxiety by containing it in his son. Harold had managed this projective identification in part by castrating his father and by denying his father's rather different and privileged position with his mother. Behind my patient's schema lay other, disavowed, stories.

What troubled me about this accounting was the absence of Harold's intentionality. Where was Harold as murderer, where was his sadism? In the course of the analysis I would find that out, as he progressively nailed me to my chair, tormenting me with my imperfections, less interested in doing for himself than in incapacitating me. The analysis flowed with the speed of a slowly melting glacier. I felt, at times, that I understood exactly what Dick Tracy had been through. At other times, Harold seemed to be enacting his version of the phallic castrated mother, the mother who, in his accounting, compensates for her castration by assuming the guise of a phallus. For Harold, being a therapist was a way of penetrating others. Had he mastered more of his sadism he might have become a surgeon—he'd imagined the possibility—but not having done so he settled for bloodless coups.

The course of the treatment is a story for another occasion, but I should at least close this accounting by mentioning a dream he described near the end of treatment. In the dream, his wife had left him for another man. I had been the one to tell him this and I had approved its happening. Perhaps it was his own fault. He described the pained hatred he'd felt toward me – it lasted well into the session – the mixture of rage and wounded longing, a hurt that would never go away. It seemed like a different accounting of the childbirth, one which acknowledged oedipal rivalry and loss, in the way that analysis moves from telling to retelling.

I present this example to demonstrate the ways in which psychic reality is assembled in childhood from events, interpretations of events, the impact of parental anxieties, and nuances of development. (While I have not discussed the point, it is also entirely relevant that this particular story was assembled during the early phallic phase). I have tried to show how constructions shape behavior, and to illustrate how stories both change and stay the same in the course of development and treatment.

NARRATIVITY

By way of this last example, I have been developing the idea that what unfolds in treatment is a story. Two stories are unfolded, actually, or, more exactly, a story within a story. The outer story is that of the encounter between patient and therapist. Much of theater has this structure – two persons meet, they become acquainted, things happen, they part, the curtain falls. Therapy is notoriously theatrical – we put on costumes, take up roles, it's always both real and unreal, both play and deadly earnest, both a part of our lives and yet separate from daily life. And just as so much of theater is about theater, so in therapy are we self-consciously examining roles, removing masks, discovering the masks behind masks. While therapy may at times resemble works from the Theater of the Absurd, with its perverse destruction of meaning, even those acts will become part of a more encompassing narrative. This narrative will be driven by a second story, the inner story, the story of the patient's life as she believes that she has lived it. (And also, less obviously, by the narrative of the therapist's life, but the nature of intentionality in therapy that is aimed at making manifest the inner workings of the patient will result in *her* narrative taking by far the leading edge).

The strategy of therapy is to use the outer story to reveal the inner one. We generally begin with the patient's telling of her story, which we assume will be a quite biased accounting, selective, distorting in ways of which the patient is both aware and unaware. The patient, of course, presents this disingenuously as the chronicle of her life, but we find it hard to listen without skeptical thoughts creeping in, alternative possibilities. Over the course of therapy, guided by the unfolding of the outer story, this internal narrative is revised. In this sense the past is reshaped by the present. Typically a major shift in the narrative is from the patient as victim to the patient as agent provocateur, although at some junctures precisely the opposite retelling will be called for (Schafer 1976).

Both patient and therapist will be swept along in this venture by the human longings for integration, continuity, and narrative closure and the human intolerance for uncertainty. At times this will tempt each of them to fill in gaps that rightly are still obscure. Despite our efforts to keep an open mind, too easily a hunch becomes a hypothesis, a hypothesis an explanation, an explanation a certainty. Beyond our usual anxieties, our folly develops at three levels. First, our belief in psychic determinism (something approaching a religious belief for analysts) steers us away from happenstance and coincidence. Second, our belief in developmental teleology biases us toward explanations of later events in terms of the happenings of early childhood to a degree that disqualifies the possibility of independent or novel motivation (Mitchell 1988). And third, our theory comes equipped with stories that can all too readily be plugged into narrative gaps to create the illusion of explicability. The tale of Oedipus, Creon, and Jocasta has been the leading contender for this honor.

Each theory comes equipped with an anthology of tales, including its myth of creation, childhood fable, family reminiscence, and legend of honor. As practitioners, we listen to our patients with those anthologies in mind, replete with story lines that we expect to find weaving their way through our hours. The greatest danger is that we will be especially inclined toward a particular narrative that happens to be the story of our own lives. Through our own analyses we hope to flesh out that plot line so that we can recognize our narrative biases as they appear. Nonetheless, even at our best we must at times wonder whether we are simply writing plays as Shakespeare did, draping new poetry on ancient tales. Too often case reports read like "word search" puzzles; the therapist seemed to see his task as rediscovering preordained themes in raw text.

Context

It will be clear to his other readers that this discussion of narrativity as the structure of the treatment process has been heavily influenced by my reading of Roy Schafer. Much of his writing on this topic is presented in *The Analytic Attitude* (1983). At this point, let me note two further dimensions of his perspective. The first is his emphasis on context. All meaning, he argues, is context bound. For Schafer meaning always develops in particular contexts within an analysis: in response to certain *questions* that analyst and patient develop; within the frame of particular *states of the transference* (and countertransference, it would seem fair to add); in relation to *other meanings* that are being developed or rejected; and in relation to the particular *intentions* of each party. No *psychoanalytic* meanings simply stand there, apart, speaking for themselves. This seems a reasonable extension of his assertion that "from the analytic point of view, there is, strictly speaking, no independent biographical material that counts" (p. 211). It is also concordant with Merton Gill's (1979) definition of neutrality as "never taking for granted that the meaning we intend is the meaning the patient ascribes" (p. 7). *Meaning* in psychoanalysis must always be derived by consensus; neither party alone can generate meaning. The lifelessness of the typical case vignette, Schafer observes, is precisely a consequence of its being isolated from context and presented as an independent truth. It is in this sense that all genera-tion of meaning in psychoanalysis cannot escape being ultimately subjective.

The other emphasis of Schafer's that I want to highlight is his position that the meaning one is aiming to arrive at in the analytic dialogue—the crucial narrative—is the story (actually *stories*) of the analytic experience. These are the only truths both parties can believe in. The patient's life story, even as it is unfolded, fleshed out, revised, and turned upside-down in the course of the analysis, is ultimately a shadow truth for the analyst and even in a certain sense for the patient. The truths about which they can develop a shared conviction are those that develop *between them* as transference and resistance are unpacked and struggled with. Although they will have their own respective versions even of that truth, it will be those narratives that will ultimately count as the product of their work together. We might think of this as the field of truth generated by two gardeners. While the pair will view their joint effort from different vantage points, there will be no mistaking that, for better or for worse, they have sown and harvested this field together. I do not know whether I am carrying Schafer's arguments further than he intended, but I have offered these last two paragraphs themselves as a joint tending.

As yet another expression of the transcendent impact of the therapeutic experience itself on our accounts, let me offer this abashed personal recollection.

During my residency training, one of our courses was devoted to listening to and discussing tape recordings of an entire brief treatment (about fifteen sessions, as I recall) conducted by the teacher. It was not until the very last class that, in the wake of some unusual developments in the case, I realized that I knew the patient, that she was a friend of a good friend of mine, someone I'd spent a few evenings and a weekend with. I believe that my capacity not to recognize her speaks to the way in which the therapeutic process that unfolds has a life, a story, of its own. In fact, had it not been for certain extraordinary eventualities, I would never have realized that this person was someone I knew. I offer this vignette as an example of the impact of context on knowledge.

Story Lines

As a way of discussing the multiple levels of psychic reality in psychoanalytic work, I will present my work with a patient as a set of four narratives that could be constructed from the treatment. I should make clear, to begin with, that while working with her I did not distinguish these as narrative lines; the possibility of elaborating the experience in this way only came afterward. Presenting this work entails special problems of confidentiality. It is necessary to include a good deal of biographical material, because part of the interest here lies in the ways that portions of the patient's personal history are owned and disowned. At the same time, to preserve anonymity, some of these very details are fictitious. In making revisions, I have tried to remain faithful to the psychological truths of the story.

The first of the four narratives that can be constructed from my work with Elizabeth is the story she would easily tell of her life if you asked her, the autobiography she might write. This report, of course, serves defensive and adaptive purposes, and it has changed a bit during her analysis in that she would now offer you a slightly different story than the one with which she began. The broad outlines would nevertheless be much the same. Every patient has such a story to tell.

The second story is actually, from her point of view, a number of bits and pieces that don't fit well with the autobiography. They are memories of experiences, or stories she has been told, which to the listener cast the first report in a different light. They don't jeopardize the first telling for her because she keeps them split off from the main current of her self-understanding. For the listener, however, they come together to form another narrative of her life, a darker, more problematic one. Every patient does not have this story to tell, in this way, because most patients do not encapsulate and isolate experience to the degree that Elizabeth does.

The third narrative can be constructed from reading the analytic tea leaves—listening to dreams, tracking associations, following the events of her life. This narrative must also be assembled by the listener, and it is composed of elements that, unlike those in the first two narratives, are not within Elizabeth's awareness. We might call this, imprecisely, the narrative of her unconscious. It is more lurid than the first two.

The fourth narrative is the one that emerges in the process between patient and analyst, specifically in the transference–countertransference unfoldings, and I have chosen to trace this from the vantage point of the countertransference. So this is an enacted story, a lived telling.

I have decided to develop Elizabeth's story by means of these four accounts not because they appeal to me on structural-theoretical grounds, but because they represent the strands through which I have specifically come to understand her. The work of analysis is that of integrating these accounts, developing their correspondences and contradictions and the ways in which they comment on and inform each other, deconstruct each other, fashioning all the while a new analytic narrative, which is never a finished tale.

First Narrative

Elizabeth thought of herself as a conforming, compliant person who cautiously negotiated her days, trying not to give offense. She believed that she kept her anxieties well hidden from others, that her friends and her co-workers at her place of employment thought of her as a happy and well-adjusted person, while from her own point of view life was a constant burden with many demands to be negotiated. Elizabeth felt hopeless much of the time. Her favorite image of herself was as the little match girl of the Andersen tale, who stood shivering outside, sadly and longingly looking in on someone else's happy family. She characterized herself as a loyal wife and mother, a diligent worker, a devoted Christian. She felt that she was defined entirely by the reflection of others, that she had no sense of herself, and that in a way there was not even a self to make sense of.

Elizabeth idealized her mother as a kind, gentle woman, never critical or angry, self-denying, self-effacing, to whom she felt she had been a burden. Her mother was a saint, a paragon of virtue. She might have added that her mother hadn't had much to do with her, but she would have immediately countered that this hadn't been her mother's fault. Her father, she said, had been outgoing, genial with friends, an imposing figure, and at the same time an insecure man who had been sensitive to slights and in need of constant reassurance. He had had a tragic past. His father had died in an institution and his mother had perished from pneumonia, contracted on one of her many trudges through the snow to visit her husband. His sister had died soon after of malnutrition in a foster home, and Elizabeth had been named after her. My patient told this story with vivid detail and I sensed that she had seamlessly incorporated into her own narrative this account of her father's.

Her birth, she related, was very difficult for her mother, who had after it been warned to have no further children (although in fact she did). As a latency-age child Elizabeth had been troubling for her parents, who considered her too stubborn and independent. With her peers, she had been a daredevil tomboy, and her childhood between 8 and 10 seemed to have been the best years of her life. But she also remembered that after she stopped living in her parents' bedroom when she was 5, in response to nightmares or bed-wetting she had regularly come into their bedroom. She had either crawled into bed between them or slept on her father's side and spent the night there, sometimes having had to compete with her younger brother for space. This had gone on for several years. Since that time, she had virtually never spent a night alone in a bedroom. Before we talked about it, she had never thought of this as particularly unusual.

The most upsetting event of her early childhood had occurred when she was 7. She had been baby-sitting her younger brother, and he had run into a bicyclist. He hadn't been injured, but she had been terrified and had forced him to get up and run away with her before the ambulance arrived. Only years later was she able to tell her parents this story.

The great transformation of Elizabeth's life had come when she was approaching adolescence. The family had moved to another state and she had suddenly felt out of rhythm and place. Boys now intimidated her. She described this as the time when her personality was transformed into its present self-effacing compliant character. During this period, she had become obsessed with the idea that her masturbation was a mortal sin and she had fought to control it. Also at this time, in what she considered the other crucial event of her childhood, Elizabeth had discovered a lump in her breast and had believed she had cancer. When a doctor had reassured her that it was probably a swollen milk duct, even though she had had no sexual contact with boys, she'd become terrified that she was pregnant. And she had felt humiliated as her father watched the exam. She had promised God that if he made her not pregnant, she'd never become pregnant again, and so it came to pass that she was infertile for many years.

Elizabeth had first fallen in love during her senior year of high school. In flight from that love, at the end of the year she had decided to join a convent, but her parents had persuaded her to enter college instead. In college she had achieved well but had tortured herself with extreme scrupulosity. She had been afraid to marry her husband but remembered her mother kissing her to wake her up on her wedding morning—the only kiss, she told me, that she had ever received from her mother. Her marriage had been conventionally acceptable; she enjoyed sex but could not initiate it. Elizabeth had finally become pregnant after renouncing the church. She had not known, however, that she was pregnant until late in the second trimester.

Elizabeth had had an earlier psychoanalysis, prompted by great concern about the appearance of her eyes, and she felt that the treatment had mainly been a failure—her analyst hadn't liked her, she said. She thought she had been an analytic flop. She was able to manage what at times was formidable anxiety by staring at an icon of Jesus in which she experienced his gaze as accusing; by meditating; and by contemplating the writings of tortured saints. Elizabeth longed for someone to rescue her but expected that that longing would be futile.

Second Narrative

The second story I assembled from bits and pieces Elizabeth related to me. Because these bits and pieces all contradicted the first narrative, she kept them encapsulated. I would say, however, that one function of telling me these fragments was so that I could hold them—they were thus simultaneously kept alive in the dialogue and repudiated. We might call this the projective identification of a narrative.

In this second account her mother was cold, rejecting, and absent. This mother had not wanted to have children and had tried to abort her pregnancies, presumably including her pregnancy with my patient. Her mother had needed her infants to be independent from the beginning and had been pleased when they could manage their own bottles in the crib. A prototypical memory from childhood was finding her mother off reading by herself, resentful of any intrusions. The one time Elizabeth remembered crying in front of her mother, she had felt humiliated by her mother's impatient response. A particularly painful image (which actually was not a memory) was that of Elizabeth's frolicking in the water at the beach, imagining that her parents were standing behind her watching, and turning around to discover that they had left. While in the first narrative her parents had managed with each other, she told me that her brother had vivid memories of them throwing furniture at each other. Elizabeth did not remember this.

Father came across in this second narrative as more incestuously tied up with his daughter, and she with him. On the one hand some memories emerged from earlier childhood suggesting a warm relatedness that she overtly denied. On the other hand there were memories of his verbally attacking her and his then insisting that they hug and kiss so that they could make up—he had been upset until she forgave him. As she'd grown into adolescence she'd felt he was obsessed with her, treating her friendships as a betrayal of the family. When she had wanted to spend a year living at college he had pleaded with her not to leave. "I felt if I came too close to him I'd die, and he wanted me that close." Then again, she remembered that she was afraid to separate from him and must have been clinging herself. Although Elizabeth did not remember seeing her father naked, on one occasion she told me that he used to dress in front of her.

While Elizabeth generally painted herself as supportive of her younger brother, she once mentioned that she had been able to scare him by staring at him in a certain way, which she did not connect to her anxiety about her eyes.

In her current life Elizabeth described her husband as indifferent and critical, and yet she mentioned to me, on various occasions, a variety of special gestures that he regularly made on her behalf. On the basis of these and other anecdotes, he seemed to me to be quite solicitous and devoted, and yet she tended to regard him dismissively. In listening to accounts of her own actions I developed the impression that Elizabeth was not quite the martyr she described. She cut certain corners at work and engaged in other minor corruptions that gave the lie to her purported saintliness.

These, then, are some of the other dimensions of her experience that emerged over the course of our work, and they can be integrated into a second narrative, a narrative composed of disavowed fragments. Disavowed, but not necessarily for that reason more likely to be true, whatever that might mean.

Third Narrative

The third narrative was put together from inferred, substantially unconscious elements and is thus less coherent. It is the story that unfolds as dreams are sifted through, associations tracked, metaphors decoded. This is standard psychoanalytic work, and it generally takes us into the netherland of childhood phantasy, sexual imaginings and theorizings, the dark alleys of passion and loathing. This narrative unfolds in the context of the transference, but I am separating it out here as the sort of story that could be told by a psychoanalyst listening only to the language, reading only the text.

Elizabeth had opened her analysis with such a story. During the summer, she'd read Tom Wolfe's *Bonfire of the Vanities*. She said that it was about someone who'd inadvertently committed a hit-and-run crime but wasn't sure he'd done it. Actually, she amended, his companion had been driving. Gradually, she said, his life became more and more exposed and ended up in ruins, adding, "I felt like I was that character." In one distortion of the novel she claimed that the protagonist hadn't realized until quite late in the story that his car had actually hit the person.

We could link this story with a dream in which she used the couple's 17-year-old cat, to which she was very attached, as bait on a fishing trip. The cat was immediately bitten by a huge fish, and she excitedly reeled it in. Elizabeth was then horrified, and mortified, when she realized that the cat was fatally wounded. She promised the cat, who was licking a woman's hand, that she would eat her to preserve her, but she felt that her own life was over, that having done such a terrible thing she could never be happy again. In a subsequent dream she fed this cat to a starving kitten and again was horrified by what she was doing. She separated the cats and put the kitten on the floor where it could find meager scraps of food. This story and these dreams conveyed a sense of guilt, hunger, and felt destructiveness toward loved ones far more vivid than anything we had heard in the other narratives. Elizabeth seemed terrified by her ruthlessness. We also get a sense of where piety might begin. From these fragments we can begin to imagine childhood scenes, another version of her relationship with her mother in which she is victimizer rather than victim, the birth of her scrupulosity.

Her dreams were very engaging, some of them seeming almost like screenplays for film noir classics. Common plots included romances with appealing men who were transformed into sadistic victimizers of women, liaisons with men that were suddenly disrupted by jealous women, occasionally with women turning the tables on these powerful men. The dreams were often sexual and richly fleshed out, quite in contrast to the demeanor of this prim, constricted woman. (I felt like a schoolboy being told dirty stories by my spinster schoolteacher!) Let me tell you a few of these dreams, just to give you a feeling for them:

> She was in bed, a man was kissing her breasts, he said he was playing a tune on them, she had an orgasm in her sleep, she woke up coughing and choking, gasping for air.

> She felt frightened, going down a long hallway to her office. Inside it was dark, scary. She decided that she was blind and would just go on as usual. A man came in, he attacked her, he laughed a weird laugh. She had her hand on his wrist, but it didn't seem like a wrist, it was soft and fleshy. She said that if he moved, she'd leave, but she knew it was a hollow threat because she couldn't leave.

> At a formal party, a man said to her, "Do I have anything that belongs to you?" She said, "No." As she talked with him she had a memory in her body (that's how she put it) of when he'd touched her genitals and buttocks with his hands, but they were talking as though they were just acquaintances. She then felt something wet on her face, he was kissing her, she felt sexually aroused and woke up.

> At a reception for President Bush she sang, "Put Your Head on My Shoulder." Bush invited her to dance and after an initial hesitancy she joined him. It felt wonderful, she hugged him, but then they stopped next to his wife and she had to walk back across the dance floor feeling humiliated and embarrassed. Commenting on the dream, she said that Bush was the last person she'd want to dance with.

Leaving aside the transference implications of the dreams, they spoke to intense longing for connection that was sexualized, to themes of sexual rivalry and jealousy, to conflicted wishes for the paternal phallus combined with impulses to destroy it and fears of retaliation. These dreams and others also evoked for me images of a child with her father feigning naiveté ("Oh what's that fleshy thing in my hand?"),

and I speculated to myself about what she had experienced and imagined those many nights in bed with her father. Incestuous themes flowed through her dreams with the sort of nuances and intensity that could lead the listener to the conviction that incest had occurred, although of course it might not have. One might also imagine a child who cannot get clear where dreams begin and reality ends, living in a twilight state, half asleep before dawn, rubbing up against her dreams or perhaps her father's body.

These are the kinds of story lines that develop as we listen to dreams and other metaphorical tellings. They may not constitute a truer narrative than the others, even though we conventionally take their source to be, so to speak, deeper. They are told with various motives in mind, concealing deception. But they do constitute an approach from a different side. We participate more actively in the construction of this narrative and so we may be more invested in it; being more obviously metaphorical than the others, it is also more plastic, more subject to warpage.

Fourth Narrative

Finally, we come to the narrative that develops out of the transfer-ence–countertransference interaction. This, of course, is the narrative we develop the deepest conviction about, because we were there, although it must ultimately be integrated with the other accountings. I would like to discuss a couple of the more striking transference developments in the analysis, taken from the early years of treatment. They do not reflect the evolution of the analysis—they are not intended to—but rather are offered to illustrate what we take to be the psychoanalytically privileged narrative.

The first parallels a development I described in Elizabeth's dreams. It has to do with our living in two different states of mind, one which was stark, broad daylight, and the other a twilight state. These two states were split off from each other, especially split apart for her. An example of this for me, which I just referred to, was my conviction at one point that Elizabeth had had incestuous experience with her father. The point I'm trying to make here is that I felt a *conviction* about this, but I didn't feel that I could say in any daylight sense that I *knew* this—intellectually, I could think that this might have been just her incestuous phantasy. I experienced this conviction as a kind of twilight, split-off knowledge. This feeling of both knowing and not-knowing, I thought, must have been an evocation of the state of mind she herself lived in so much of the time. This state of mind might have developed for her as a way of managing the provocative situation of being in bed with her father. By a splitting of awareness, a hysterical dissociation, she could consciously disavow the incestuous dimensions of the experience while keeping it alive in her unconscious. This, in fact, was what she was putting into me: an experience of being divided, of simultaneously holding two realities, and of feeling driven a bit—or in her case, more than a bit—crazy by that.

Closely related to this was another countertransference experience, a sense of split-off seduction. I was seduced by her dreams, fascinated by these erotic gothic tales, but not by her as a person. Again, I felt a sense of a radical split between these two experiences of her, which I could imagine paralleled a split she felt in her experience of me (and, I imagine, of her father before me). As matters heated up between us, she reported that on one occasion, while lying in bed, she was startled to find herself imagining that if I were in her house she'd desperately want to go to me sexually. This seemed an impulsive thought that had come from out of nowhere. What was most striking was not the feeling itself, but the sense that it was so alien to her.

My predominant countertransference experience during the early years, however, was of a different sort. I felt increasingly controlled by Elizabeth, deprived of agency or will. At one point I began to recognize that our sessions had become burdensome and confining, a ritualized performance on both our parts. She'd wait for me to look at her to begin, and then would announce that she had two dreams to tell, which she would describe in detail and to which she would offer associations. I might ask a question or two. It was always two dreams, never more, never fewer. She never made interpretations herself, for two reasons. First, it would represent an unconscionable taking of initiative, comparable, I think, to initiating sex or committing murder, which I also thought were in some sense equivalent for her. Second, she was creating a test for me. About thirty minutes into the session she would fall silent. It was now my job to speak. If I did not speak— and it didn't much matter what I would say, as long as I spoke— Elizabeth would decide that she had done it wrong, that she had bored me, that she was a failure, and she would become withdrawn, hopeless, despondent, and reproachful. She would not say this, however, unless asked, and was capable of remaining silent for the rest of the session.

Furthermore, my words came to have ominous power; they defined her experience, although her hearing of them generally did not carry the meaning or implication I had intended. Let me give an example of this. She had a very lengthy menstrual period, which she thought might be a harbinger of menopause. Elizabeth both minimized this and also felt sad about it. In a dream a flower bloomed in the desert, and I interpreted this to represent both something hopeful developing in our work together and also a wish not to be infertile. During the next hour she told me that it had felt good to have me see the desert come to life, but that having me see the flower as just a wish felt depressing. This was exactly the kind of statement that I'd come to experience as extremely burdensome, because she was informing me that I had such an enormous capacity to define her reality. My comment about the flower had actually been somewhat offhand, sort of a marginal thought, not a grand interpretation, and yet she had taken it both to elevate her mood and to indict herself. It wasn't particularly that I felt criticized for the comment—more that I had such relentless power over her.

In writing this, I have the thought that Elizabeth fashioned my cast-off string of words into a noose, which she draped over her neck and which she then used in an effort to strangle herself. Of course you can't succeed that way, you just tire yourself out—you have to tie the rope to the ceiling and jump off the chair. As a matter of technique, I think I would have liked to have expressed at least the first half of that thought to her—hinting of course at my wish to strangle her at those moments—but I then felt too guilty when I was with her to allow myself such an aggressive feeling. Elizabeth had made analysis into a perfect closed system in which she defined all meanings; I was left without role or identity. The main task of the analysis became that of curing me of my begrudgingness. If I succeeded in undermining that operation for a moment, she then pirouetted and told me that she was utterly unable to act in any other way, that our work was hopeless. At times I certainly felt that myself. Her most perverse—although not exactly inaccurate—reading of the situation was that I was trying to coerce her into being spontaneous, and that she would have to contrive a spontaneity to appease me.

I understood the setup in this way. I believed that the controllingness had to do with her experience with both parents. Schematically, Elizabeth felt that neither one had empathically engaged with her and that she mainly had learned how to comply with them. She felt that she had submitted to their reality and to their needs. It seems likely that in time she had tried to coerce them into submitting to her, as she tried to coerce me. At times I was the oppressive parent. At other times, or even at the same time, she was the parent and I was the oppressed child. At moments this seemed to defend against warm feelings toward me, as though a mother lurking outside the door or across the bed could not tolerate her feelings for her father and she had to disguise her longings. At other times, this resentful relatedness seemed a way of hatefully engaging with a mother. And at still other moments, it felt like a depressive link to a father, I imagine to the orphaned father who told and retold the story of all those deaths. She had an uncanny sensitivity to any hint of depression in me. This, then, exemplifies the kind of narrative that unfolds in the evolution of the countertransference and transference.

A Fifth Narrative

The degree to which these alternate versions of the story can be teased apart was unusual, and actually suggested a fifth, integrative narrative in which I was to be the container for Elizabeth's dissociated versions of herself and her life. Her unconscious intention was for me to wrestle with her fractured experience; I was to drown or find a handhold in the swamp. The separating of the strands, in this telling, was part of my effort to adapt to this disorganizing situation. I then wondered whether this had been Elizabeth's fate as a child: being made container of her parents' split experiences. There was much to suggest this.

As analyst my task was to clarify for her the dissociative process itself, not to try to make the integration for her, for that is something that one person cannot do for another, try as she might wish I would. I did understand that the dissociation served primarily to keep at bay her experience of herself as a destructive person (her range of what constituted destructiveness being, to put it mildly, extensive). One step along the way to appreciating this was a resonance she felt with the bananafish in a story by J. D. Salinger (1953). The life cycle of the bananafish ended when it found itself in a small cave filled with sea fruit: after eating all the food it was swollen too large to leave through the cave's opening, and it starved to death. Elizabeth believed that her hunger was so voracious that, left unrestrained, she could devour her entire inner object world, leaving her unbearably alone. Dividing experience was a way of preserving her inner world.

Although Elizabeth's capacity to dissociate narratives was unusual, all of us split and encapsulate experience. The sort of splitting I am describing here is different from the splitting of self, object, and affect states that Kernberg describes as central to borderline conditions (1975). It is more a matter of splitting narratives (and we might see multiple personality formation as an exaggerated version of this). Psychoanalysis has long acknowledged one aspect of this process in asserting the repression of oedipal conflict—the primal disavowed telling. But that repression is only one instance of a much broader trend in human experience toward divorcing narratives. And the divorcing of narratives does not always, as in this case, depend only on repression. In this sense the work of analysis is not only to flesh out the narratives but also to integrate them. In the course of this the patient comes to view herself no longer as the victim of many hit-and-run drivers, but as perpetrator, author, the driver at the wheel.

This exploration of treatment as constructed narrative highlights the problem of subjectivity. The subjective complexity can only be multiplied when we discuss the cases of other practitioners. It is to the myths of case reporting that I will now turn, hoping to sharpen the issue by approaching it from a different vantage.

7

Therapy as Narrative: Storytelling

Wolf Man: Well, how did Freud explain it? You know better
            than I.
Obholzer: Better than you? No, no.
Wolf Man: It's paradoxical but that's the way it is.
                                    —Karin Obholzer (1982, p. 52)

I do not know how my colleagues work. I am not there, and I listen to
their descriptions of their work with skepticism. All accountings, mine
included, are tendentious, and none less so than the case report. To
further sharpen the issues raised by our consideration of narrative,
this chapter explores the relationship between patient, therapist-
writer, and reader. Along the way, we will encounter one price of
making the figurative literal.

The case report, since Freud, has been the favored way to share our work with each other, but case reports, since Freud, have always been written with an agenda in mind, a point to make, and the data are organized to make that point. Not, of course, that we could do otherwise. In presenting the story of our work with a patient, we must always both organize the work and be selective, presenting one aspect and not another, and generally presenting the work as we eventually come to understand it, not as we understood it at the time. But we are always organizing our experience with our patients, from the first moment we see them. And that organizing is always as much about us—us as the analyst, us as the person—as it is about them. Case reports are never, in fact, about patients. They are always about treatments, about our view of an interaction in which we have participated, no matter whether we have chosen to recognize or to conceal this.

Actually, analysts rarely present their clinical work in detail; case reports are usually focused on a particular aspect of the treatment about which the analyst wishes to write. It is equally rare that a course of treatment will be presented in our professional meetings and classes. The preservation of privacy is at stake, we are told—in truth the analyst's as well as the patient's. That caution is not unwarranted, because the analyst foolhardy enough to risk such exposure reliably gets shredded. Conventionally we understand the shredding occurs because the material is always open to many interpretations, because people have axes to grind, and because we are relentlessly competitive. However, I believe that we also go after each other in this way because what we are being offered is a view into an intimate experience, a primal scene. At once anxious about being drawn in and enraged by our exclusion, we force ourselves in and destroy the scene by appropriating the case. Alternatively, we revise the scene, making ourselves the protagonists. The exception to this rule, not unexpectedly, is the participants' experience in case discussions in small study groups that have been meeting over a course of years. In that setting the members' regard for each other, and their investment in their group, counterbalances the narcissistic tensions generated by feeling too drawn in or too left out.

FOSSHAGE AND HIS CRITICS

A recent issue of *Psychoanalytic Inquiry* (Miller and Post 1990) was constructed by asking a group of clinicians to consider a protocol consisting of four consecutive analytic hours framed by a bit of background material. The discussants represented a variety of psychoanalytic orientations: classical, self psychological, developmental, relational, Kleinian, British Independent, Lacanian, and neurobiological. The presenter, James Fosshage, is a self psychologist. After discussing the project with his patient, Fosshage tape-recorded their sessions for a month. He reports that he was in sufficient conflict about the venture that he did not tape two of the meetings, and the notes from those sessions represent two of the four hours in the protocol.

Each commentator considers the material from his or her own orientation. The most consistent criticism of the work has been that Fosshage did not pay enough attention to the ways in which the process was unfolding between him and his patient, that he was being guided too much by his theory (by what he expected his patient would be feeling) and was not listening closely enough to what his patient was saying. The respondents did not make a great deal of the decision to tape her, perhaps because they had also agreed to take part in the project and thus were, in some sense, co-conspirators. More significantly, they responded to the protocol as though it were unprocessed data, an open view of a week's analytic work—as open, that is, as a written protocol can be.

In my reading of the case report, I thought that Fosshage was shaping the material, both in its framing and in the conduct of the hours, to advocate the usefulness of a self psychological orientation. It seems preposterous to me to think that the hours reported fairly represent psychoanalytic work, for analysis must always be such a profoundly dyadic interaction.[1] Fosshage's critics were surely, so to

---

[1] This dilemma is also present in the supervision of analysis in training, a matter I will take up in a later chapter.

speak, in the room with him, a third party to the transaction. A couple of the respondents picked up on the frequent appearance of the number three in the material: the patient was in the hospital at age 3, it was three days before her mother arrived to visit her there, her sister slept for three days in a dream, her first analysis had lasted three years, she was in the third year of her current analysis, which until recently she had been attending three times a week. One discussant remarked that the analyst hadn't made anything of three as a phallic or oedipal symbol. I believe that he was onto something, but that he was excluding himself from the omission. No one considered that the many threes *in the protocol* might be related to both the patient's and Fosshage's burdensome experience of being part of a threesome now— patient, therapist, and critics. The framing of all the discussions in a dyadic context seems consistently defensive to me, a turning of the blind eye.[2]

Early in the protocol, Fosshage described an interaction in which his patient reported having seen a Cadillac outside his house and was horrified by the thought that it might belong to him. She considered it an old man's car. Fosshage responded to her insistent anxiety about this by telling her that indeed the car didn't belong to him. The respondents, predictably, treated this as a feast set before their eyes and made mincemeat of the event, accusing Fosshage of ducking the patient's rage. Fosshage, of course, knew precisely what he was setting out on the table—it wasn't turkey, it was a red herring. I imagine that that outrageous action (not the decision to tell the patient, but the act of including that session in the protocol!) represented his intention to take on the critics of self psychology, and, I think, to deflect them from more subtle criticism of his approach. He elaborates more fully in his concluding response to their comments his rationale for the way he handled that moment; he indicated, in fact, that he would also have told the patient that it was indeed his car had it belonged to him.

I don't think that Fosshage succeeded in distracting his critics, for

---

[2]For a wider consideration of this dynamic, created from the point of view of Oedipus himself, see Steiner (1985).

their discussions of the case are quite rich and thoughtful. But I do suspect that at some level this whole project was, for him, a desperate piece of business. The reader senses the desperation in the mounting intensity of his response to the discussants—what could he have possibly expected in a setup like this? None of the respondents raised the question of what it meant that Fosshage had agreed to participate in this project and, specifically, that he had chosen this particular patient to do it with. Ordinarily a clinician chooses a case to write about because he believes that he has made certain discoveries in the course of the work that could usefully be shared with a readership. While there may have been unrevealed motives involved—a favor owed, for example—in the absence of such knowledge we must wonder where anyone could find the courage to expose his work, in *relatively* unprocessed form, to this sort of scrutiny.

I will offer a wild conjecture about this, one that returns us to the number three. Fosshage may have intuitively sensed that his patient, for all the progress they had made, was unconsciously heading for another reenactment of her fateful abandonment by her mother at age 3. I put aside whether she was actually left alone in the hospital at 3 as she reported it, for this is, in any event, how she constructs it. Just as she had left her first analyst in the third year, thus recreating the trauma with roles reversed, she might have been on course to repeat the enactment, all against her best intentions. Were this the case, Fosshage might have been unconsciously engaged in a heroic attempt to save the treatment by taking his patient with him out from the darkness into the light of day, where spectators could have a look at the couple and interact with them. Even the Cadillac incident would be defiantly held up to view. This would have been in stark contrast to the covert romance the patient had conducted with her father, which had aborted when he symbolically shunned her in public by refusing to acknowledge the special photograph of her that he kept in his wallet. In any event, Fosshage and his patient survived their third year, he reports in his epilogue, and are now approaching the end of the fourth year of a very useful treatment. My speculations in this matter cannot be offered with much conviction because I don't have enough data to support them. But I do believe that a response to the case should include thinking through the matter of the *choice to present* itself. The reader is not being offered a script of a play; he is being given a narrative about the writing of a play, in which the plot of the play is embedded, and it is *this* narrative that is the appropriate target for discourse.

CASE REPORTING

I find a case report useful if it persuasively demonstrates to me an idea that I can apply to my work with patients or if it assists me in my own model construction. I may find the report unconvincing if its internal logic seems faulty, or if I can offer a more satisfying explanation of the clinical events. I won't *know* that my interpretation is more accurate— I can't know that—but plausibility will carry the day. I will also fail to find the report useful if I can't align it in some measure with my own conceptual models. In one sense that is my problem, not the author's, and yet dismissal is so often the fate of theorists who construct their own metapsychologies—only those with a cadre of loyal friends survive (perhaps this is the reason Heinz Kohut has thus far succeeded where Harry Stack Sullivan failed). I cannot imagine taking the treatment material of others as data from which I could build a testable alternate theory because the material is densely encased in its author's interpretation, and at most I might come up with only contrary interesting hunches.

Persuasiveness will be determined by the author's ingenuity and rhetoric. Stanley Fish (1980) tells us that works acquire their authority when they are well received by their interpretive communities— success is determined by the appeal to the audience. The power of Freud's rhetoric, Schafer comments, is attested to by the amazing way he can "be felt to be holding up his end of a lively and invariably refocusing conversation" (1992, p. 10) with subsequent generations of readers. Donald Spence (1987), on the other hand, is deeply concerned about the way we work our rhetoric. He urges us to provide more of the relevant data, explain our rules of inference, and avoid the narrative smoothing that conceals cracks in our argument, so that alternative hypotheses can be constructed. He accuses us of trying to sneak into the scientific community by concealing the hermeneutic basis of our work and presenting our findings as if they were based on deductive logic. Spence's effort to dispatch our wanton seducers to a convent is misguided. As savvy readers, we generally know when we're being handed a line. The problem, as both Spence and Schafer point out, is that too often the hustlers seem compelled to dress in mourning clothes, hoping that we'll be impressed by their sobriety when what we really want is to be engaged.

Then again, being engaging can backfire. Janet Malcolm (1987) points out that Freud got himself into such trouble over the Dora case because of the vividness of his telling. The facts, she reminds us, are Freud's facts—he chose, for example, to believe Dora's account of the seduction over Herr K.'s. I'll let Malcolm tell the story herself:

> As Freud structured his account of it, the truth and good-
> ness of the girl and the falsity and badness of the father and Herr
> K. are as unarguable as are the traits of princesses and ogres in
> fairy stories. The feminists . . . who charge Freud with insuffi-
> cient understanding of and sympathy for the beleaguered girl's
> plight at the hands of the creepy men around her—should
> understand the extent to which their own understanding of and
> sympathy for the girl are artifacts of Freud's rhetoric.[p. 98]

Contretemps of this sort, framed within the inherent subjectivity, dramatic structure, and intimate privacy of the therapeutic encounter, have prompted many critics to think of the better case reports as well-constructed fictions.

This idea receives a useful application in the hands of Jonathan Culler (1981), who examines the relationship between story and discourse and shows the interrelationship between taking the reading as discourse (narrative) determined by story (events), and story shaped by discourse (the meaning of events created by their rendering). This parallels the dialectic between present and past in the clinical situation and lets us see from another vantage point how we are simultaneously driven by the structure of events and by our effort to narrativize the events in our work.

The problematic aspect of considering case histories to be fiction is that to do so blurs the issue of referentiality. Although we cannot know what actually happened to Dora by the lake, we read the case knowing that something in fact did or did not happen, however Dora and, in turn, Freud chose to remember and understand it. We will form our own ideas about that, and about all the romantic entanglements in the case, and will find Freud's account more or less plausible in relation to structures of meaning based on our sense of how people work. While structures of meaning will also inform our reading of a novel, the question of believability has far different implications. It matters to us whether a case history is believable, partly because we want to be able to use what we learn from it. In fiction, believability is a parameter of style. That we are always working with *psychic* reality only means that we have a less tangible referential field, but my fantasy of revenge is as real as the car that cut across my lane.

We might define reality, for these purposes, as that which can be located in history. Why do we have such difficulty allowing for the referentiality of psychic reality? Are we afraid that its elusiveness means we're more likely to be conned? Do we fear that there is no mast we can be tied to to protect us from the Sirens' call? If we feel uneasy about Freud's persuasive powers, Stanley Fish (1986) warns us that we should be. Patrick Mahony (1984), in an exhaustive and remarkable study of the Wolf Man case, demonstrates that Freud, through devices of rhetorical wizardry, sold us (and for over a half century kept us in the thrall of) a thoroughly implausible reconstruction of a primal scene putatively witnessed in astonishing detail by a malaria-struck 1½-year-old. Mahony argues that Freud's writing mimes in various stylistic dimensions both the Wolf Man's symptomatology and Freud's theories. As one example, the issue of the deferred effect of a trauma is represented in the ways in which Freud moves backward and forward in time in his report.

Fish, however, turns it the other way around, and argues that the case reflects the telling. Freud, he says, is quite caught up with persuading us while denying that he is doing so, and constructs the case, or at least his telling of it, to enact that conflict. To wit: "The real seduction in this chapter . . . is the seduction not of the patient by his sister, but of both the patient and reader by Freud, who will now be able to produce interpretive conclusions in the confidence that they will be accepted as the conclusions of an inevitable and independent logic" (Fish 1986, p. 936). For Fish, all is persuasion, but Malcolm challenges this, pointing out that Fish was not persuaded. On the contrary, I imagine that on first reading he was thoroughly seduced, and that a subsequent unease brought him back for a deconstructive reprise, an undoing of the spell. Mahony links Freud's overidealization by the analytic community to his rhetorical facility. Fish takes as an epigraph for his essay the Wolf Man's thoughts during his first hour on the couch: this man is a Jewish swindler, he'd like to use me from behind and shit on my head. (Fish's point is that the Wolf Man got it right!) According to Jones, however, Fish got it backward. Citing Freud's letter to Ferenczi, Jones (1955) reports: "He initiated the first hour of treatment with the offer to have rectal intercourse with Freud and then to defecate on his head" (p. 274). In his effort to persuade us (and to create a great epigraph?), Fish made the victim into the perpetrator.

THE WOLF-MEN: A CAUTIONARY TALE

As noted earlier, one response to the absence of case reports has been our interest in taking on the cases reported by others, most notably by Freud (amply demonstrated above). To be sure, part of the motivation for this work comes from the need each analyst has to take his own measure of Freud, to destroy and resurrect him, Freud being every analyst's father and straw man cluttering the road to professional growth. And what better way to take on Freud than at the heart of his practice? In another sense, those cases *are simply there*—Dora,

Schreber, Little Hans, the Rat Man, the Wolf Man—like Everest, Mount Fuji, and Annapurna, peaks demanding to be scaled. My ambition here is more modest: to take on the mountaineers.

The Wolf Man chronicles read like a gothic novel. From Freud's case report onward, we follow the transformation of this man from a troubled young Russian in Vienna to an artifact of the psychoanalytic profession—from person to persona. The 88-year-old pensioner we encounter in the German journalist Karin Obholzer's interviews and the one in Muriel Gardiner's later reportings (1971, 1983) is a man wrestling to reclaim himself from his proprietors. From reading Gardiner's accounts of what begin to sound like pilgrimages to Mecca ("I received many letters, from analysts and others, wishing to meet him, asking his name and address, asking me questions about him or requesting some information from the Wolf Man directly. I was often in a quandary as to what to do" [1983, p. 876]), one senses that the Wolf Man had become a talisman for psychoanalysts, a magical link to Freud. Kurt Eissler spent many hours tape-recording interviews with him. While according to Gardiner, Eissler's purpose was primarily diagnosis and research ("One cannot consider this an analysis" [1983, p. 888]), the Wolf Man complained, not without admiration, that Eissler could not stop analyzing him, apparently in the sense of interpreting childhood sexuality and unconscious process. Reading of Eissler's doggedness with this elderly, fading man, who considered himself by this time to be well beyond help, I sensed that he might have felt uneasy about simply taking from the Wolf Man for archival purposes without offering something in return, whether helpful or not. Perhaps Eissler recognized that he was part of an outrageous business that was turning analysis on its head, and was trying to rescue his calling. We work in this remarkably fragile profession.

The Wolf Man (1971) begins his memoirs with a description of strange happenings on his father's estate:

> The estate was well known throughout the surrounding country-side, because part of our land was used as a marketplace where fairs were held every now and then. As a small child I once

watched one of these Russian country fairs. I was walking in our garden and heard noise and lively shouting behind the garden fence. Looking through a crack in the fence, I saw campfires burning—it was wintertime—with gypsies and other strange people clustered around them. The gypsies were gesticulating wildly, and everyone was loudly shouting at the same time. There were many horses and the people were evidently arguing about their price. The scene created an impression of indescribable confusion, and I thought to myself that the goings-on in hell must be pretty much like this.[pp. 4–5]

This haunting description is in sharp contrast to the banal renderings of childhood events that follow. The opening chapter, we learn, was written at the end, and only in response to concerted pressure. In fact, the Wolf Man finally put pen to paper only when he was told that the book would go to the publishers a month hence, with or without the childhood accounting (*another* deadline, as Gardiner observes). One can imagine a variety of reasons for his reluctance, certainly including the difficulty in writing about the era that was the heart of Freud's report. In later years at least, the Wolf Man was troubled by the sense Freud had made of those early times; he and Freud had always seemed to have divergent views of the analysis. But beyond that, I imagine that the Wolf Man was disturbed by the imminent public revelation of his affairs. The story of the country fair is foreboding: it speaks of intruders, riff-raff on the estate, strange commerce, "indescribable confusion," the gates of hell opened on earth. He wants us to know what this is costing him, this presentation of a life lived as another's creation.

Harold Blum (1974) thought that "the analysis was more enriching for Freud than it was for his famous patient . . . possibly . . . an indication that the analysis was primarily elucidated and organized in the mind of the analyst" (pp. 721–722). Blum thus reflects a typical experience of the reader—that he is being dazzled with an astonishing tour de force, which sailed right over the patient's head. Janet Malcolm (1987) comments that only Freud is alive in the narration; the

Wolf Man appears as an anesthetized body (dream, free association, enactment) undergoing surgery. Others argue that Freud, to follow the dream's metaphor, was barking up the wrong tree. They claim that he ignored the relationship with the mother, or that he missed the Wolf Man's paranoid (Meissner 1977), narcissistic (Gedo and Goldberg 1973), psychotic (Frosch 1967), or borderline (Blum 1974) psychopathology. Balancing these depreciations of Freud's work, yet others remind us that the Wolf Man came to Vienna "in a pitiful psychological state" (Gay 1988, p. 285), "unable even to dress himself or face any aspect of life" (Jones 1955, p. 274), and, in Freud's own words, "in a state of complete helplessness" (1937, p. 217). The Wolf Man, this argument goes, with the help of Freud and later of Freud's analysand and student Ruth Mack Brunswick, was eventually able to carry on a self-sufficient life in spite of substantial external hardship, including the loss of his family's fortune: he married, worked competently at a career, enjoyed painting, and developed intellectually.

Efforts to vindicate Freud by emphasizing the Wolf Man's recovery are doubly misguided. In his interviews with Obholzer, the Wolf Man claims that statements of his incapacity were great exaggerations, passed on uncritically within Freud's circle. Though this assertion also cannot be taken as the last word, one senses in reading his autobiography a vitality in the child and adolescent that suggests the Wolf Man's breakdown in late adolescence or young adulthood was probably traumatic in origin—a response perhaps to his gonorrhea, or more likely to his sister's death, and later, his father's. The Wolf Man himself thinks that in seeking out Kraepelin he was trying to find a replacement for his father. By this reasoning, it was likely that the Wolf Man would have in time recovered in any event, that Freud had not miraculously rescued a drowning man. (This would not, of course, deny the Wolf Man's substantial character pathology, however one chooses to characterize it.)

On the other hand, Freud's treatment, as presented in his report, does not require absolution. Freud made it clear that he was not by any means presenting us with the entirety of the treatment, but that he was selecting certain aspects of the work to elaborate for purposes of articulating his clinical and developmental theories. His assertions about infantile sexuality, the impact of the primal scene, deferred action, unconscious homosexuality, the role of reconstruction and of forced termination, and his conjectures about fantasy and reality stand or fall as they are supported or refuted by experience with new cases. These ideas can hardly be proven or rejected by this case, because ideas are never in fact proven by an author's cases.

In reviewing the various sources, furthermore, the reader might reasonably conclude that Freud *did* help the Wolf Man, although not in the ways he believed he had. To conclude from reading the Wolf Man's autobiography and the interviews that he had assimilated Freud's formulations about his infantile sexual conflicts, one would have to stretch both faith and the imagination. On the contrary, however, one can imagine the Wolf Man being obsessed throughout the treatment with his relationship with Theresa, the main issue for him being whether Freud would permit the relationship, just as during his later years he tortured everyone who spoke with him (Obholzer not the least) with the question of how he should deal with the woman who he then claimed was persecuting him, the woman Obholzer calls Luise. He says that he went to Freud in the hope that he would be given this esteemed man's permission to see Theresa (a relationship everyone else in his life seemed to oppose), and it's not clear that he ever got much past this. The reader senses, however, that the Wolf Man found himself in a meaningful relationship with a person of intelligence and integrity who was determined to come to terms with him, at least on his own terms. This affirmation, internalized as a relationship with a supportive other, seemed to sustain the Wolf Man over the years. Such support is often understood as the nonspecific therapeutic aspect of analytic treatment and is simply attributed to the analyst's commitment, reliability, and presence. In reading these accounts, however, one hears something more at work: a relentless effort to reach understanding that brooked no evasion. The Wolf Man seemed grateful to Freud (and later to Brunswick, Gardiner, and Eissler) for pursuing that.

The problem that the analysis created for the Wolf Man was that he swallowed it whole and came to see himself through Freud's eyes, not his own. It seems impossible to tell whether this happened in the course of the treatment or after the publication of the case report, but in any event we hear the Wolf Man offering formulations of his character and his illness that ape Freud's language. He himself has not internalized an understanding, he has taken in a persona: he is Freud's most famous case, the Wolf Man, the man who had the wolf dream, the man who witnessed his parents copulating as an infant, and so on. It becomes almost uncanny how much he sounds like Freud when he discusses psychology: "Theoretically, it is interesting how insidious the 'id' can be. How it can dissemble, apparently following the commands of the 'ego' and the 'superego,' but in secret preparing its 'revenge' and then suddenly triumphing over these higher courts" (1971, p. 337). The literate world has become fascinated with him, but not him as he truly is, rather as the man who Freud made him out to be. This is the cloak that he obsessively tries to fit on and to tear to shreds. His life becomes, in large measure, the unwinding of his analysis.

The Wolf Man is not the only one, however, who has come to confuse person and persona. Subsequent analysts take up Freud's interrogation, not recognizing that they are not analyzing Sergei Pankejeff but Freud's Wolf Man, a creation of Freud's analysis. What is available for scrutiny, of course, is a rendering of a psychoanalysis. This can relevantly be approached with the tools of literary analysis, which might lead to a critique of Freud's capacity for representation and communication.

Some writers have tried to strengthen their arguments by including material from the Wolf Man's memoirs, as though this were a primal source and not itself a tendentious representation, the Wolf Man as seen through the eyes of the Wolf Man as transcribed by Sergei Pankejeff, if you will. (The memoirs could easily be read, for example, as a reproach to Freud that Theresa was what mattered in his life after all—apart from the opening paragraphs, this is the only section I find poignant.) Nor are the reminiscences of the Obholzer interviews, for that matter, simply liquid truths. Behind their ingenuous surface lie levels of refraction—Obholzer's agendas and editing, the Wolf Man's agendas in permitting the interviews, and his transference to her and hers to him, to name a few.

It has been argued, by Mahony among others, that the Wolf Man used the various psychoanalysts who had contact with him as selfobjects. While this seems plausible, it also seems plausible that in so doing he was mirroring their use of him as a transitional object, a link to Freud. Those of us who have analyzed the Wolf Man have kept it unclear, because we ourselves have been unclear, whether we were talking with Sergei Pankejeff or the Wolf Man. We have left it ambiguous whether we were speaking of a person or a creation—which is how, as Winnicott told us (1971), transitional objects are experienced. (Remember that Winnicott instructed the mother that she was not to ask her toddler whether he had created the object or received it, for it was always to be both and neither.) Laboring between our ambitions regarding Freud and our refusal to accept the inaccessibility of another practitioner's patient—our refusal to accept the Wolf Man as a narrative creation—we have given birth to a monstrosity: the Wolf in Sergei's suit.

And so, we have one Sergei Pankejeff, but many Wolf-Men. Who are the wolves—our renderings of him or ourselves? This brings us to the heart of subjectivity and transference—transference being the great conception psychoanalysis brings to our understanding of subjectivity. Ironically, one senses that Freud was too determined to be the master, too intent on making psychoanalysis into an objective science, to allow himself to appreciate the depth and power of his conception, and thus it remained for him a conceit. One senses that he could feel chagrined when misled by a patient, but not shattered, in the way in which we now understand that we must bear shattering so that we can recrystallize an understanding. How else, for example, could he bear to tell and retell the story of his encounter with Dora? Or, for that matter, with the Wolf Man? To be more generous, as Schafer (1992) certainly is, we might say that Freud did not yet have the tools to fully understand himself.

There is a remarkable locution that has crept in around the Wolf

Man case. It begins with Freud's footnote at the end of the report, added a decade later, in which he comments on the Wolf Man's brief return to treatment with him toward the end of the First World War: "After a few months' work, a piece of the transference which had not hitherto been overcome was successfully dealt with" (1918 [1914], p. 122). Referring to the case in "Analysis Terminable and Interminable," Freud comments on the brief attacks of illness that brought the Wolf Man to treatment with Ruth Mack Brunswick: "Some of these attacks were still concerned with residual portions of the transference" (1937, p. 218). Brunswick (1928) echoes this in saying that "the source of the new illness was an unresolved remnant of the transference" (p. 264). The phrase "unresolved remnant" becomes standard fare in discussions of the case, as though we were considering a scrap of cloth Freud had accidentally mislaid. But the Wolf Man himself is hardly so sanguine here. He comments ironically, changing metaphors, "Mack [Brunswick] thought there was a little grain, as it were, that had remained undissolved, and that grain was paranoia" (Obholzer 1982, p. 57). "Transference," he assures us, "is a dangerous thing" (p. 31).

For the Wolf Man, late in life and speaking retrospectively, his transference to Freud has been the bane of his existence. By "transference" he meant helpless dependency on another, a state of mind that he felt had suffused far too much of his life. He saw his dependent relations with subsequent figures as extensions and displacements of his transference to Freud. And he used this perception to blame others and exculpate himself: had it not been for his transference to Freud, he argues, he might have returned to Russia and rescued his fortune. Transference, of course, is never a little bit of anything; it is always all of everything.

For Freud, the treatment was an exercise in reconstruction, the reinterpretation of childhood memories and especially of a childhood dream. The Wolf Man's transference is treated as an obstacle to this unfolding, a resistance to be gotten rid of through education and limit setting. And so the crucial information that emerged in the last stages of treatment became available because "Under the inexorable pressure of this fixed limit his resistance and his fixation to the illness gave way"

(1918 [1914], p. 11). We might now say that Freud did not work through the Wolf Man's transference but manipulated it to create a state of compliance. In fact, he comments that "the patient gave an impression of lucidity which is usually attainable only in hypnosis" (p. 11). Despite Freud's engaging presentation, the absence of an analytic process, as we now understand it, makes this case report ultimately unsatisfying to the contemporary reader.

Consider, however, the possibilities—the wolf dream, for example. Freud does not tell us the context in which the patient remembered the dream, presumably because he considers the context irrelevant. Yet the telling of a dream, like any act in an analysis, occurs in a transference setting. Encoded within the reporting is a communication about the analysis. In reading the Wolf Man's memoirs, I was caught by this passage: "[Freud] was a genius. Just imagine the work he did, remembering all those details, forgetting nothing, drawing those inferences. He may have had six, seven patients a day" (1971, p. 32). I immediately thought of the dream's wolves in the tree—the Wolf Man had said there were six or seven— and of Freud's speculations about the meaning of those numbers and of the uncertainty. I wondered if the wolves represented for the Wolf Man Freud's daily patients, six or seven, depending on whether he included himself. We are aware of his intense rivalry with his sister for his father's affection, and it is easy to imagine that he felt a similarly intense competition with his analytic siblings. He asked Freud about the people he saw coming and going, and Freud identified them to him by occupation and circumstances, although not by name. At the point at which Freud finally sought to analyze this dream, might the Wolf Man have been retelling it because he was facing rejection by Freud, imagining the siblings poised outside the consulting room door, motionless, ready to spring, a projection of his own wish to break in on Freud's life and make his claim—a protest against the exclusions, both the forced termination date and the Sunday absences, the one day of the seven Freud didn't receive him, the omission blurred by the phrase "six or seven"? This is all, to be sure, wildly speculative, but it is evocative and brings the treatment to life.

If the dream can be understood as an elaboration of the transference, it can become part of an analytic process. Perhaps "six or seven" was a locution the Wolf Man habitually used, picked up in childhood, entirely incidental to the possibilities I am suggesting. But perhaps not. In the spirit of full disclosure, I should report that the theme of rivalry with a sibling for a lost father is hardly irrelevant to my own life. Does this create my interpretation as a projection of my own competitive strivings, or does it sensitize me to recognizing something present in the treatment? That is an unanswerable question, and the appeal of the interpretation, as always, will depend on the resonance it evokes in other readers.

The lesson of transference is that we cannot stand outside a subjective position. My choosing to use the case of the Wolf Man as a vehicle for exploring these issues is dense with personal meanings, only one of which I have briefly acknowledged. I do not begin to imagine that I could sort out my countertransferences understood as my own distortions of the material from my countertransferences understood as empathic responses to the material. In the literature on treatment, the capacity to make this distinction is held to be absolutely critical, and yet it will always elude us. Every moment in an analysis is created by two minds, two psychologies, two lives intersecting. The notion that we could perceive our patients without our own transferences is unanalytic. Bion's conception that we should approach our patients without memory and desire I take to be his acknowledgment of the absolute impossibility of that task. We hesitate to share our cases because we know they reveal as much about ourselves as about our patients. One rhetorical tactic has been to more fully expose cases we treated when we were in training. Those patients, we imagine, were treated by someone else.

Each reader will create his own Wolf Man, as each analyst, each interviewer, and each author has done. The irony, in terms of received theory, is that we do find ourselves more engaged in certain treatments and in certain readings, where we have more personally at stake, and are less clear about our bearings; these are probably the treatments in which we have the potential to be of greatest use, and the readings to which we can best respond with our own interpretations. In any event, and in all events, we work by adding our own meaning to the layers of meaning that existed before us. If what we have to offer is useful, it will be added to the fabric of meanings already created. In contrast to Freud's vision of analysis as archaeology or sculpture, a process of unearthing and subtraction, I understand analysis as a process of addition, in the way that an artist might return to a painting and see a new possibility, add new paint to the canvas, reach a new synthesis.

8

Therapy as Mourning

From another outlook, we might describe the work of therapy as mourning. In every treatment, as in every life, there is much to be given up: great expectations, grievances, avoidances, prejudices, habitual ways of managing anxiety, and problematic forms of relatedness, just to begin a list of the possibilities. Freud's concept of the analyst as lightning rod, as attractor of transferences, is apt here. All that has to be given up will be made manifest in the transference, as wishes, hopes and fears, perceptions, and styles of interacting are brought to life in the space between analyst and patient. The thrust of transference interpretation is to bring these states of mind into the light of day, to expose what must be relinquished. My patient's capacity to make use of interpretation thus depends on her ability to mourn, an ability that will be in part already established, and in part developed in treatment.

The transformation involved in mourning may be dodged in a variety of ways. Some patients insist upon their own constructions of reality despite our best efforts. We may eventually sense that we have been of use to them primarily in refining *their* efforts, helping them to manage a little more efficiently within a quite restricted scheme. Others offer surface compliance while concealing their perverseness and their passions. What previously has been acted out may continue as a silent guiding phantasy. Manic and depressive solutions are both flights from mourning: the former pretends to do away with all need, the latter grudgingly refuses to let go. Externals may be altered while what's inside is preserved untouched. A colleague who treats alcoholism told me that alcoholics will give up anything, including alcohol, to preserve the freedom to drink. That principle has broader applications.

Every transference–countertransference enactment, whatever else it might mean, serves to abort mourning.

How do we understand the act of mourning? Freud emphasized the process of detachment from the object. His conception was that each of the libidinal ties to the object—each memory, each longing—is intensified, and then the spell is broken, the bond can be untied (1917 [1915]). I discover here a parallel to our idea of how treatment works: we bring problematic ways of functioning into the transference so that they can be recognized and then relinquished or revised. A casual reading of Freud might suggest that mourning means severing all connections. We know, of course, that we don't stop caring about that which we have mourned, but that we care in a different way. Our caring now acknowledges the reality and the permanence of the loss. In depression loss is protested, in mourning it is recognized (Smith 1971).

Mourning signals a shift in attitude toward the object: it is no longer part of the present, it can be placed in the past. In this way man creates himself as a historical being. By contrast, in the refusal to mourn time stands still. When we are lived by our transferences—when, for example, I experience my analyst as though he actually is my father—I destroy historicity, I exist only in the present. When I recognize a transference feeling, I am a maker of meaning. I have shifted from the realm in which everything only *is* what it appears to be, to a world of symbolization, in which things *evoke* one another without being each other.

Winnicott (1971) taught us that symbolization begins for the infant in the intermediate space between mother and child. The crucial developmental experience for the child, along these lines, is its relationship with its transitional objects. The teddy bear or security blanket is an object the child uses to find its way toward separateness in its relationship with its mother. In intermediate space objects are both *me* and *not me*, not experienced definitively either as the infant's creation or as the creation of the mother. It is precisely that ambiguity that makes negotiating the transition toward aloneness possible. Not being committed to a state of individuation or to primary identification with the mother, the infant is freer to experiment, to try things on for size.

The analytic situation can be understood as an analogue to this experience. The analyst tries to help the patient to enter a state of regression in which transferences can be tried on for size. When captured by the intensities of her transference neurosis, which we might conceptualize as an encounter in intermediate space, the patient experiences both the factuality and unreality of her transferences. Her analyst both is, but also is not, her mother. To the extent that patient and analyst can create this space, renunciation, mourning, and acceptance can take place. The capacity to make use of treatment, the capacity to mourn, is measured by the patient's capacity to make use of transitional experience.

The act of mourning itself can certainly be accommodated in a one-person psychology; in fact, we inevitably do much of our mourning on our own. The way in which mourning occurs in psychotherapy, however, is more clearly captured by a two-person framework. Insofar as parenting and treatment create an intermediate space for symbolization and enactment, the space is created by two parties, whether mother and child or therapist and patient. Both must be able, to a degree, to lose themselves in the regressive experience that lies between separateness and oneness, where embedded resistance can be pried free and brought to life. Therapy is the place for the mourning one cannot do on one's own.

Considering mourning as symbolization makes the process sound excessively cognitive. The double edge of treatment is that it simultaneously creates a phantasy of fulfillment, of dreams being realized, at the same time that it institutes relinquishment. In this sense, therapy is a tease: desire is both enticed and cruelly thwarted. The ways in which we lead our lives are the ways in which we have known love, for better and for worse. We are invited to bring our passions to life in treatment so that we can give them up. But we are not asked to give up being passionate, and—again, paradoxically—it is by bringing passion into our lives in treatment that we become alive, releasing the numbing grip of transference repetition. Smith (1991) observes that desire arises from "necessary lostness," making use of the title of Judith Viorst's book, *Necessary Losses*. In the act of mourning, desire bursts forth again.

Then again, we might say that treatment and mourning lead us into a condition of reminiscence. Where longing was, there nostalgia shall be. In quiet moments we appreciate that our ancient dreams cannot be fulfilled in the ways we had originally intended, and we might even come to know this with some affection for ourselves. We also recognize the ways that those dreams, transformed, live in our present intensities, and transference then acquires a new meaning: the transference of desire.

Loewald (1962, 1973) reminds us that mourning leads to internalization, by which he means that the useful parts of lost relationships become part of ego and part of character. He takes as his model for this the internalization of the superego at the end of the oedipal phase. With the renunciation of incestuous and aggressive ambitions, the child accepts and internalizes the parent's authority. Internal object relations are projected onto the transference screen so that they can ultimately be relinquished (more precisely, the passions embodied in them can be relinquished) and transformed into psychic structure.

To continue this discussion, I will now present three examples from clinical work: with an individual, a couple, and a family. In each instance a crucial part of the work to be done involved mourning; in all three cases it was only possible to go part of the distance. In the way that we often learn more from our partial failures than our complete successes, these stories are particularly instructive.

ILLUSTRATIONS

The Dying Child

The first case is a relatively brief family treatment that I supervised.

> The Turners were facing the imminent death of their 4-year-old daughter, Nancy. Many surgical procedures had failed to rectify her congenital heart defect, and her condition had weakened to the point that a common cold might cause her death. Nancy had been conceived as part of an effort to save her parents' failing marriage. Once the pregnancy was under way, they had considered aborting it.
>
> Mr. Turner was a rigid, authoritarian man who said that he had spent his childhood trying unsuccessfully to win his critical mother's approval. He remembered that he'd always tried to stay one step ahead of her to remain in her good graces. His alcoholic father had deserted the family when he was a teenager. Mr. Turner was responding to the present crisis by withdrawing from the family and immersing himself in his job.
>
> Mrs. Turner was in her third marriage, and Nancy was the fifth of her children. One of the children was the product of an affair she'd had with a married man during her first marriage. This paternity was concealed, and the child believed that she was the daughter of Mrs. Turner's first husband.

One begins to get a horrific sense of the extent to which the parents treated these children as extensions of their own needs, to be conceived, aborted, or lied to as needs demanded. In each of these acts and intentions, an aspect of history was to be denied—that the parents' marriage had turned sour, that they had conceived a fetus, that Mrs. Turner had had an affair. The children, in their existence, were to embody what could not be mourned. Nancy's illness put a great strain on a fragile adjustment.

> The Turners could not face the reality of their daughter's condition, particularly because it reverberated so painfully with their feelings of guilt and inadequacy. Mr. Turner felt a special sense of failure since he, as the father, expected himself to provide for the security and safety of the family. His helplessness turned into anger at his daughter, whose dying exposed his ineffectualness to him, placing him at the mercy of his hateful, demanding maternal introject. This internal attack was now being defended against by means of emotional withdrawal.

The terminal illness of a child will inescapably evoke overwhelming feelings of helplessness, and the parents will attempt to manage these feelings in various ways. What, for a long time, is most unbearable is the capricious nature of fate, the realization that terrible things can happen for no good reason. A common defense is to search for someone to blame, but what is really being searched for is causality. The work of mourning begins with having to bear the loss of omnipotence, to recognize that there are eventualities from which one cannot protect one's child. I imagine that also embedded in the search for causality is an unconscious phantasy that if the cause can be found it can be reversed. For a time, the finality of death cannot be borne.

Mr. Turner's internal self-accusation may have arisen as a defensive response to murderous feelings aroused in him toward the internal mother who had failed him—failed him, that is, by allowing this catastrophe to occur. Living in the company of a persecutory maternal introject and without an adequate internalized holding capacity or supportive family structure, Mr. Turner was at the mercy of forces beyond his control. The addictive nature of such internal object relations is remarkably impressive. It is based, in part, on the person's fear of abandonment by the object. Abject submission to the internal imago thus defends both against the temptation to destroy the object and the danger of being discarded by it. The object can hardly be released at a time of loss—it is felt to be all that one is sure one has.

> Mr. Turner's 15-year-old stepson, Teddy, whom he had once tied to a chair when he would not sit still, was clearly feeling the stress of the situation with Nancy and asked to be sent to his grandparents. When this was refused, he ran away, planning on living by himself in the woods. When Teddy was discovered, his father told him sadistically, "I'm not going to punish you now. When you know why you ran away, I'll punish you." His mother added, "Your running away could have given your grandmother a heart attack! It could have made me unable to take care of Nancy! It could have caused your father to lose his job!"
>
> A few weeks later the family canceled their therapy session because the parents had decided to be remarried in the church. In context, it seemed like another form of running away. Nancy, barely able to walk, would be the flower girl.

The family was using the remarriage to create an illusion of hope in the face of despair. The despair, however, was not simply over the child's imminent death. More significantly, I think, the despair was over the family's inability to provide support to its members in this time of stress. The hopelessness was a response to the sense that the guilt and anger aroused in the parents was destroying all love in the family, as experienced in the family's vengeful response to their son's running away. Teddy's elopement expressed the father's flight from the family—we could imagine that Teddy was driven to enact this for his stepfather. In attacking Teddy, the parents could disown their own feelings of disloyalty and rage and project them into their son, whom they would now control and punish. Mrs. Turner could say to herself: I don't cause heart attacks; Teddy does. Father's statement, "When you know why you ran away, I'll punish you," reflected, I think, his own need to not know why he himself was running away, since not knowing might spare him terrible self-punishment. The family needed to have Teddy desert them to protect the parents' marriage.

One truth that the family needed to bear and not run away from was that they were not strong enough to provide one another support. Acknowledging this might have helped them to feel a measure of freedom—freedom from the burden of failing at what was for them an impossible task—and to experience sadness. Great catastrophes offer families a view of their resources; times of grief become times of reckoning. But so often failed expectations seem to be resolved not by mourning but by divorce.

The family's shared unconscious belief was that Nancy's illness was their fault, a fulfillment of their sense of inner destructiveness. The guilt could only be dealt with by projective identification into Teddy and manic flight away from therapy and into the remarriage festivity. The canceling of the therapy hour had left the therapist feeling useless and discarded, and wondering if he had been destructive in trying to help the family face its withdrawal and denial. The family was disowning its feeling of destructiveness and projecting it into the therapist, from whom they then had to flee. His feeling of inner badness, and, perhaps more poignantly, his feeling of futility, mirrored the central conflicts the family was struggling with. His attention to his own responses could have led him to a clearer understanding of their struggle.

The end point of mourning might be thought of as reconciliation. *Reconcile* has two meanings—I reconcile myself *to* something, or I reconcile *with*—acceptance and reunion. For the individual, reconciliation means the self-acceptance that can come with self-knowledge. I accept myself as the person I am, accepting the harm I've caused along with the good I've done, accepting my limitations and bypassed opportunities along with my achievements and my remaining possibilities. Without that reconciliation I have no meaningful freedom or autonomy. The reunion achieved is with the disowned parts of myself. For the family, reconciliation means acknowledging the family's historical reality, and that includes recognizing the injustices that have been done, and the motives behind them. It means relinquishing the shared self-protecting illusions. It also means accepting the inevitability of the family's past and the consequences of that past for the future. The reconciliation possible might not be a tearful reunion, for that might be inauthentic given the shared reality, but it would include a shared understanding of what the family's life has been about. And that reconciliation may be greatly liberating for the members of the family. Had this objective been clearer to the therapist and his supervisor at the time of the treatment, they might have been of greater use to the Turners.

The Lost Child

My second story is about a man who shed many tears but was unable to mourn. After telling you a bit about him, I will present excerpts from a series of sessions to highlight these issues at the level of therapeutic process.

> John, age 45 and a successful cardiac surgeon, initially came to see me because he had lost interest in his wife. They had been childhood sweethearts and life had flowed easily in the early years of their marriage, but with the succession of children they had drifted apart, becoming more immersed in their careers and avoiding spending time together. He'd found her loss of interest in him when she had the babies intolerable; he said it had made him feel like a "Chinese peasant." By the time we were working together he felt intensely aversive when he was with her; he was acutely uncomfortable even touching her arm.
>
> A crucial series of incidents had occurred toward the end of John's oedipal years. The first pair of events are confused in his mind. He had an image of his parents being off on a vacation together while he was left with a maid, and a memory of his father suffering a stroke while sending John off on a trip with an aunt. Thus an image of being left out by his parents was mixed up with one of his father being hurt. Within the year his mother's father also had a stroke, and she left home to take care of him, being gone for much of the next year. John, an only child, was sent off to spend that summer with a friend's family. His first night away, watching the friend's mother play with her sons, he felt overwhelmingly sad and cried himself to sleep. By the next morning he had put his mother

out of his mind and he never thought of her again all summer long. When he returned home, his grandfather had died and his mother was back home, severely depressed. John has a memory from that time of looking at his mother's naked back in her bedroom and feeling a wave of nausea. His mother never recovered from the loss of her father, and as the years passed she became remote, hypochondriacal, and embittered. John had lost his great pal. In the years that followed, his father became progressively disabled, both by a series of mild strokes and by an accompanying depression. This remarkable captain of industry, who had been John's great hero, became a shell of his former self, as he remained today. By adolescence, John was occupied with propping up his father. And by this time his mother was only a distant presence for him.

By midlatency, John had become an independent, resourceful child, although something of a loner, spending hours by himself playing fantasy games in the woods. He achieved extremely well in school, holding himself to rigorous standards. He went after the medical career his parents had hoped he'd pursue, with a vengeance. By the time I met him he was one of the foremost practitioners in his field and had made several significant contributions to surgical technique.

When he was present, John worked hard at his analysis, keeping track of his dreams and dredging up memories. Like everything else in his life, he wanted to do it well. He mostly kept me at arm's length, treating me like a wise, avuncular mentor. He valued my intelligence but felt unable to feel a warm connection to me—I was like a stone wall to him, he said. On my own side, I felt more than a bit stonewalled by my earnest patient. We'd been able to construct a narrative of his life that hung together and explained a good deal, some of which is presented in précis above. I understood that he experienced his life as a pleasureless compliance to a series of masters whom he resented—his wife, his children, his work, and me.

When, for example, John was with his older son, of whom he was especially fond, he was repeatedly chagrined to find himself keeping an eye on his watch, wondering when he'd have devoted enough time to fathering. I also understood that he would not get angry—that to do so would be uncivilized. And so he simply missed half his sessions with me, all the absences ostensibly being necessitated by his work. I, of course, found this exceedingly frustrating, for just as we'd be building up a head of steam, he'd turn off down a private track. I thought that he was ducking both his embryonic feelings of dependency on me and his suppressed rage at me for controlling his life. I told him that he was giving each of us half a loaf, that that was his compromise between surrendering to us and totally shutting us out. I think that my putting it this way, not speaking only to our relationship but expressing the thought in a plural form, reflected my feeling of not being special to him. The half loaf that was missing in his marriage and in the analysis was his passion, or perhaps I should say his heart.

John expressed his anxiety in an unusual way. He would fill the session with a string of daydreams, which had the quality of sleeping dreams. They weren't the usual wishful fantasies or fears one finds in daydreams—the contents were more disguised. He would experience this as working hard at his analysis, but I would usually find it very difficult to make any sense of the images. They seemed like the equivalent of obsessional thinking—an effort to keep other thoughts, or feelings, at bay. Once I realized that this was going on, I would interrupt him and ask him what he thought he was anxious about. The behavior was a microcosm of his leading defense: distancing disguised as devotion. Until I recognized the pattern, I had felt a little uneasy about my lack of gratitude.

I liked John—I admired his forthrightness, his industry, and his honesty. I envied his ambition, his capacity to work for days on end while getting virtually no sleep. While I am hardly a slouch, it seemed to me that he fit twice as much into a day as I could. He never trivialized the analysis, even though he avoided it. I sensed a mutual respect. I also felt a palpable sympathy for his predicament that apparently had no solution: he was unable to feel comfortable with his wife, try as he might, and yet he did not want to leave his children, who were still quite young. Thus he was obliged to go through his days with no hope for love, left only with memories of lost loves from his youth. At the same time, the analysis felt a bit sterile to me, too intellectualized, too far away from feelings. I felt that I couldn't quite connect up with John, and when he complained about my remoteness I wondered whether he wasn't right, that I couldn't let myself get close to him. And so self-doubt began to seep in.

For our purposes here, I would like to highlight the failure of mourning. As a child, John's working-through of his oedipal ambitions had been disrupted by his father's stroke and by his mother's absence and depressive withdrawal. He'd lost his chance to test and measure himself against his father during adolescence, as his father had progressively declined. In the face of his mother's absence, he had adopted the defense of indifference—he would never hold her in his heart again. Unable to mourn the failure of his oedipal ambitions with her, he had attempted to deny desire.

Desire, of course, will have its way, and during adolescence he was quite taken with sexual fantasies about a woman his mother's age. Those feelings seemed to transfer next to the woman he married, whom he experienced as being quite like his mother in appearance and temperament (the mother, that is, before the fall). He was never able to surrender himself to this woman, although the disturbing feelings did not develop until she had children. The paradoxically necessary step in development is that desire for the mother must be given up and mourned, but also kept alive for infusion into the loves of adolescence. The mother as object of desire must be relinquished while desire for the mother is preserved, awaiting transformation into less incestuous longings for others. In this sense, it is the loss of an ambition that must be mourned—a narcissistic loss must be endured. Unwilling to risk hurt again, John kept his distance—from me, from family, from friends. In three years of analysis I never heard about a meaningful ongoing involvement with a pal.

His experience of his father's strokes, and his father's progressive decline, made it difficult for John to work out a comfortable aggressiveness. Although his work offered a competitive outlet, he noticed that he was unable to get forthrightly angry. He kept his father idealized as a latency-age child's hero; he was not able to bear subjecting this experience of his father to the ordinary wearing away of adolescent disillusionment. It seemed like any move in that direction might quickly lead to tearing his father to shreds, so vulnerable did his father seem. In trying to understand the confusion of childhood images that I mentioned near the outset, I imagined that he might have experienced his father's first stroke as the realization of hateful feelings he felt toward him over taking his mother away on the special vacation. This might have been experienced as a frightening realization of the power of his fantasies. The situation of so early exceeding father, always traumatic for a boy, could not be mourned. He kept the omnipotent father as a talisman.

Finally, his difficulty with realizing both erotic and aggressive feelings made ambivalence impossible (or, in a different sense of the word, made ambivalence universal). He was always torn between preserving and destroying his objects. He began his surgical practice by joining with a group of senior surgeons and quickly became the most productive member of the team. During treatment, he rather abruptly decided to leave them. He had been so loyal and hardworking as a member of the group that they were shattered by his decision to leave. Feeling violently betrayed, they sued to stop his departure. I thought that the intensity of their feelings was a measure of the intensity of his ambivalence. I also thought that, in some measure, this was a displacement of an attack on me. That was to follow.

The following excerpts are taken from sessions toward the end of the third year of analysis.

I had a nightmare last night. I was in an old building . . . a haunted house? There were spots of light on the wall, a larger and a smaller one. I looked to find the source of the light, but there wasn't a source—I put my hand in front of the light and there was no shadow. I realized that these were ghosts whose presence was on the wall! They moved a bit. I became very scared. It would be hard to accept that I was talking to a guy who died fifty years ago. [My ears perk up. I've just turned 51.] Then I saw a stampede of ghost horses coming toward me. I started moaning and woke up.

The image I've had of you is like talking to a wall. [He backs away from this, and after a while, knowing of his enthusiasm for the movies, I ask him if he's seen the recent film *Ghost*.] Yuh! I was crying and crying. It really affected me. How much they loved one another. Not being able to be with one another. The movie was cruel to people who did lose a loved one. It gives a cruel hope to someone who desperately wants to deny death.

[Putting the movie between us has allowed him to open up a bit about his longing. The ghost nightmare makes me think about the return of the repressed—actually, the threatened stampede. I have the thought that he's sealed his feelings for his mother and father in that wall. Like Poe's entombed cat, they're trying to break free. The ghosts are stirring. Affected by his thoughts about the movie, and reflecting on the juxtaposed spots of light, I comment on his fear of being in touch with his longings, in particular with his longings for me.] I had the thought that I was touching my father. I have an image of an army obstacle course. I wasn't strong enough to pull myself up over the wall. [I thought that he'd missed having a father's help and wouldn't now let himself use my help, and so he'd blocked my attempt to reach him.]

Mourning makes it possible, in Loewald's (1960) phrase, to turn ghosts into ancestors. The inability to mourn left John haunted. He could not bear facing his disappointment with his parents, but he was living it out now as a dissatisfaction with me. (And I discovered in the next hour that he'd stayed away from telling me that his father was now acutely ill.) The following is from a session a few days later:

What's happening to my father is what I'm afraid will happen to me— that I'll become marginally incompetent, unable to deal with the real world. This is heightening my feelings about the slow progress we're making in this analysis. After my session with you yesterday it just seemed very frustrating. I had no better sense of what it is that's confronting me, how to better express it, deal with it. I feel like I'm talking into a void. The meaningful benefit isn't there, it's not worth it. But I don't feel angry. [I replied, "You *seem* angry."] I don't feel any rage. I've had these thoughts for some time, but I haven't expressed them before because I didn't want to offend you, didn't want to make you feel bad, but if I can't tell *you* this, who *can* I talk to? I guess I'm angry, but all I feel is a knot in the pit of my stomach.

The scene from *Ghostbusters II* is in my mind: the underground stream of liquid evil flowing through the city of New York, you could walk along the street and not know it's there. I feel there's this stream of liquid evil coursing through my veins. [These are vivid images, but, as John speaks, there's no palpable feeling behind them. It all seems intellectualized, to both of us. I did think that in part he felt angry at me now because I wasn't protecting him from the explosion of rage that he feared. I say this, but it feels too cerebral even as I write it.]

In the hours that followed I heard about John's fears of being vulnerable and about castration anxiety: memories of masturbating his first girlfriend and being terrified afterward when he discovered blood on his fingers, fantasies about a switchblade his father brought back home from a trip, revulsion at seeing his wife naked in the bathtub without a penis, dreams of alligators and medieval tortures. I thought that he wanted to counter his feeling that he was losing his grip in the analysis, that he was sensing that his ability to keep his ambivalence warded off was breaking down. Would quitting be the only solution? In retrospect the memories seem compelling, but at the time I felt impotent. My words felt mechanical to me, as he sapped the life blood from the treatment.

I did begin to hear a bit about violence—childhood torturing of animals, imagining banging a woman's head against a board while having sex with her, wishes to retaliate against rivals—but I heard also his fantasies of being able to withstand tortures, of being indestructible.

I have an image of being in a small room. The purpose of going in there was to flail the skin off an arm. I put my arm in a device. There was a grip at the bottom that you held tight. There were metal and knives inside, but you didn't feel anything. The knives suddenly came up the arm and flailed it; I did it. I didn't scream. I didn't see any purpose to the device. A little boy, 2 or 3 years old, wandered in the open door, he peeked in. I said "Don't go in there. You can get hurt. We should keep the door closed."

[I imagined this as a child's primal scene phantasy: the 3-year-old boy's castrating mother. He had no associations to the toddler. I remembered him telling me that when he was 2 or 3 a house across the street burned down, killing all the children, but I wasn't sure that this was relevant. But his associations led to a movie in which the hero, stakes in his chest, was suspended over a fire as a test of his manhood.

A fire to be survived. It was an Indian rite of passage. I interpreted that he was trying to manage his anxiety about my treatment of him by considering the analysis also an initiation to adulthood.]

I make the analysis a rite of passage because it's pointless.

[Again, I felt disarmed.]

I had the passing thought that John was a bit like the child who murdered both parents and then begged the court for mercy because he was an orphan. Unable to mourn the ways in which his parents had disappointed him, John had eradicated them from his mind, or at least had reduced them to pathetic invalids in his custody. The psychic murder, however, raised further guilt, beyond the survivor guilt intrinsic to his childhood, and his need to flee from this guilt further compromised mourning. Without being aware of it, and in an externally quite composed life, John was always secretly in flight. Despite our efforts, and some earnest maneuvering on both our parts, the analysis ultimately seemed more successful as a documentation of a flight path than as an effort to change its course.

An honest treatment relentlessly highlights the tragic aspect of existence, goes beyond the inevitable lostness to the necessary lostness, recognizes that we work our ways through life by negotiating losses. This is not to say that therapy is only about tears and never about joy, but it is to say that there are always tears with the joy, that even with every taking up there is inescapably a letting go. The ironic edge of treatment keeps us aware that because it can't be otherwise we needn't feel so devastated, that we will survive the losses even against our will, that because we know we have a final curtain to face we needn't make the other drapes into mourning shrouds. Treatment helps us to expect a little less of ourselves, and thus to resume our journeys. The failure to acknowledge the tragic and ironic dimensions of existence leaves us paralyzed, alone on a barren passage with a faceless clock.[1]

---

[1]For a rich consideration of the comic, romantic, tragic, and ironic dimensions of psychoanalysis, see Schafer (1970).

The Haunted Marriage

My third story is about a couple I worked with for a few years. They were referred to me by a colleague who was seeing the wife in psychotherapy twice a week.

I found Peter and Carol immediately likable. Their marriage seemed on the fringe of divorce and I felt, as I don't recall ever having felt before, that it would be tragic if they broke up. They seemed like such a natural couple. He was tall, manly, handsome, articulate, and decent, and he wore his heart on his sleeve. Carol was pert, vivacious, witty, and smart, but a bit arch, more guarded than he, less openly vulnerable. As I said, I liked them both, but beyond that, and more unusual from my point of view, I cared for their marriage. Most marriages that I encounter in my work I could, from the point of view of my own sensibility, take or leave. And so, in the early months of treatment I was unusually willing to extend myself to see them at odd hours to accommodate Peter's business travel—on occasion we met on weekends or at hours well into the evening.

It was about a year into the work when I realized that Peter and Carol were also the most diabolically matched couple I'd ever encountered. They had the capacity to hurt each other with surgical deftness and precision, to unleash savagery in the flick of an offhand remark. And the hurting seemed effortless, intuitive. Once I appreciated all this I reported my experience to them: how I found them at once so exquisitely well- and ill-matched, perhaps the best and the worst marriage I could recall having encountered. Peter replied, "It's two sides of a very thin coin."

Two months before they came to see me, Peter had told Carol that he'd had an affair with a colleague. On Carol's birthday, 2 weeks later, he surprised her by telling her more: it hadn't just been a one-night stand, and the woman was now pregnant. The repercussions of these disclosures had prompted them to consult me.

Peter and Carol had been together for ten years, having met as young professionals working on an assignment. Her earlier relationships had mainly been based on sex—she said she had found that easier than being intimate or talking. Sex had become a way of guarding her privacy. With Peter something else had seemed possible, a kind of love she'd never known before, a new beginning. He had lost his erection their first time together and, to her surprise, it hadn't mattered to her.

After their first child, a couple of years into the marriage, sex had become more difficult. The episiotomy had been botched, making sex very painful; more surgery was required to repair the defect. Carol felt completely scarred and thought she would never enjoy sex again. As matters developed, sex wasn't so painful now, but she was less interested in sex than Peter was. Their solution was that Peter masturbated, as much for relief as for pleasure, it seemed. When his feelings of rejection became troubling enough to her, Carol would have sex with him, but then she would feel used, as if she'd been a prostitute. Carol now wondered whether Peter had liked her before they first had sex. I recognized that she had never felt sure he loved her, his assurances notwithstanding. Peter countered that he thought he was living with a wife who was seething with resentment and that there was too much hatred in bed.

Carol's pain about the affair seemed more a matter of shame than betrayal. On the one hand she was intensely concerned about who knew about it, perhaps because she was afraid they would think she'd been naive. Being exposed as a person capable of being fooled seemed, at moments, the worst part to her. On the other hand, she was consumed by invidious comparisons with the other woman—who was more attractive, who was better in bed, who was better at conversation, where and when had he done it with her and how did that compare with where and when *she'd* done it with him. Carol pressed Peter for accountings and sometimes he was willing to tell her, to inflict the pain. At one point he tried to reassure her that "big tits and a tight pussy aren't a basis for a relationship." (The other woman had "big tits" and, being childless, "a tight pussy.") The comment was hardly reassuring. It made Carol feel even more inadequate and she shoved the remark back at Peter again and again in the months that followed. But the other woman hadn't been the only other woman, and certainly she hadn't been the most important one.

Peter had been involved with Shelley for eight years before he met Carol. The relationship had had violent ups and downs, although it had been on again at the time he met Carol—they had been engaged, actually—and he subsequently had to break it off with Shelly for good. Two days before Peter and Carol's wedding, Shelly had staggered into Peter's bachelor party, uninvited, lethally intoxicated by a massive overdose of sedatives. She had emptied out the bathroom cupboard. Efforts at rescue were to no avail and she died in the hospital the next morning. There was no suicide note. The next day, as planned, Peter and Carol were married. After Carol had heard the news, she'd asked Peter if he wanted to put off the wedding. She later thought that this had been the first blow and that she'd struck it.

Carol thought that she had stayed with Peter out of guilt over Shelley's death. She had also been afraid that her mother would view her as a failure if she left the marriage. And Peter had sensed that.

Shelley's death haunted their marriage. Carol developed a pain in her right side that couldn't be explained; she underwent x-ray examination and exploratory surgery. While recovering from the operation she discovered that she was pregnant, and the radiation and anesthesia now prompted the question of whether the fetus could have been inadvertently damaged. They decided to stick with the pregnancy, although Peter had deep forebodings that it wouldn't turn out right. Their daughter, Evie, was born with a birthmark, and Peter decided that this was the sign of Shelley's curse on their marriage. Evie seemed to have early learning difficulties, and they took this to confirm the curse. Peter spoke about his relationship with his daughter: "I have a volatile relationship with her and I can't control that at all. [He is crying.] I feel much closer to her than to Carol. I punish her much too much. Then I overcompensate and feel I'm just destroying her. She's not very clever, and I try to teach her things she can't do, and I lose my temper. Carol is disorganized with Evie, which makes it worse, but she's a much better parent than I am and she gives her stability."

Peter said he thought that by having the affair he had eroded whatever moral basis he had in their relationship, that he had excluded himself from the possibility of any real relationship with Carol. We were then in our third session together and I felt clear enough about certain ideas to put them forward. I said I thought that his guilt about Shelley's suicide had been an important motive behind the affair. By having the relationship and telling Carol, he had created a situation where he would get punished by a woman for hurting her. This would externalize the internal self-attack for Shelley's death. At the same time I thought that Carol's frequent rejection of him had been a factor in provoking his affair. The affair had then served to punish her for her role in the suicide, for taking away another woman's man. Thus for her the affair would also externalize a self-attack. The fighting about the affair seemed to me a flight from the unbearable guilt about building a home on someone's grave.

Over the months that followed, Peter seemed more able to think about this, and he frequently brought us back to Shelley's death. He thought that the woman he had the affair with had looked like Shelley around the eyes. He had felt very aggressive in their sex, and he thought that the aggression had been meant for both Shelley and Carol, Shelley for the suicide and Carol for the ways he felt undermined by her, for her resentment of his successes. For her part, Carol had been having a recurrent dream in which she was driving around in a car with a body in the trunk. She linked having the dream to not talking with anyone about Shelley's death—it was something she had to carry inside her. And the dream had now taken a new twist: Peter was off cutting up the body and she was washing herself obsessively.

There and been another tragedy, one they rarely spoke of. On their honeymoon in Argentina, driving through the countryside in a taxi, the driver had struck a young girl who had been either killed or at least seriously injured. They didn't know how it had turned out, because they had given the family a great deal of money not to press charges against the driver. The driver had been unwilling to take the child to the hospital for fear of arrest. When I returned to this incident at one point in our work a year later, saying that their guilt about this death must have merged with their guilt about Shelley (I had said "death," forgetting that the outcome had been unclear), they both said that they didn't feel much guilt about that accident. Carol said, "Why should we? We gave them a lot of money." She told me a story about an acquaintance who had accidentally caused the death of a cyclist by opening her car door just as the biker was approaching. This woman didn't feel guilty, she explained; it hadn't been her fault. I did not think that these were callous people; I just thought the knife had cut too close to the bone.

Carol felt that she had lost track of herself in the marriage, that she had become wishy-washy, paralyzed. It was time to tell me a bit more about herself. Her mother had become pregnant with her when she was just married and only 19 years old. Apparently it had been a difficult birth, and her mother had lost a lot of blood. Carol was the oldest of several children and had been very competitive with the next child, a brother, whom her mother thought to be the sensitive, loving one. I found it hard to get a clear of picture of Carol's relationship with her mother. She described her mother as a subtle presence, but over bits and pieces I came to sense that she felt her mother had placed her own ambition in her, and that she had then tried to achieve to please her mother. She had also come to resent her mother for that. Carol had been quite successful, getting into a top university and then securing a professional job usually open only to men.

Two memories from her childhood caught my ear. Her mother had had a favorite cradle; boys had stolen it and it was later found in the marshes, ruined. Carol's sense was that this was a metaphor for her mother's experience that something perfect had been spoiled. Growing up, she had thought that her own being perfect could make it all right for her mother. The other memory, from early adolescence, was of her mother coming to a special service at their church terribly overdressed, which mortified Carol. She hadn't acknowledged her mother's presence, and for this her mother had never forgiven her.

Carol had been closer to her father. She said he was like Peter Pan, always running away from things, very gregarious and clever, and she had been his favorite, but not obviously. There had been suicides in his family.

By the end of the session they had wended their way back to the marriage. I said I thought that she wished Peter would treat her the way her mother had treated her brother, not the way her mother had treated her. At the same time, I knew that Carol had set up in the relationship precisely the tensions that had characterized her relationship with her mother — insidious, competitive, envious dealings. But I was aware that she also longed for something more. When they had been planning the wedding, her mother had reproached her: "You don't care about my relatives. They're always second best." A few years later

Carol had told Peter that he was second-rate. In the ensuing fight he had mashed spaghetti into her hair.

In the years that followed, those words reverberated in the relationship. I understood that Carol, the first born, felt second best, thus second-rate: second best to both her brother and her mother. I guessed that she had been the recipient of her mother's projections of second-ratedness. Identifying with those projections, imagining herself as inferior and paralyzed, had served to keep her in check, to defend against murderous feelings. Carol was treating Peter the way her mother had treated her, making him feel second-rate, and he was prone to feel that. She achieved a small triumph in the process. (I would speak to this later in the work, but not now, for if I did she could only feel that I was putting her down, making her second-rate.)

Peter thought it was his turn to make an accounting of himself. He began by telling me that his mother had said that he would always fly off the handle if he couldn't do something right away; "Any criticism has always made me virtually want to cry and lash out." Both he and Carol were very sensitive to criticism, and I found myself couching rather carefully whatever I intended to say.

Peter's first memory was from age 3, standing outside the hospital, looking up at his mother and newborn brother. He said that his brother couldn't take milk or formula and almost died; infant and mother had spent weeks in the hospital before they had been able to come home. Peter's rivalry with his brother, like Carol's with her brother, was intense. When he was 5, the story goes, Peter watched his 2-year-old brother floundering in the lake, about to drown, and didn't move to save him. His parents claimed that by standing still Peter had tried to kill him.

Peter said his father had demanded that he jump through the hoop, but his father also had said that the hoop was absurd. The father, a writer who worked at home, was a thundering presence, critical of young Peter. His mother once said, to appease him, that she should have married him rather than his father, Peter told me. He actually thought that he was more like a daughter to her than a son. She had taught him to cook, and in fact he had done much of the cooking for himself and Carol early in their marriage. Peter's parents were lower middle-class, but at age 10 he was tricked into taking a special exam that qualified him for boarding school. He had tested well and was shipped off. He couldn't do math and cheated at it tremendously. These appear to have been lonely years. At college he had his first affair, with a woman several years his senior, the girl friend of one of the faculty. He had felt overwhelmed, had developed terrible headaches, and had cried all the time. A therapist suggested he drop out of school, but he continued. He referred to this as his "breakdown." Since that time, his father has stopped criticizing him.

"I used to tie up my testicles and hide them behind my legs. I pretended I was a girl, but it also gave me the feeling that my testicles were larger. It hurt, so I guess you'd say it was somewhat masochistic. It made me more *aware* that I had testicles. I'd crawl out the bedroom window and hide in the garden beneath my parents' window and masturbate with my testicles tied up.

"I had a hydrocele [a scrotal swelling] when I was 14. I'd been aware of something being wrong for two years. I suppose it came from tying up my testicles. My father was a peacock until he got sick. He'd take me out with him to the tailor and he'd have clothes made for both of us. The tailor asked me which side I wore my wallet on—my testicles, he meant. I assumed that the hydrocele must be visible and that I couldn't keep up the pretense any longer, so I told my father and he was very upset. He got me a jock strap—was it to keep my testicles from falling off?" Peter had had surgery to correct the condition, but he had continued to tie himself up afterwards anyway until he met Shelley.

I wondered whether Carol's seeing him as a beast increased his sense of manhood. He said that Carol found it more exciting when he just *took* her. It seemed that Carol both inflated and castrated him; did he accept the castration as the price of inflation? Did the castration relieve the guilt about the self-inflation? He replied that she flattered him, but not for very long: "She kind of builds me up and then cuts them off." I imagined that both the inflation and the cutting-off reenacted aspects of his relationship with his father, and that he was probably the bearer of his father's impotence. On another occasion he told me that his father seemed a little hollow at the center, that he thought his mother propped his father up. His mother would say that Peter had to be treated with kid gloves, but he thought that she was confusing him with his father. In any event, with Carol feeling second-rate and Peter feeling castrated, and both adept at evoking these feelings in each other, we had a well-matched pairing.

"I'm not at all like his mother," Carol said. "I don't think Peter likes me very much. What attracted him to me if I'm so unlike her? I'm not very meek and mild, and she is. She's utterly repressed and she just wants to please—I guess I was like that once." Peter replied that his mother had great vitality, a sense of what was important and worth getting and a desire to get it, a drive he himself lacked. Carol continued, "I'm frightened of being flirted with. I only let wimps—feminine men—flirt with me. I do find very obviously sexual men attractive and frightening. Sex is better when Peter ravishes me, when there's less fiddling around, but he loves to fiddle around." Peter thought Carol hated him for being a man and despised him for not being enough of a man.

I sensed that I was hearing more about how destructive they both felt, and about how frightened they were of their power. In part I believed that they were castrating themselves, or provoking the other to castrate them, to defend against that anxiety. But once they were weakened, powerful envy would set in, especially for Carol. I imagined that she felt quite conflicted about competing and asserting herself. She had not worked since the children were born, and she felt ambivalent about this. She seemed to resent Peter's successes and to derive some satisfaction, although not pleasure, from putting him down. She had felt vindicated by his failures until she felt guilty about them. I thought that she was quite confused about succeeding in relation to her mother, that she felt that her success would simultaneously confirm and destroy her mother, and that this left her totally stuck. In this sense, I think that she feared that her success would also destroy Peter.

During the sessions I felt Peter's rivalry. He was quick to pick up on my moments of glibness and therapeutic pomposity. Interestingly, this didn't bother me beyond brief embarrassment because I generally thought he was right. He could be easily hurt by Carol in the sessions, but rarely by me. Carol, on the other hand, found me intensely critical. She was constantly demanding to know whose side I was on (or, as she would put it, which of them was in the right). It was as though I were a mother who was incapable of taking her side in anything, and at times I did indeed feel that way. At the same time, she told me that she thought I didn't realize how valuable I was to her; she offered me her diary, which included an account of the treatment, to make that point.

Carol had resumed painting, an interest she had set aside for many years. She had been encouraged by a well-known artist who had seen one of her canvases. To her delight he had offered to serve as a mentor. Peter and I hoped that this opportunity would relieve some of the competitive tension, but at least in the short run it did not have that effect. I suspected that she felt both that her success would hurt her marriage and, at another level, that she was implicitly having a clandestine affair with the painter, betraying her husband.

The feeling I couldn't shake when I was with Carol and Peter was that I was in thrall to their relationship. There was something exciting there, and while I didn't feel entirely excluded, I felt on the periphery of it. An edge of excitement and tension saturated the experience—would they stay together, would he storm out of the hour, would he mash spaghetti in her hair again, would they get rid of me? I'd gird myself a bit before each session, not knowing quite what to expect. They seemed larger than life to me.

Issues of being special and being excluded were crucial for both of them. Both had, in a fashion, fairly explicitly won their opposite-sex parents (his mother's confession that she would rather have had him as a husband; her close relationship with her father). And yet both felt very much that they were outsiders. The image of Peter's masturbating all tied up outside his parent's window stayed with me as a vivid expression of a feeling I thought was general in his life. He felt shut out by his wife, never allowed to be part of the private dialogue she carried on with herself. Carol also felt estranged—it seemed to her that intimate relationships were not to be her lot in life. This went beyond the particulars of feeling excluded from her husband's exciting work, from his affair, from his fated relationship with Shelley. Even being a mother didn't seem to foster a feeling of belonging. I had the impression that her relationships didn't seem substantial to her.

The way that this played out in the treatment was not, however, that they felt excluded from my life, or that I was particularly paired with each partner against the other, although there were moments when this was in the air. The main setup was that I was the one on the outside, fascinated—figuratively, masturbating—looking in. I felt, in a certain fundamental way, obsessed with their relationship and unable to enter it. At the same time, paradoxically, I thought that I was the marriage's custodian. It was my job to see that it survived. That might have been a child's feeling—needing to keep the parents together so that the child could have something to be a part of. At one point, under the pressures of these tensions, I unwisely tried to force my way into the relationship by interpreting transference aspects too aggressively, with near-disastrous consequences for the treatment. The balance was restored only when I withdrew to the outside.

I then began to address, with more focus, their feelings of exclusion, elaborating my understanding of the fate of the triangular relationships in their lives. Peter left midway through a session, believing that Carol had maliciously attacked him, thereby leaving us alone as a couple and himself rejected. This put me in a quandary as to whether to continue the hour—I didn't like taking part in the enactment of exclusion, but I also didn't want him to have the power to unilaterally destroy our work. Hoping that he would return, I decided to continue the session; in fact, he did not rejoin us. The next hour he announced that it was all hopeless, that they should quit therapy at the month's end. I spoke both about his ostracizing himself from us and then about the deeper sense in which I thought that they both believed that loving and being loved was a hopeless cause. It seemed to me that they had both brought this view of themselves to the marriage, that while it was a part of their relationship it certainly hadn't started there, that they were just living out a preconceived destiny. It had been my role, I said, to carry the positive feeling about the relationship for the two of them, which had left them free to abuse each other. The weekend after this session went unusually well. In the next hour Carol was able to reflect more perceptively on her relationship with a female friend that was filled with rivalry and envy, and to volunteer the parallel to her relationship with her mother.

During this period, Carol remembered a dream. She was in someone's house; someone had died there. She read a Latin inscription: *Rosini—casus et belli.*

She wasn't sure what the Latin meant. Did *casus* mean battle? Death? The suffix *-ini* was a diminutive. I wondered if they were thinking about having another child; they admitted that it had been on their minds. Carol said that in medieval times the first *row* of soldiers going into battle knew they'd die. She wondered whether they'd felt despair or ecstasy. Carol and Peter used the word "rows" to mean fights.

I interpreted the dream to mean that the threat of separation and loss was the cause of their fighting. Feelings of threatened abandonment were defensively covered by their battling. I was particularly impressed that neither could bear feeling empathy for the other's experience of loss—whether the loss be Shelley's death, the loss involved in the affair, or the childhood losses. Carol replied that she felt unloyal to Peter, that she hadn't helped him enough with his work—perhaps she was like *Cassius*.

I came back to thinking about the idea of another baby and I conjectured that the "cause of the belly" would be pregnancy, but that their little rows were the only intercourse they could bear without guilt. Having another child would be more a celebration of life than either felt entitled to. Peter said that when they had sex he imagined that he was making love to a dead woman in a casket. I thought that complicating the issue of exclusion was the guilt they both felt about what they'd managed to get for themselves in their lives—the interest of a parent, a career or talent, each other. Certainly Shelley's suicide needed to be mourned, and the treatment had been of use in that regard, but they both also needed to come to terms with their own motives in relation to her, to their parents and siblings, and to their marriage—those motives needed to be mourned also. I thought that I had reached a useful juncture when I realized that I was trying to do the impossible—to carry their relationship for them. Accepting my own limitations seemed to facilitate an opening up for them. The idea of having a baby represented believing that they could create a family that they might be able to belong to.

In these three treatments I believed that mourning was a particularly central aspect of the work. In Peter and Carol's case the issue of Shelley's suicide provided a central focus for the mourning, which then drew in a much wider range of issues. For the Turners, the approaching death of their daughter was the core from which a host of other conflicts radiated. It is particularly difficult to talk about a catastrophe that is about to happen; the family's defensiveness was such that they seemed only able to face the last month of Nancy's life with denial. In such terrible situations, denial may be the best way of coping for a time. Perhaps after her death something more would have been possible, some measure of reconciliation. For John the issue of mourning was not focused on a single trauma, but involved a number of troubling issues from his childhood, conflicts recreated in his marriage. When it became clear that he had decided to end the treatment because he felt I could not help him further, I felt, within the range that I feel such things, devastated. I had been extremely invested in our work together and felt the rug pulled out from under my feet. My own mourning, at some level, became the unconscious focus of the ending, and I will continue the story later in this text.

Rather than our seeing the work of therapy mainly as accomplishing the mourning of necessary losses, we might see the task as helping the patient develop the *capacity* to relinquish, to let go of what is best left behind. Therapy is, after all, about learning how to live a life. The therapist's own mourning must stand as a model for that capacity. There is so much for each party to mourn in any deeply engaged treatment. Both start, to a degree, with expectations that will not be fully realized. And the ending is so often a greater loss for the therapist than for the patient. When therapist and patient leave the gnarled fairyland forest of their shared regression and return to the sun-drenched highway, a taxi will show up to take the patient off, but the therapist will have to find his way back to his own car alone. These complications of ending are an issue I will take up in the next chapter. Thus, for these reasons also, the process of mourning in therapy makes sense only in a two-person framework, a matrix that will be dissolved.

PART 3

BOUNDARIES OF TREATMENT

9

Beginnings and Endings

This chapter and the three that follow it take up various issues that relate to the boundaries of the treatment relationship and the therapeutic process. Negotiating boundaries could be considered the pivotal point of our work, although we are not accustomed to framing our efforts that way. These chapters focus particularly on negotiating the intersubjective junction—at the two ends of treatment, within the process itself, in the presence of a third party, and in the larger contexts within which therapy is conducted.

At the opening and closing boundaries of the therapeutic encounter, the two-person aspect of the experience is highlighted. In the beginning, two strangers must come together to participate in a shared venture. That joining will be implicitly structured in large measure by established social codes. But the two parties will need to find their ways into the roles in which they will conduct their work with each other—the roles of patient and therapist—and this process is not automatic, nor can it be taken for granted.

At the other end of the encounter, termination, the interpersonal dimension is again highlighted. While in one sense the two participants will remain patient and therapist until the end, it is also true that they will separate from each other as two individuals who have, if all has gone well, been engaged in a deeply meaningful piece of work. The patient's success at internalizing the experience will be affected by the way the two parties negotiate their separation. For the termination is a real loss for both that will take them beyond their experiences in the roles of patient and therapist.

BEGINNINGS

To begin with, both therapist and patient must be able to imagine the other as a suitable partner. At the extremes, I have certainly had both the experience of taking an immediate liking to someone over the telephone and of straightaway starting to calculate how I can arrange things so that the person never enters my office. I am sure that my callers have had a similar range of experiences.

It is a common practice for therapists to hedge about their availability to a prospective client, to claim that at the moment they have time free only for a consultation, reserving the option to discover time available for ongoing treatment if they find the patient suitably treatable or, perhaps more honestly, likable. This is not a completely invidious method, because the other two alternatives are arguably worse – directly telling a patient that you feel you can't work with him (because this might actually speak more to one's own idiosyncrasies of agreeability, but this will never be understood as such by a client, who would almost certainly feel profoundly rejected), or taking him on despite your not liking him, and trying to make the best of it. A prospective patient and I once resolved what I think was probably an initial *mutual* dislike by getting into a fight over whether I would provide him with duplicate copies of his bills. This conveniently sank our ship before it left the harbor.

Among the problems involved in the practice of seeing the patient ostensibly only for a consultation, and then offering treatment, is that the patient may decide that he was specially chosen, or that he succeeded in a seduction, or that he gulled the therapist, or that he masochistically submitted to the therapist's authority and manner to win his favor, or that the particular self-presentation of that first hour needs to be recreated to the end of time to assure the therapist's continuing willingness to see him. This might not be fatal to the treatment, and it could potentially be brought into the arena of discussion as the work continues. In practice, for reasons not hard to imagine, it rarely is. It then remains an unacknowledged context of the treatment, which is now without a solid foundation, a house constructed on ice.

It is, on the other hand, remarkable how easily therapists engage with a huge range of prospective clients. At times it seems extraordinary to me that I am apt to find myself identified with the struggles of almost anyone who comes to my office for help. In part this is a function of my intentionality: when I meet someone, I want to be able to make contact, and withholding patients are simply challenges. In part it's a consequence of the person's wanting to make use of me. Seduction works both ways. (It has been said that the therapist's goal in the first hour is to make possible a second one. Perhaps this is actually true for both parties.) The occasional patient whom I won't be able to bear is the person whose demands on me to do something for them, right here and now, are impossibly extravagant.

Openings

The opening moment may have a profound impact on the relationship in other ways. A colleague described listening to a teenager's initial call on his answering machine; her voice was full of enthusiasm and life. When he returned the call he found her sullen and withdrawn, and so she appeared on her first visit to his office. The girl was afraid to look at him and was scarcely able to speak. Holding in his mind, however, another vision of her, the lively child he had heard on the answering machine, he was able to reach out to that potentiality in her by the end of the first hour and make contact.

As in any negotiation, the two parties take each other's measure in their first encounter; they determine the proprieties of their relationship. I remember being called by a fellow who wanted to see me with his wife. Having four different hours open the next Monday, with the last being at 6 P.M., I offered him his choice of the times. Replying with a slight air of petulance, he asked if he could see me at 6:10. In this instant he eloquently revealed to me the issue we would have with entitlement. I decided it was the last choice I'd ever offer him. (I also think that someone else might have made the same request in a different way, and that I wouldn't have found it outrageous. Which might not necessarily have been to his benefit.) In the past few years I have found that patients are more apt to ask, in their initial call, if I can see them in the evening. If I can, I do. But I also imagine that I am being asked something else—will I impinge on their lives? Patients wish for bloodless surgery, even though at the same time they know better. (The end point is represented in the cartoon in which the patient is pointing a gun at her analyst. She tells him that he's been a great deal of help, she profoundly appreciates what he's done for her, but she's sorry, now he knows too much!)

A Shared Task

Once therapist and patient get past the issue of initial comfort with each other, the larger question becomes whether they can develop a shared sense of task. I believe that in a good deal of treatment, patient and practitioner are working at cross-purposes, even, in some instances, when they both seem to be on the same side of the street. Our patients generally want us to do something for them—help them make a decision or take an action, console them, take away their anxiety or depression, make it better—and we want to help them to find the means and the courage to take responsibility for their lives, especially for their inner lives. In writing about the Wolf Man I commented that I imagined that he and Freud had never developed a shared sense of purpose: the Wolf Man seemed primarily determined to secure Freud's approval of his relationship with Therese.

Whole therapies and analyses can be conducted without a mutual accord on their purpose ever being reached. These situations can be divided into two broad categories. In the first, the patient insistently holds onto a view of how treatment is to operate that doesn't fit with an ordinary therapeutic modus operandi. In the second, the patient is determined to destroy the treatment. The latter could be considered a more malignant version of the former. But while the first is often amenable to influence, the latter, all too often, is not.

Let me take up the patient's effort to define and control the treatment first. There are two common ways in which this can happen. The patient may hold out for a particular activity on the therapist's part that the patient is convinced is necessary behavior if he is to be helped. He may, for example, insist that the therapist provide direction or, perhaps, affirmation. The issue here is not that the therapist won't, at times, in the ordinary course of treatment, provide guidance or support; these patients insist (some directly, others covertly) that this is what the entire treatment should be about. Some of these individuals will not be helped by our offering words that carry meanings—what we have to say to them will be scanned only for its implicit approval or condemnation. While these patients can be relentless in their efforts to control us, my experience is that they usually move between this position and another space in which they are more available to work with us in the ways in which we are accustomed to working. But in some situations I do think that the client offers a surface compliance, while privately holding onto other agendas.

The other manner in which patients oppose us is by shutting us out, and they do this in a variety of ways. Most totalistically they may remain silent—even, rarely, for weeks, months, and years. More commonly they take control of the treatment by refusing to grant us authority. These people self-assertively spend hour after hour dominating the conversation, pursuing the lines of inquiry that they have determined will be relevant, and treating our thoughts dismissively.

One such patient had decided, after reading a book about adult children of alcoholics, that his problem was that he was excessively controlling. He was determined that this would be the focus of his analysis, and he spent hours relating incidents in which he might or might not have behaved in too controlling a fashion. The role he assigned to me was to tell him whether or not he'd been controlling. My efforts to describe to him his determination to control me through this form of interaction fell on deaf ears. To be more precise, he politely listened to me and then continued on his way.

For appalling lengths of time, I would counter by shutting him out—I'd let my mind wander elsewhere. When I held myself to the task, I felt furious, because this ostensibly reasonable man was allowing me no role in the sessions, or at least no role that I could accept.

Some of these patients just want us to be their audience and will cheerfully fill up hour after hour with stories, accounts of their lives, even dreams, with little interest in having us participate. It is as though the self is an elaborate sandcastle, needing constant protection—our words, if let in, would wash it away. The shutting out can occur, however, in more subtle fashion.

A patient who had been sexually abused as a child went through an entire analysis in what appeared to be a customarily useful fashion. She explored her feelings, told me her dreams and fantasies, let herself be drawn into various transference positions, and worked with my observations. And her life outside treatment perceptibly improved: she was now able to do things she had been unable to do before. I believe that we had a very useful experience together. And yet I also believe that her secret underlying mission was to be able to go through an entire analysis without ever feeling that she had really yielded to my power. She would succeed with me where she had failed with her father (or, in phantasy, she would defeat me where she had been unable to defeat her father). The impact of this on me was that I felt that I was never really being allowed to be an analyst. I always thought that I was a bit of a fraud, a party to a cover-up, a partner in a "pretend" analysis.

Thoughts along this line occurred to me during the treatment and I tried to explore them, but never with great success. I think, in retrospect, that my patient might have gotten even more from the treatment if she had been able (in a certain sense) to yield to me—if she'd kept me less at arm's length. It might have led to an even deeper understanding of her experience with her father—in particular, to a sharper understanding of how their interaction had led to the confounding of her own experience of desire. I believe she had found the prospect of making that inquiry with me unacceptably dangerous. Nearer the surface, it would have been humiliating. Deeper, her intactness as a person would have been at stake. And we did come to understand something of this during the treatment. But in this particular way that she considered the treatment a success, I considered it an enactment, and thus, at least to that degree, a failure.

Experience in this first category of cross-purposes is generally mixed. Patients' positions usually aren't entirely inflexible. At times of stress they barricade themselves behind their reliable ramparts, but in sunnier seasons they come out in the open and we have commerce. Analysis of the needs for these defenses tends to shift the balance, sometimes decisively in our favor.

With the other category of experience, results are rarely so felicitous. These are the patients who often become labeled *negative therapeutic reactions* (Freud 1923) when they terminate treatment either untouched or worse off. We understand that they are loyally committed to self-destructive internal object relationships. But beyond that, I believe that many of these patients—and perhaps all of them—are determined to live out specific tragic narratives, and that we have no power to disrupt their enactment of destiny. The destruction of the treatment—and the defeat of the therapist—is a central part of the narrative. Generally, a childhood drama of rejection is being recreated, with the patient and therapist simultaneously in both parent and child roles. The patient both triumphantly abandons the therapist and at the same time feels like a forsaken child. These therapies need to be distinguished from other treatments in which sadomasochistic entanglements are endlessly played out. The latter are not necessarily intractable, but when they are intractable they tend to be interminable.

In the dramatic instances of negative therapeutic reaction, the patient fights the process almost from start to finish. Sometimes the encounter is brief, lasting only one or a few sessions (which should not be misunderstood to mean that I think that all aborted treatments reflect the patient's pathology). Occasionally the therapy will go on for years with the patient resolutely insisting all the while that the experience is of no use and eventually quitting. More frequently the negative therapeutic reaction is one aspect of the treatment.

> The patient I discussed earlier (see Chapter 5) who had had nightly incest with her brother, and whom I believed might be able to seduce me, ended treatment in an act of self-defeat. We had spent several months working toward a planned termination date, and the end was only a week away, when she decided that she wanted me to give her a gift. All efforts to make sense of this wish were to no avail, and no symbolic equivalent was to be sufficient. She ended the last session on a note of bitterness. I felt hurt and disappointed, for I thought that we had done a great deal of useful work together and I would have liked to have ended on better terms.
>
> It was not possible to understand definitively the meaning of the enactment, because the patient carried it through and left. I imagine, however, that she was recreating the loss of her brother as an incestuous partner when she was about 6. Just as the actual incest had breached the symbolic order of incestuous phantasy, making the realization of oedipal longings an enacted reality, no symbolic exchange was to be sufficient between us. Instead she created a situation in which, from her point of view, I was forced to reject her. I believe she was absolutely certain that I would not give her a gift—even if by some odd chance I had felt so inclined, the nature of her request would in any event have made it impossible for me to do this. By this construct, she could guarantee her scripted ending. I also imagine that her brother's rejection of her was itself a repetition of the earlier rejection she had felt from her mother. I suspect, too, that many other levels of loss were contained in her enactment with me.

As patient and therapist proceed to work together, they develop their own particular rhythm and balance. Although we believe that ultimately every nuance of the relationship is potentially subject to investigation, in fact therapist and patient will—and must—work out a mutual accommodation, a way of being together that provides space for the patient to make manifest his difficulties and for the therapist to respond to him. The adaptation may be a quite lopsided one for a while (in the extreme case even for many years), especially as the therapist may need to submit for a long time to the patient's dictatorial regime.

It is in this sense, to return to an earlier theme, that therapy resembles marriage. Like spouses, therapist and patient find a way to coexist, each side making certain concessions (some within awareness, more outside it), each knowing, eventually exquisitely, the other's vulnerabilities, both enduring rough times and misunderstandings, finding moments of intimacy and losing them again. Like marriage, therapy develops both a modus operandi and a history. Unlike marriage, this modus operandi and history will become primary objects of scrutiny—therapist and patient are to be not only participants but also observers: participant-observers, we might say.

ENDINGS

From a different standpoint, the question of purpose has bearing on the problem of ending. I would venture to say that few patients actually enter treatment with anything approaching a formed expectation of what they can get out of it. They begin with ambitions, with dreams, with transferences, and with agendas, but they cannot reasonably have a sense of what they might actually be able to accomplish, any more than a person who has never dined on curry could imagine the taste of Indian food. As the work proceeds, however, such expectations do develop—one goal seems possible, another hopeless, another always feels as if it lies just beyond reach. At moments in the treatment the patient will speak to these prospects of hope and failure, and at such moments the speaking to them may unmask the lurking opposite, the fear that the hope will actually be realized, or the comfort being sought in failure. But for the most part these expectations are unvoiced, for a long time even unthought.

In a sense, the termination process begins when this question is honestly faced (and, to be clear about it, this may occur early or late in the course of the treatment). For the adult facing the midlife crisis, the new recognition of death as the termination of possibilities creates a boundary around life and defines what lies within and beyond our purview. Similarly, the patient's awareness of termination implicates the question of what the bounds of treatment will be. The actual decision to end reflects a completion of that dawning of awareness. At the risk of belaboring the obvious, expectations about the future are not a special category of experience that exists outside the complicated nexus of human motivations. Those anticipations are hardly free of neurotic influence, perversity, and transference, but to simply treat expectations about the treatment as a disqualifiable locus of meanings (something more to be analyzed!) will disenfranchise the patient and make therapy interminable.

A patient and analyst were having a remarkably difficult time disentangling their lives. Their relationship had started with an enormous mutual idealization, but over time the patient had begun to feel relentlessly controlled within the treatment, pressured to become her analyst's disciple, and she had decided that it was time to leave. The therapist refused to acknowledge the actuality of his patient's plan and continued to interpret what he understood to be his patient's destructive motives as manifest in her threatening to stop. When this refusal continued unabated even in the session that the patient had declared would be their final hour together, the patient said that she had impulsively brought a sharp gardening tool with her to the session. The therapist finally got the point and agreed to end.

I'm not suggesting that the analyst should have accepted the patient's decision, or that he shouldn't have continued to try to explore its meaning, but I am saying that this needed to occur in a context in which the reality of her intention was mutually understood. It could be said that the patient had unconsciously found it necessary to become concrete in the face of the therapist's inability to symbolize an ending. But intentions and endings are in fact the objective aspects of an

intensely subjective process. Their acknowledgment slashes the fabric of
that process, awakening us from a dream.

The therapist also has expectations about the treatment, visions
of its future. In part these will be generic, based on his notions of the
potential of therapy, and in part particular, based on his experience
with the patient. As therapists grow older and wiser, they tend to
become more modest in their ambitions, more appreciative of life's
great intractabilities. Freud was struggling with these limitations when
he wrote "Analysis Terminable and Interminable" (1937) at the end of
his career, but Freud had never been overly impressed by the therapeutic potential of psychoanalysis. The idea that analysis has suffered
from being oversold by the early generations of analysts does not do
justice to the citizenry's desperate enthusiasm for new cures, or its
anger when it is betrayed by its own unworldly expectations.

Apart from the ambitions of patient and therapist, the future of
each treatment will be bounded by potentials, limitations, and needs
intrinsic to the life cycle. With a young patient, the therapist may
simply be interested in freeing the child up to the point at which she
will be able to make use of normal developmental opportunities, while
recognizing that important aspects of character have remained untouched and may require treatment at another time. This more
modest goal will be set with the recognition that internal developmental forces have healing powers of their own (particularly for the
young, but in some measure throughout the life cycle). Conversely, in
working with individuals past midlife, therapists are more cautious
when assessing their patients' psychic flexibility. While some people in
their seventies and eighties are able to make use of insight therapy to
work through core psychological issues, others, even in their fifties,
have consolidated their psychic lives into forms of compromise adaptation that will remain untouchable in the face of even the most gifted
of therapeutic approaches. To these latter individuals, therapists
(especially more experienced therapists) are prone to offer words of
encouragement or reassurance while tactfully suggesting that treat-

ment would not be advisable here (which is often heard as "Treatment is not needed here"). While this practice has something to do with therapists wanting to make the best use of their time (more so for the senior therapist who is attuned to the time limitations of his own career), it also respects the realities of human development.

Separation and Internalization

At the intrapsychic level, termination is concerned with the bearing of limitation. Interpersonally, it involves negotiating a separation. Successfully negotiating the interpersonal dimension makes intrapsychic mastery possible. Our objective with our patients is to effect an internalization, to keep what has been going on between us alive as a process inside them (Edelson 1963), and it is to this process that I now turn.

It is a special hardship of our craft that we cannot view the finished product. The experiencing and subsequent integration of the ending, of the separation of patient and therapist, is a crucial phase in the treatment from which we are, by definition, excluded. And the way in which the patient works through the separation will be an important determinant of the treatment's benefit. Several writers have suggested that, whatever one's opinion of posttreatment social relationships, it is useful that contact be minimal for a period of time, perhaps a year or two, after termination. (Gabbard and Pope [1989] note that in a study by Buckley et al. [1981] of ninety-seven psychotherapists who had completed therapy or analysis, thoughts about the therapist did not reach a peak until five to ten years posttreatment!) Implicit in this recommendation is the idea that an internalization of the therapist, or the therapeutic experience, is proceeding, an experience that requires sufficient aloneness and time. In a sense, this process should be considered part of the treatment itself, separate from the posttreatment self-analysis that one might continue, with more or less intentionality, for the remainder of one's lifetime.

Throughout his writing, Loewald stresses the crucial difference between the impact of repression and internalization, respectively, on the psyche. Through repression, the individual maintains a secret internal experience of the relationship with the object in a primitive (repressed) state. Because the repressed does not get worked over by its contact with new experience, repression paralyzes development. Internalization, in contrast, transforms the person's experience with the object into his own self-organization. And the object relationships themselves that contributed to this structure formation are destroyed. The crucial instance of this process, for Loewald, is the internalization made possible by the individual's mastery of the Oedipus complex. In "The Waning of the Oedipus Complex" (1979), he emphasizes that in successful development the complex is not repressed—it is destroyed, in an act of parricide, and reconstituted in the superego. What had been in the mind as a father's injunction, for example, is now internalized as the person's own morality, and the internal parental voice disappears.

> [I]t is no exaggeration to say that the assumption of responsibility for one's own life and its conduct is in psychic reality tantamount to the murder of the parents, to the crime of parricide, and involves dealing with the guilt incurred thereby. Not only is parental authority destroyed by wresting authority from the parents and taking it over, but the parents, if the process were thoroughly carried out, are being destroyed as libidinal objects as well. . . . The organization of the super-ego, as internalization . . . of oedipal object relations, documents parricide and at the same time is its atonement and metamorphosis: atonement insofar as the super-ego makes up for and is a restitution of oedipal relationships; metamorphosis insofar as in this restitution oedipal object relations are transmuted into internal, intrapsychic structural relations. [p. 389]

In psychoanalysis the conflicts of childhood are revived with the analyst now as object. Internalizations have been undone (life has been breathed back into structures) to make this reexperiencing possible. What had been internalized as the nature of one's personality is now alive again as transference. Then, in the ultimate resolution of the transference neurosis, the patient must renounce the analyst as incestuous object (more effectively than he renounced his feelings toward his original oedipal objects) and transform the experience back into a new internalization. The reawakened dead are again laid to rest. This also is a parricide, requiring mourning and atonement, and the outcome is the modification of psychic structure.

If in the process of termination this necessary parricide is impossible (if the loss of the analyst is not bearable), feelings of rage, anxiety, and helplessness overwhelm the patient. Internalization is not achieved, and thus the useful aspects of the experience with the analyst cannot be transformed into one's own adaptive ways of functioning. The former patient remains dependently addicted to the analyst, in the form in which he holds him in his mind. This identification serves to contain and control the analyst, in phantasy, but no enduring mastery is achieved. The analyst is then not thought about, because memory is painful, reminding the patient of the actuality of the loss. In Loewald's sense, the analysis has not been destroyed, but rather repressed, and the patient stays haunted. One wonders about individuals who claim that they never think of their ex-analysts. Although conventionally analysts consider this a satisfactory outcome, we might question this. Mourning does not mean removing from memory. As I noted while exploring mourning, what must be let go of is not the felt tie to the object, but rather the possibility of restoring the object in actuality.

Adolescent Relationships as the Structure of Termination

In the termination phase we are thus trying to separate from our patients while concurrently working to promote a consolidation of the internalization processes that have been developing during the treatment. I have two ideas to propose about how this occurs. The first is that for the *patient* the termination experience recapitulates crucial aspects of late adolescent development. The second is that the *therapeutic relationship* during the termination has as its substructure the adolescent separation process, in the same sense that earlier phases of the analysis have other childhood developmental issues underlying them.

The adolescent must relinquish his parents, both in their deeper unconscious connection as incestuous lovers, and in their actuality as ego support. And so must the patient release his therapist. During both adolescence and treatment, the patient's ego deficits may be concealed through reliance on the parents' and therapist's adaptive ego functioning. The possible consequences of the disruption at leave-taking are well known for teenagers, but less well studied for clients. In one sense the situation may be worse for the patient. The analyst has provided a consistency of presence, support, and empathic contact that is essentially unparalleled in human experience. Ambivalence, inconstancy, and conflicts of needs inevitably complicate ordinary life. Analysis may thus mask ego weakness more than adolescent–parent relatedness does. In development, the work of consolidation occupies the late adolescent moratorium and takes place after separation from the parents (Blos 1967, 1977; Erikson 1968). Therapeutic consolidation similarly continues into the postseparation period, as the patient organizes a definitive integration of the experience, including its ending.

What I am arguing here is that termination will regularly find its echo in adolescent experience. It is certainly true that the prospect of separation may awaken crucial anxieties from any phase of development. Conflicts over castration and intactness, dominance and submission, homosexuality and heterosexuality, gratification and restraint, idealization and contempt, omnipotence and helplessness—the list seems endless—may all take center stage for a given patient. But it is also likely that these particular conflicts were central *in that patient's adolescent Armageddon*, and their occurrence at termination will reflect a sympathetic response not only to their first appearance and elaboration, *but also to their adolescent reworking.*

Anna Freud (1958) and others have commented on the difficulty in reviving adolescent conflicts in the transference. Lampl-de Groot (1960) suggests that this may reflect a tacit conspiracy on the part of patient and analyst to experience conflicts as between a young child and an omnipotent parent, not between a developing adolescent and a more vulnerable mother or father. She points out that adolescent aggression is more refined, and adolescent criticism more telling; both parties feel more comfortable avoiding this. As Loewald points out, the parent does die a bit with each step of his teenager's individuation, and, for patient and analyst, there may be a mutual interest in denying this.

I would like to expand the exploration of these issues by presenting the termination phases of my work with two analysands, a teenager and a young adult. While adolescent themes were present in both endings, the contrast is instructive.

Termination with a Teenager

I will first describe my experience completing treatment with the college student briefly discussed earlier, the patient with whom I negotiated a change of fee.

> At the beginning of his fourth year of analysis (which was also his senior year at college) Anthony talked about finishing up. The impetus seemed to come both from his sense of his progress and from the phase-appropriate inner pressure toward individuation that develops in late adolescence. I accepted this as a possibility, thus setting in motion a process that led to his ending treatment eight months later.
>
> Throughout this period I was quite conscious of our approaching the end. I was in a slight, but definite, state of mourning throughout the year, which was focused on my having to accept the limitations of this treatment. Although in many respects he was functioning better, he still seemed to lack a sufficiently healthy self-esteem, was still too prone to fall back on grandiose fantasies. I knew that I would not be making a major impact on this problem in the remaining time we had together, and this was a loss for me. At times, during the year, I pushed those feelings into the background, but at moments I felt keenly the restriction. My own unconscious phantasy of being able to remake Anthony into my image for him was at stake here (this being *my* grandiosity). In a subtle way I'd joined him in imagining that he was an unborn child. I

think that my mourning was like what parents of separating adolescents go through—having to accept the limits of what's possible, having to realize that your child won't be all you had dreamed he would be.

Anthony's initial response to my not challenging his decision was to feel unprotected. He helplessly missed sessions and arrived late, trying to provoke me into a controlling response. Once the crescendo had subsided he felt ashamed of himself for using me that way. Subsequently it seemed that the knowledge that he was ending left him freer to be both more assertive with me and unabashedly closer to me. He said (with deliberate irony) that he felt more married to me than to his girlfriend.

Anthony was fearful that his success would injure me. In a manic (and displaced) effort to reassure himself that he wouldn't hurt me, he felled a large tree without damaging a house close by. He told me he had broken someone's arm in football once, an event he had previously concealed. Anthony tried to reassure himself that I wouldn't suffer financially with his departure—his father was facing bankruptcy and borrowing money from him. Shifting to the maternal transference, he feared hurting me by letting me know how eager he was to be liberated. He remembered feeling he'd exploited his girlfriends by discarding them when he had no further use for them. Overall, his fear of doing harm to me reflected his initial projected anxiety in the analysis—that I would make him into a warped, destructive animal. One winter morning I failed to shovel the snow off the walk and he criticized me, saying that he had a right to that anger, and adding that perhaps I was trying to provoke him. He did not feel intimidated about challenging me directly now.

Another theme was his feeling deflated by the recognition that he could not live up to his ideals. (This mirrored my own struggle.) Anthony said that I was forcing him to accept mediocrity. Depressive anxieties surfaced: he complained that life was too short, that he'd wasted too much time. (I could certainly agree with that.) As we moved into the final months, he pushed me away with a counterdependent self-sufficiency. When I seemed distant in return, he felt discarded. There were also moments of acceptance: his feeling choked up before a session that I canceled, and feeling more disappointed in his mother and therefore less angry at her. Anthony began distinguishing between the analysis, which he would keep with him, and his relationship with me, which would end. At the same time he wanted to insist that this had been a "successful analysis," as though that acknowledgement would serve as a talisman for him.

Persecutory anxieties were manifest in a dream: he and a friend stole someone's food, shot someone who had seen them, were spotted by the police and feigned nonchalance, and then were taken to a religious prison where there was no chance for escape or for contact with their families. I thought Anthony felt deprived by me now and experienced his leaving me as murderous retaliation, concealed behind feigned indifference. The dream implied that he was afraid I would punish him by making him serve out his term with me without help or caring. After worrying that our ending would be marred by "rampant needless expression [of bad feelings]," Anthony told me how disappointed he was that we hadn't been more warmly connected. He was sure that he would have felt more rapport with the analyst who referred him to me. (Listening to this, and experiencing my own limitations, I felt some real pain. I always feel that I don't let myself get close enough.) He went home and "puked [his] guts out." Recognizing his sadness that analysis was just analysis, I acknowledged his courage in telling me that, and pointed out that his stomach upset was a consequence of feeling he'd hurt me. With his comment about the referring analyst in mind, I also said that he was wanting me to experience what it felt like to be second best—this was a familiar feeling for him, I knew. In our final week he mainly externalized the problem. Anthony had been pushing his girlfriend away, making her feel the loss *for* him, and she reacted by having a brief affair, enraging him. I thought that the externalization had made the ending more bearable for him, since events indicated that he would win his girlfriend—but not me—back. We parted affectionately.

Throughout the treatment I felt I was part analyst, part parent. In a characteristically adolescent manner, Anthony repeatedly tried to provoke me into a holding-on position against which he could rebel. On many occasions I had to actively confront his acting out, especially his missing and coming late to sessions. Often it seemed only actions mattered, and that Anthony simply paid lip service to my words. The negotiation of the fee raise seemed the crucial event in the analysis. In retrospect, I believe that until this issue was addressed I had actually been infantilizing him. Now I was no longer getting in the way of his need to take responsibility for himself and for the analysis. Apropos of this, I felt brought up short in the unshoveled walk incident in a way that I never had by his more outrageous complaints: he was acting as an equal, not as a child.

In emphasizing the centrality of adolescent experience in termination, I do not mean to minimize the importance of earlier—and especially oedipal-phase—conflict. Typically, however, the earlier conflict appears in the termination phase in the form of its adolescent reworking. Anthony had felt out of control as a 5-year-old. In response to his brother's birth and illness he had thought his world was shattering. He had reacted with tantrums and fire-setting, which his parents had seemed unable to control. Anthony had recapitulated this as a teenager, when he had compensated for being unable to compete effectively with his classmates by succeeding in the drug world, where he could charm and intimidate his peers, threatening violence when necessary. His father had again been ineffectual—for example, returning a pound of marijuana to Anthony instead of confiscating it.

It was the *adolescent* experience that Anthony reenacted in the analysis, and this was especially vivid at termination, when, initially out of control, he wanted me to restrain him. Throughout the termination phase Anthony was concerned about harming me through his self-assertiveness and aggression (which he had difficulty distinguishing), and at the very end he was worried that he would become rampantly, needlessly destructive. Yet this concern was in the context of his adaptive effort to move his life forward, to overcome his fear of standing up for himself. In telling me of his disappointment with me, he recognized both that he needed to tell me this, as well as that I could hear it without retaliating. He understood that both he and I were strong enough to manage that. These are the concerns of an adolescent, not of a 5-year-old child. For the child, parricide is a phantasy. For the adolescent and his parents, it is, so to speak, a reality.

Thus the termination phase seemed the most "adolescent" part of this analysis of an adolescent. I felt very much that Anthony was trying to grow up through mastering the separation. He was trying to find a new place for his parents (and, internally, for his analyst) in his life. He seemed aware of the consequences of growing up, for himself and for me, and didn't want to hurt me more than was necessary. And Anthony felt quite pained about his own limitations. Two months before ending he offered his own understanding of how experience is internalized:

> I don't think I've identified or taken anything particular from you, as a person, but I have because analysis is not really something tangible. Your ability to understand a situation, to seek out alternatives . . . I learned how to do it for myself. This is something that's not embodied in a person, it's not enacted before me—they're things I picked up that I've made distinctly me. There are parts of me that I do identify with other people. If I act charitably I would attribute that to my ethics and my religion and my father. So when I feel altruistic, helping an old lady carry her groceries, I think of those days. The things I got here I don't think of in the same way. I never followed you in analysis, in the same way of patterning my life after you. . . . There seems to be more of *me* involved, it's not just copying.

In the process of working through the termination, Anthony had appropriated our experience and had made it uniquely his own.

Termination with a Young Adult

> Jonathan, the only child of refugees, sought treatment in his mid-twenties for help with what seemed to him an impossible dilemma: he wanted to marry outside his faith in opposition to his parents' wishes. Holocaust survivors, they had barely escaped extermination, and their parents had not. An effort to save the father's parents had failed, and they had fled leaving the mother's parents behind. In America, the parents established residence in a situation that reversed their earlier experience: they were lords of the manor in a ghettolike setting, attended by disabled servants. While Jonathan's father was able to seal the experience over enough to be able to become a successful profes-

sional, his mother remained depressed, preoccupied with the Holocaust. Their child was the light of their lives.

Jonathan's father seized the initiative in parenting and was intimately involved in every aspect of Jonathan's life, guiding, encouraging, and controlling him. He chose to send his son to a school known for its high concentration of aggressive and violent young men, and Jonathan learned there to immunize himself against anxiety. His consequent fearlessness kept him in constant danger during his teenage years. He lived at home during college and then chose a professional school on the basis that it would allow him to stay near his father. During his professional training, Jonathan went camping one weekend with his parents and slept between them in a tent. The experience so disturbed him that he avoided them for the next two years. At this point, wanting to marry the young woman he'd stolen from his best (and only) friend, he sought treatment.

Jonathan was an extremely well-behaved patient. He was scrupulously on time for sessions and straightened the napkin on the pillow before lying down. He filled the hours with dreams and fantasies and psychological speculations, listened carefully to my bright ideas, and never caused trouble. Jonathan wanted to protect me and decided that I was definitely in need of protection. He imagined himself repelling invaders at the door, deflecting missiles aimed at my head, leaping off the couch and springing into action. In the community, he was the Great Avenger, righting injustices and protecting the weak. When I began seeing him he was spending more hours a day bodybuilding than working at his profession. His torso definitively outlined, he swaggered down my walk and imagined himself a cartoon superhero, The Hulk. I quite enjoyed working with him.

Over the course of our four years' work, although he never turned forcibly against me, enough of the sadism bound up by Jonathan's reaction formations became unglued to allow for a warming-up in the transference. His relationship with his parents continued to be difficult. His father responded to his announcement of wedding plans by immediately having a serious heart attack. The marriage went forward, parents in attendance. After months of controlling her, Jonathan increasingly allowed his wife to function as a separate human being. At the beginning of the fifth year he talked of wanting to finish the treatment. Although I did not agree with him that the ending was imminent, it did seem to me as I listened to him that what lay ahead for us would be his work at separating from me, and two years later we reached a mutually acceptable conclusion.

Over the course of the termination period, I felt that I was in a subtle but continual tug-of-war with Jonathan. It took the form of his insistently restating his intention to end and my continuing to interpret what I understood as the underlying meanings of his communications. He wasn't prone to act out, and I never felt any real danger that he would terminate unilaterally. I did continuously find myself questioning whether I was holding onto him out of my own needs, either my need for perfection or my own dependence on him. At a manifest level, I did think that more of the dependency was on my side (much like the parent's experience as the teenager is moving toward leaving home). I worried about being selfish. But I also felt that my agreeing to quit would be just surrendering to Jonathan's insistence, acting like the parent who throws his hands up in the air in response to his teenager's ordinary rebellion. And so I gritted my teeth and stayed with it. At some moments I felt like a controlling father, at others like a depressed mother, and at still others like a stubborn teenager.

Upon raising the termination issue, Jonathan initially felt exhilarated and closer to me. He responded to my not accepting the proposal with three dreams, each of which spoke to a different aspect of the conflict. In the first, a man driving a car made what Jonathan thought was a wrong turn, but Jonathan didn't challenge him. He supposed that this reflected his disagreement with me about our ending, but his associations also led back to an exciting time when he was caught in a snowstorm with his father. Thus he managed his anxiety about our conflict by sexualizing it. In a second, terrifying, dream, he and his wife drove off the edge of a cliff. His thoughts led back to the summer resort he and his parents had frequented, the site of primal-scene phantasies, and to later trips he made there as a teenager with girlfriends, when he drove too fast and almost went off the road. Here I heard the leave-taking as an adolescent oedipal victory, perhaps ending in a catastrophe. The third dream hinted at phantasies of sadistic attacks on women. Intercourse was represented as a crossbow attack, and as an injection of saline causing an abortion. I thought that the abortion aspect of the dream implied Jonathan's deeper anxieties about his internal relationship with his mother, which were now prompted by the threat of separation.

Relentless reminders of his intent to leave me were accompanied by unabashed confessions of his affection for me. Jonathan bought a house in my part of town and made plans for our post-termination friendship. He imagined himself inside a Nazi gas chamber, feeling conflicting urges to sit down and surrender, and to viciously claw his way over other bodies to the top of the human mass to gasp the last breath of air. He felt that he couldn't have a baby with his wife until after he terminated with me, just as he felt he would never be able to have a decent relationship with his mother until after his father died. I pointed out to Jonathan that he seemed to feel that he could grow up only by actually experiencing an adolescence with me, by struggling as father and son through a pro-tracted leave-taking. He treated any interpretation of this sort as itself an attempt to hold onto him. He had short-circuited his adolescent devel-opment by never leaving his parents. Even now he worked part-time in an unrewarding job at his father's firm, not needing the additional in-come, avoiding contact with his dad, but delighting in the mistaken calls he and his father received for each other.

At the same time, his father's old accusation that Jonathan had once tried to kill him by dropping him off on the far side of a busy street still rang in his ears and was alive in current versions. And he certainly believed—not without reason—that he would kill his father if he made a further break with him. I commented on his extreme efforts to avoid feeling guilty about his wishes to separate from me. He told me the story of an Indian puberty ritual. The boy has to go out alone into the night and have a "correct" vision. If the boy's vision is improper he has to live as a woman and be a sexual object for the braves. Thus he regarded his choice with me: submit or submit. He pointed out that I would only agree to finish if he stopped wanting to! At the same time he felt increasingly excited to be with me, and I began to hear exquisitely tender memories of times with his father. They would get up on a weekend morning, don their identical outfits, and go riding together in the forest. His father would teach him all about the natural world. Swimming underwater, they would look at each other, eyes open, face to face. He thought his father had worshiped him then.

At another point a dream of a fast, frightening ride in a Fiat Spyder with a psychiatrist driving suggested to me the combination of exciting and claustrophobic maternal aspects of the transference. I had a series of minor illnesses during the year, which he unconsciously picked up on with an eerie accuracy, and yet he seemed oblivious to positive developments in my life. All this suggested a special link to his mother's depression. He also intuited that my wife was pregnant again and seemed determined to terminate before what he thought was the due date. The maternal conflict came to dominate the transference as he variously experienced me both with great longing and excitement as an object of desire, and as an ensnaring figure (a spider, by fiat) that he determinedly wanted to get away from.

Overall, as the work progressed I experienced Jonathan increasingly as my equal, as did he. He felt freer to criticize me and to consider the way in which he might prefer to be different from me. It occurred to him that he might rather not have a friendship with me after finishing. By this time, I could imagine us ending.

While Jonathan's termination, like Anthony's, represented an attempt to enact an adolescent separation, with the conviction that *actual enactment* was necessary for growth, here I felt less pressure to respond parentally, and I thought that my words mattered as much as my deeds. In this case I was indeed analyzing an *adult* whose transference neurosis contained important conflicts from the adolescent period. The distinction between transference and present developmental conflict was clearer.

Jonathan's father's ability to actually respond with a heart attack to wedding plans he didn't approve of (and this was not an isolated event) seemed to me in reality to give the issue of separation a life-and-death quality. It seemed impossible for Jonathan to bear the possibility that his leaving might in some way diminish me, or that further steps in his development might more than diminish his father. This is the parricide guilt of which Loewald spoke. Driving home to his wife in a snowstorm and leaving his father to fend for himself, Jonathan passed a car on fire. He was terrified that it would explode, sending shrapnel into his car and killing him. The next day, having to choose between work and seeing me because of the storm's aftermath, he chose to stay at his job. In neither instance could he feel guilty—in the first case the danger was projected, in the second the choice was rationalized and guilt repressed. Nonetheless, this man who was so afraid of feeling anxious had let himself feel scared. When I commented on his problem with guilt and mourning, Jonathan remembered a time in gym class when he had been required to perform an unfamiliar maneuver for a test and had been frightened that he would break his neck. He was indicating that I was expecting the impossible. But as he worked through the aggressive conflict, he was able to feel more freely affectionate as our analysis proceeded to its close.

Actualization

In writing this chapter I found myself repeatedly tempted to use the word *actualizing*. In regard to termination the therapist must step out of his role as interpreter to make a decision with his patient about ending. This change of stance is unique in the treatment. The therapist is inescapably leaving his intersubjective position, his place, we might say, in the intermediate zone, and making a judgment about the patient. This is so whether therapist or patient initiates the issue. And this judgment—that treatment will end—will have great consequence in the patient's life. The therapist is now no longer simply a commentator; he has taken a decisive and fateful action with the patient, and this is an *actuality* that profoundly affects that which is to follow. Disengagement is now not only from the therapist in his transference meaning, but also from the therapist as the person who has agreed that the treatment will end.

I am suggesting that one important force behind the shift to adolescent themes in termination is the fact that patient and therapist are now involved in a real event, the mutual decision to separate, which breaches the boundary of subjectivity; its referent is the adolescent leaving his parents. One-person clinical theory cannot apprehend the consequences of this change in function for the treatment. Furthermore, this change in function contributes to—but also sets in motion—the problem of internalization, outlined earlier, which the patient is faced with at the end of the analysis.

The question of how treatment achieves its therapeutic effect lies beneath the issues I have raised here. In summary, I am making two main points, which I will frame here in terms of psychoanalysis, although I certainly think that the application is broader. The first is that termination recapitulates adolescence, both for the patient and for the analytic relationship. Put another way, the transference neurosis will highlight adolescent conflicts and the therapeutic alliance will have adolescent separation as its understructure. I hope that the reader will have found the case material convincing in this regard. The second point is less easily demonstrated. I am proposing that the working-through of the analytic separation, on the model of late adolescence, contributes to the internalization of the growthful aspects of the analytic experience, much as a well-worked-through separation will contribute to the personality consolidation of the adolescent. In this light, the work of the termination phase is another mutative factor in psychoanalytic treatment. With late adolescent patients who have not completed this developmental stage, the analyst will be in the position of actually taking a new developmental step with the patient. For patients who have traversed adolescence, for better or for worse, the analyst will be to a greater degree analyzing an aspect of the transference neurosis. And the adult patient's original success in negotiating adolescence will have bearing on the shape of the analytic termination.

The process of assimilation continues through the ending and beyond. During the analysis, the patient organizes a personal historical continuity. That which has been lost to the self is brought back to life. The initial adolescent consolidation, in which parts of the self had to be disowned, may now be reorganized in the service of the adaptive needs of the adult. And the consolidation continues after the ending, in that only then can the experience of the separation itself be integrated—or disowned. Alas, our own wish to know the ending is thus denied us as this final task is carried out in privacy. For unlike the adolescent's parents, we say goodbye for good.

10

Desire

We encounter our patients with our desire. It could not be otherwise.
We might say that our desire has two aspects—adaptive and neurotic.
In the adaptive category we include the ordinary desire to make
something of one's life and profession, a developmental drive. Dismissing the received wisdom that being paid should be sufficient
incentive, we know that we could not realize ourselves as analysts and
therapists if none of our patients benefited from our efforts on their
behalf (although our self-actualization should not require success in
every case). On the other side, we have the neurotic desire that
informs our career choices (as well as all our other choices). To one of
us, being a therapist might mean curing, by proxy, a parent, or
knowing the secrets of humankind, or being offered a manageable
intimacy, or a secret love, or having a measure of control over the life
of another, or being part of a secret fraternity, or being offered
voyeuristic pleasure. Some motives are more likely to get us into
trouble than others, and certainly the degree of sublimation of the
underlying conflict counts. But I think it is fair to say that to some
extent the choice to be a therapist is always a compromise formation,

the symptomatic expression of a conflict. We struggle with these tensions within ourselves as we work, and in the final chapter I will explore the ways in which these exertions evolve over the course of a career.

Here, however, I want to take up the impact of our desire on our practice. For purposes of exposition, I will divide these matters into two broad categories: the desire to cure and the desire to be cured. I recognize, remembering the remark of a patient cited earlier, that these are also two sides of a very thin coin. In what follows I will be elaborating another dimension of the issue of boundaries. We hold the maintaining of boundaries to be crucial to our work, and we also understand that one focus of understanding and interpretation is precisely our encounters with our patients at those interfaces (Shapiro and Carr 1991). Transference and countertransference are, from this point of view, boundary phenomena, the place at which the clear distinction between self and other is lost. Interpretation of transference, and the silent interpretation to oneself of countertransference, acts to clarify this boundary distinction by sorting out the reasons for the confusion. It is thus desire, the heartbeat of transference and countertransference, that brings us to the edge . . . and beyond.

THE DESIRE TO CURE

Let us consider the therapist's refusal to take "No!" for an answer. In one sense, the insistence on finding a way to move forward has led to great discoveries. The invention of free association was born of Freud's failure to make sufficient headway with hypnosis, suggestion, and pressure. As Jones points out, Freud was helped to this insight by a patient who complained about his continually interrupting her with his questions (cited in Searles 1979). Kohut's (1979) fleshing-out of self psychology was spurred in part by his efforts to find a way to work with Mr. Z. I can imagine that most all efforts at modifying mainstream technique have been prompted by failures *at treating particular patients*. And yet there has been a general uneasiness about efforts at

revision, a tendency to characterize such ventures as acting out. This
has particularly been the case when the new practice is a relatively
more active sort of involvement. In the idiom we have used to describe
the process, trappers have always been in vogue, while hunters have
always been suspect.

Ferenczi was a case in point. By about 1920, this earnest disciple
of Freud was arguing for a shift in treatment approach toward a more
active stance, in which the analyst might insist that the patient either
undertake or renounce certain activities, where the prior avoidance or
participation on the patient's part had been serving neurotic ends.
Ferenczi's experience with insisting on these injunctions was that the
patient, blocked from the usual symptomatic solutions, now brought
forth previously repressed material that advanced the analysis.
Having chosen this course of action, Ferenczi pulled out all the stops.
While treating an inhibited musician, he heard that her tyrannical
sister had been in the habit of singing a particular melody.

> I did not delay in asking her to sing the song. It took her
> nearly two hours, however, before she could bring herself to
> perform the song as she really intended it. She was so embar-
> rassed that she broke off repeatedly in the middle of a verse, and
> to begin with she sang in a low uncertain voice until, encouraged
> by my persuasions, she began to sing louder, when her voice
> developed more and more and proved to be an unusually
> beautiful soprano. . . . [She then confessed that her sister sang
> the song with gestures, which she awkwardly tried to imitate at
> Ferenczi's urging.] After endless spiritless partial attempts she
> showed herself to be a perfect *chanteuse*, with all the coquetry of
> facial play and movement that she had seen in her sister. . . .
> Presently memories of her early childhood, of which she had
> never spoken, occurred to her. . . . [1920, pp. 203–204]

In less florid form, such practice has become part of mainstream
technique, in that phobic patients are encouraged to confront the
situations they avoid and acting-out patients are directed to contain

themselves, so that, in both situations, the underlying anxieties can be addressed. But Ferenczi's own involvement expanded. As Roazen (1975) relates it, "By 1931 Ferenczi evidently was kissing patients and allowing them to kiss him, all part of the motherly affection he thought patients needed. . . . Freud worried whether 'pawing' might not be next on the agenda in the work of future adherents of Ferenczi's views, and then maybe 'peeping and showing,' and so on to the ultimate sexual act" (p. 367). Ferenczi did not write from a deficit model perspective, making any justification for this activity difficult to understand. Simon (1992) argues that the extent of Ferenczi's misconduct was probably exaggerated. In any case, Ferenczi's last paper was controversial for other reasons. Ironically, in consideration of his own conduct, he returned to an abandoned position of Freud's, claiming that sexual traumatization of children (a "hate-impregnated" love) was a vastly underrated pathogenic factor in mental illness (1933). Although modern practitioners might find much in the paper quite contemporary, Freud was deeply upset with it, and Jones claimed that their colleagues would find it scandalous (Jones 1957).

In my own experience, Ferenczi stood as a discredited figure. In the course of my training, and subsequently, I had heard his "active therapy" disparaged as misguided enactment. I was surprised, when I encountered his writing for myself, to find so much that made good sense. In a recent article, Simon (1992) suggests that Ferenczi represented to Freud his own disavowed capacity for engaging in "wild analysis." To Simon's understanding, what troubled Freud most about the seduction issue, ultimately, was his fear of his own seductiveness. He worried that he had put ideas into the minds of his patients to support his theories. Discrediting Ferenczi would have been one way of managing that conflict.

And so Alexander, with his emphasis on taking a role that contrasted with the behavior of the parents, thus creating a "corrective emotional experience" (1954), and Ferenczi thus came to be icons of bad practice. Within the psychoanalytic mainstream of that period, any suggestion that the noninterpretive aspects of treatment might have developmental benefit for the patient, or that an interpretive dialogue might have profit beyond the specific content of the interpretations, had to be carefully couched with assurances that one was not advocating something that resembled cure by love. Belief in the vested authority of interpretation has remained the litmus test for psychoanalytic practitioners.

What, we might ask, are we so scared about? The difficult boundary line, it seems to me, is between being a consultant and a parent. Consultancy is a useful model for the traditional concept of the therapist's role—it suggests that one is being hired to help the client reach an understanding about a problem. The consultant, while not indifferent to the question of outcome, is generally content to provide the most comprehensive insight he can reach about a problem. This seemed to be Freud's notion of his role. As we reread his case histories, we sense the interpreter at work. He offered his patients articulate formulations of their conflicts—framed, of course, within the model he was using—and didn't seem excessively preoccupied with how matters turned out for them. (We might even say that at moments he seemed a bit too content with the brilliance of his formulations, a bit too dispassionate about his patients' fates.) On the other hand, by contemporary standards Freud's treatments were brief and, in a sense, less ambitious than our own. When work with the Wolf Man threatened to drag on, Freud arbitrarily set a termination date. Because we do not feel free to think that the operation can be a success even though the patient expires, we dig our heels in and refuse to let go. And so the envelope of the consultancy role is stretched. Much as we claim to believe that success is to be measured by criteria internal to the therapeutic process, we do take note of what our patients are doing with their lives and feel disheartened when nothing is going forward. And, at that point, we try harder.

Trying harder puts us on the slippery slope. Perhaps Ferenczi skidded off. Parenthood has its limitations as a model; as mothers and fathers we put a great deal of ourselves into our children, and investing ourselves in our patients to that degree burdens them. And yet to an impressive extent, and far more than we feel free to write about, we are determined that our patients get well. We negotiate our position, in each treatment, somewhere on the continuum between consultancy and parenthood.

The issue is joined most emphatically with our more severely character-disordered patients, our borderlines, and our psychotics. Within psychoanalytically oriented outpatient practice it tends to be our patients' narcissistic pathology that most determinedly challenges us, their insistence that we take them on their own terms. These are the patients we feel we must *confront*.

Some years ago I read an interesting collection of essays on confrontation in psychotherapy (Adler and Myerson 1973), put together in response to a symposium on the topic in which several of the contributors had participated. Reflecting on the conference, the editors observed that "there was less disagreement among the panelists about when they use confrontation than about what they mean by it" (p. 10). The reader senses that the authors of the essays are uncomfortable with the topic, that they feel the behavior they're describing goes against the grain, at least against the grain of their training. The writers seem to be straining to make sense of their actions in a way that they can integrate into their understanding of the general principles by which they practice.

While there is considerable diversity in the articles, and a few writers even use the term *confrontation* in idiosyncratic ways, I find enough commonality among them to allow me to make certain generalizations. The authors tended to confront patients when they felt stymied by them. Typically the therapy was stuck, and often, although not always, the patient was being obnoxious. At the point of confrontation the therapist generally seemed to be angry, or at least the reader imagined that *he* would be feeling angry had he been in the practitioner's shoes. Usually the confrontation was intended to forcibly direct the patient's attention to something that he was avoiding or denying—something, that is, which the patient could potentially notice. And though the confrontation was usually accompanied or followed by the practitioner's plea to work toward understanding, it contained the unmistakable implication that the patient was expected to change his or her behavior as a condition for staying in treatment.

It was this last aspect that made the writers most uneasy. Welpton (1973), for example, offered a distinction between angry and empathic confrontations. The former, he argued, tend to promote submissive compliance; the patient conforms for fear of being abandoned. On the other hand, describing the empathic confrontation, he noted that he probably felt freer "to confront patients in this caring way when I feel free from the need to change them" (p. 258). While I believe that Welpton was making a useful distinction between two modes of response (and he recognized that these were end points of a continuum), I also think that he got snarled in the issue of change. In reporting the clinical example of an empathic confrontation, he explained:

> I said that, while I knew how afraid she was of me for fear I would not like her and had observed how she bolted into and out of my office [thus trying to avoid any spontaneous contact with him], I felt that she was really keeping distance between us in a way that made it harder for me to like her. I said this in a calm, gentle tone because I felt general acceptance and liking for her and because I only wanted to understand with her why she behaved in a way that elicited from me the opposite feelings from what she wanted, and I said this to her in our discussion that followed the confrontation. [pp. 259–260]

Whereas I have the impression that Welpton was not being particularly forceful with this patient, and that he might not have been angry with her, I can't imagine that she didn't believe that he wanted her both to handle her entries and exits differently and to be generally more direct with him. His follow-up comment to her that he was only trying to understand her behavior seems a bit disingenuous to me, albeit in that regard typical of remarks made by several of the contributors. He continued to wrestle with this at the end of the essay:

> It is not that the empathic therapist does not want to help his patient change, but that the change he is working toward is to help his patient accept himself for what he is. . . . A therapist who

helps the patient work toward greater acceptance of himself for what he is helps to free his patient from this demand to change into a different person and facilitates the patient's becoming more tolerant and understanding of himself. [pp. 266–267]

I believe that most of us tend to be of two minds about all this. On the one hand, we do think that self-acceptance is the great objective in treatment, and is ultimately the best bulwark against adjustment by compliance—that being the largest threat in the therapeutic situation. On the other hand, we also believe that self-acceptance will lead to developmental change, more adaptive functioning. In that sense, we're all developmentalists. I don't think that we would sit easily with the end result that the patient seemed more at peace with herself but was as dysfunctional as ever with her friends or family or in her work. This is the paradox the authors were often struggling with. As Mann (1973) commented in his essay, the freedom to choose is precious, and confrontation, no matter how tactfully or lovingly done, tends to undermine that freedom.

Many of the authors stressed that confrontation would inevitably miscarry if it did not take place in a context of caring. As Corwin (1973) remarked, "If no element of love is discernible by the patient, then the confrontation can be taken as proof by the patient that in the end the analyst will be just as cruel, rejecting, demanding, punitive, or unnecessarily harsh as the negative side of the parent in the transference" (p. 85). Putting this another way, Adler and Buie (1973) suggested that "a therapist can best make a useful confrontation, even though angry, when he has no wish to destroy the patient, not even his sick side" (p. 160). There is a good deal to be said for an honest encounter, and it doesn't even seem inevitable to me that the therapist's anger will generate social conformity. As Myerson (1973) points out, the therapist's anger may communicate in a way that nothing else does his deep commitment to his patient. He even argues that at just this point it might be helpful if the therapist isn't too preoccupied with examining his countertransference, for this might make the confrontation seem more stilted, more an exercise than an authentic engagement. Overall, we find it harder and harder to frame these states of mind in a consultancy model.

The issue of confrontation highlights for me the problematic nature of the desire to cure. I have tried to illustrate how our ambivalence about this desire leads us to trip over ourselves when we articulate it. We know that our hearts are in our work, but we're a bit embarrassed to acknowledge this. Part of our hesitation, I think, results from the proximity of this issue to my second subject, the desire to be cured. The boundary between these issues is well fenestrated.

THE DESIRE TO BE CURED

Near the beginning of this chapter I mentioned a few of the nondevelopmental motives that might have prompted us to enter this line of work. In the sense that choosing to be a therapist is a symptom, engaging in therapy must represent an effort toward cure. Searles proposes that "innate among man's most powerful strivings toward his fellow men, beginning in the earliest years and even earliest months of life, is an essentially psychotherapeutic striving" (1979, p. 380). This seems to me to build on Winnicott's (1948) emphasis that the toddler, in developing the capacity for concern, benefits enormously from having actual opportunities to contribute to the caretaker's well-being. Searles contends that frustration of that effort is a substantial cause of mental suffering, so that a successful outcome for treatment hinges on the patient's having the opportunity to function as a therapist to the person treating him. At this level, the therapist's desire for cure is matched with his patient's need to treat him. Using another developmental analogy, we might say that the therapist's desire to be cured expresses his search for what Bollas (1987) has called "the transformational object," the representation of the mother's preverbal facilitating functions.

In a useful treatment, negotiating this vector might be both a large undercurrent of the work and, at certain points, a matter for deliberate attention. Searles (1979) believes that the therapist's tacit rejection of his patient's therapeutic endeavors may reflect a need to keep the patient ill (so that the therapist's treatment won't be interrupted) and thus contributes mightily to treatment impasses. He goes on to detail some of the particular character flaws that his patients have brought to his attention. At this point we might gather that insofar as the therapist does not resist the patient's efforts too strenuously, the desire to be cured will not land the therapist in hot water. One caveat, I suppose, is that the patient's contributions would have to remain within conventional interpretive boundaries.

How, then, do difficulties arise? In this formulation, the problem would surface when the therapist is unable to make use of the patient's interpretive efforts and tries to recruit the patient to actually enact a problem solution. To choose the most ironic example, the patient might have to get well to enact the therapist's need to cure a disturbed parent. The patient's ostensible cure would then be an act of compliance, coerced by projective identification. As a further complication, however, this could never be an unconflicted solution. Because we are always moved to recreate the past, as a way of feeling connected, as well as to undo it, the therapist would feel estranged if his patient actually got well and would thus need also to have the patient continue to manifest her disorder. I believe that my own failure to recognize my patients' progress and my unwillingness to let go of them, especially an issue in the earlier stages of my career but to some extent throughout it, is an example of this dynamic.

The most dramatic instance of failure must be when therapist and patient join in a sexual relationship. Given the prevalence of the problem (at least one in ten psychiatrists is an offender, according to various surveys, with psychologists not far behind [Gabbard 1989]), it is impressive how relatively little has been written or understood about the phenomenon, especially from the point of view of the practitioner's psychology. In particular, we do not have case reports detailing the kind of understanding that could be reached in the course of in-depth psychotherapy or psychoanalysis of the sexually enacting therapists.

Rutter, a Jungian analyst who has become very active in this area, offers detailed elaborations of the dynamics at work for both male therapist and female patient (1989). His theorizing, however, seems to be primarily supported by anecdotal evidence such as consulting interviews; he does not offer material from patients worked with at length. Explanations are framed in terms of what each party brings to the encounter, including the consequences of cultural pressures and developmental trauma. What I find missing is the way in which pressures *intrinsic to the treatment* also play a role in leading the participants to this form of anxiety management. Rutter explains his decision not to report on his own cases this way: "I felt that asking my patients to allow me to use their stories in this book might raise issues of exploitation and fuel the hidden obligation to take care of the therapist that so many patients feel. Therefore, with only one exception, none of the cases I describe involves patients from my own practice or betrays confidential case reports given me by colleagues" (pp. 43–44). In one sense I can understand his concern because he was writing this book for the general public. On the other hand, I wonder whether he might also be excessively identified with the patients' concerns about betrayal. The stunning paucity of writing about the enacting therapists' experience in treatment leads me to consider that concerns about betrayal may be a broader issue, reflecting at a deeper level the ways in which we find our own experience resonating with that of the offending therapists we treat.

Searles (1979) suggests that patient–therapist sexual involvement may be driven by the therapist's rage at his failure to cure his patient by ordinary means:

It has long been my impression that a major reason for therapists' becoming actually sexually involved with patients is that the therapist's own therapeutic striving, desublimated to the level at which it was at work early in his childhood, has impelled him into this form of involvement with the patient. He has succumbed to the illusion that a magically curative copulation will resolve the patient's illness which tenaciously has resisted all the more sophisticated psychotherapeutic techniques learned in his adult-life training and practice. [p. 431]

This explanation seems more persuasive to me with regard to work with the more severely regressed patients who populate much of Searles's writing, although he may also have it in mind as applying to a broader population.

I imagine that the patient's effort to cure the therapist might also be a factor here. Much has been written about our loneliness, and the choice of this career direction as an effort to escape it (e.g., Buie 1982–1983). Twemlow and Gabbard (1989) describe the lovesick therapist, whom they believe is responsible for at least half the cases of therapist-patient sexual involvement. Building on Searles's thinking, I wonder to what degree the sex is prompted by the patient's despairing efforts to cure the therapist in this way when all else has failed. While this would ordinarily be concealed behind a surface presentation in which the patient was yielding to the therapist's desire and power, it would be consonant with the observation that often therapists had been discussing the distresses of their personal lives with their patients for a time before sexual intimacies began. Of interest, according to a major study conducted by Gartrell and colleagues (1989), is that almost half the incidents reported by enacting psychiatrists took place at least six months after treatment had ended. While this data seems a bit suspect to me—it's quite inconsistent with the reports of therapists who have subsequently treated therapist-abused patients—it could be taken to confirm the idea that all previous efforts on the part of the patient to treat the depressed therapist had indeed failed, and that this was the only avenue left open. As a sole explanation, these ideas seem much too simplistic to me; as part of a larger understanding they seem plausible.

In the sense that the desire to cure and the desire to be cured are so closely intertwined, I would expect that therapists who are unable to accept their patients' failures to get well would be more likely to wend their way into these sexual encounters. I suspect that it is extremely rare that a substantially successful treatment ends in an affair—or, for that matter, a marriage. The sexual enactment may point to precisely the place of impasse. This would make dubious the claims, at times from both parties, that the basis of the relationship is now true love.

Interpretation, from both sides, has failed. In Lacan's terms, we move back from the realm of the Symbolic to the realms of the Imaginary and the Real. Bollas (1989) points out that in incest the father destructures his function as provider of the symbolic order. This is parallel to the way in which incest represents a breakdown of symbolic play, a collapse of transitional experience.[1] The wishes to cure and to be cured are probably always, in a sense, at the heart of incestuous experience.

---

[1]This way of thinking about incest is elaborated in Winer (1989).

11

Politics

Although the practitioner's conceit is that therapy is a pristine encounter, we all know better—this is only the hysteric's pose to protest our virginity. I would like to briefly enumerate a few of the many political contexts in which we work. Therapy occurs in institutions, financed by third parties, supervised by administrators and teachers, as part of professional training, under the scrutiny of the patient's employer, in fulfillment of requirements for professional certification, at the insistence of the courts, in response to the importuning of a spouse, as an adjunct to another's treatment, or even to a second treatment of one's own. Perhaps half of the patients I see live in fear that someone (even *anyone*) will discover that they are in treatment, to their potential disadvantage. While this will likely stem in part from unconscious irrational fears, our patients believe that there are also real interpersonal consequences to being known to be in therapy. For them simply attending therapy is, at least at some level, a political act. Halpert (1985) points out, as one example, that in 1981, according to the *New York Times*, the Reagan administration proposed that American intelligence agencies should have the authority to get access to, among other things, private medical records.

None of these political contexts make therapy impossible, but they add particular dimensions that affect the treatment in ways that should be—but only rarely are—kept in view. I will take up the issue broadly here and address supervision separately in the next chapter. The message of these investigations is that even the two-person view of treatment is actually an illusion. For beyond our transference anxieties there are always others, in the shadows, who have their eyes on us.

STRUCTURAL ASPECTS OF TREATMENT

Consider, for a start, a few of the problems inherent in treatment that is entered into as a requirement of professionals' training programs in psychoanalysis. They might include the following:

If the patient (the psychoanalyst in training) acts destructively, both parties' advancement will be affected, but it is unlikely that the analyst will feel comfortable making the observation that the patient is toying with the idea of slashing his wrists in the hopes that he could thus ruin his analyst's career, even though this might be true and absolutely to the point. The analyst could easily be afraid that such a complaint might appear too self-protective. The patient might understand all too well that his analyst was being put in this quandary.

If the patient wishes to change analysts, he may fear that this will reflect badly on him with the training committee, and thus he may compromise his treatment needs by remaining in an unsatisfactory situation. An essential aspect of any analysis is that the treatment is entered voluntarily and that each hour might always be the last hour if either party so desires. That freedom is then lost. This restriction is virtually never acknowledged as a parameter of training treatment. The failure to discuss the issue will also prevent the two from grappling with the transference issues that will be involved in this state of mind; the patient simply considers it an undiscussible reality.

The patient will have a continuing relationship with his analyst after treatment ends, because they will both remain in their institution. This obviously alters somewhat the nature of termination, but it may also affect their capacity to be free with each other within the treatment, knowing that they have a future to contend with.

It seems to me that some analysts become more invested in the future lives of their patients who are trainees than they do in their patients who are not therapists. This probably reflects, among other things, an identification with the patient (the analyst was once a trainee himself) and a wish to protect the analyst's patient from the institution. The patient may unconsciously respond to this, but it is unlikely that it will be addressed, and it may simply contribute to the patient's unanalyzed idealization of his analyst.

I have heard colleagues express the fear, most often in retrospect, that if their analyst had known how crazy they were, they wouldn't have been allowed to stay in training. While this is virtually always an unrealistic fear and could potentially be analyzed, it is not voiced because in reality the treatment is occurring in a political context, the dimensions of which the patient cannot assess. Some training institutions have actually given the analyst a role in determining the trainee's status. It's not unusual for analysts to have second analyses after they complete their training in the hope that this time they will feel freer to make full use of the opportunity.

Ordinarily the analyst is not familiar with the important other figures in the patient's life, but this is not the case in training analyses. Reports of one's colleagues' idiosyncrasies, made in the course of free-associating, may affect their careers if the analyst is in a position of authority in the institution (and most analysts in training positions are). At best, the information reported will be held in confidence. Even then, it must still color the analyst's view of the person. In some situations the analyst may be able to disqualify himself from institutional deliberations, but this will not always be possible. In a practice inconsistent with the asserted privacy of the analytic situation, a great variety of disclosures are actually shared between analysts in training situations while keeping the identity of the patient who made the disclosure concealed. The idiom is to refer to the matter as something heard from the couch. And thus treatment becomes a vehicle for revenge.

While all these aspects of the political situation can potentially be brought into the discourse by either party, this rarely happens because the political side is an actual dimension of the treatment, an aspect of its frame; and the frame of the treatment, if it is stable, tends to be taken for granted. Fee arrangements, once set, are rarely discussed if the patient pays his bill on time. It has been my experience that it is very difficult to treat adult patients whose fees are completely paid by their health insurance companies. In this event, the basic quid pro quo of treatment—that the therapist provides his expertise and the patient pays him for it—is lost. It is true that the patient pays for the insurance, or receives it as a part of his salary for working, but he would have the insurance whether or not he is in treatment, and this undermines for him the sense that he is contributing. The impact of the situation, in my experience, has been that the patient then defensively devalues the treatment. Something similar often occurs when patients are seen at reduced fees—*they* tend to feel devalued and respond either by behaving in a more helpless manner or by depreciating the treatment.

What tends to make these situations uninterpretable is that they are part of the structure of the treatment. If the therapist is traumatizing the patient by accepting a reduced fee (I may be taking this as an example for its shock value), it is problematic to interpret the impact of that action while one continues to do it. In any of the political contexts under consideration, the therapist is at least a collaborator, if not an instigator, in the arrangement. For example, one chooses to analyze a trainee, or one agrees to treat a patient knowing that he is coming only as an act of compliance with his wife. It is a generally accepted principle of technique that one cannot interpret while one is a partner to an enactment. One must first disentangle oneself from the enactment before one will be experienced by the patient as being entitled to have a voice. It is in the nature of all these political contexts that one is participating in an action; this is what defines the situation as political. While it may be inescapable that this restricts the freedom of the treatment and puts bounds on the freedom to interpret, this in itself can at least be acknowledged and kept within the field of inquiry.

Another structural aspect of the treatment situation, which I will address at greater length in the next chapter, is supervision. I would like here to take up briefly the issue of supervision as part of training. Luber (1991) discussed a case he had treated as a candidate in which, at the time of his transition from trainee to graduate, the patient's flow of ideas indicated that she had been harboring various feelings about the fact that her analyst was discussing the treatment with a supervisor. During my years of training students, I don't recall ever hearing about patients having such thoughts, and I have distant memories of dreading that my training cases would raise such an issue with me. In working with my own training cases, I was acutely aware that the hours that immediately followed a supervisory session were distinctly different from the rest of the meetings in each treatment. It is impossible, from my present vantage point, to imagine that my patients did not notice that Tuesday, for example, was routinely different from all other days of the week.

In searching the psychoanalytic literature, Luber found only a couple of articles in which cases were reported that even included the supervisor's existence as part of the material. He thought that the omission spoke to the conspiracy between patient and analyst that took the form of not inquiring into each other's secrets. Even in those few cases where the issue was discussed, however, the patient's feelings about the supervisor were explored essentially for their transference meanings as reexperiencing of childhood conflict. The patient's experience of the analyst's actual embarrassment—a virtually inevitable experience for the analyst, given the vicissitudes of training and human propensities to shame—was not mentioned. For Luber, the jump away from the present transference intensities to the childhood historical situation seemed a bit premature and thus defensive. I agree with Luber that the treatment then institutionalizes a blind spot, as the patient is not allowed to take his measure of the treatment situation as a whole.

AGREEING TO TREATMENT

The decision to join in a treatment is a political act for both parties, both in relation to the participants' culture and society and in relation to their circle of intimates. Given the values of the culture, entering treatment may range, for the patient, from being an act of courage to being an act of conformity. The analyst chooses each day to continue his work as an analyst. As a minimal but not irrelevant example, the analyst may choose on a given day not to cancel his patients and take part in a political action for a cause he believes in. (This example may seem too minimal to be relevant to this discussion in late twentieth-century America, but it seemed less minimal to some practitioners in the 1960s.) He makes a choice—choosing to work is a moral and political decision. But other, less dramatic, examples also come to mind. A man who is a member of a racial minority came to see me; he was depressed, enraged with his employer, who had been blocking his advancement. He was countering his boss by being ill and refusing to work, and I expected that he would use the fact that he was seeing me as leverage in his battle with his white employer. He would do this even without my overt collaboration—his employer, as it happened, would believe that he was in fact seeing me without my attesting to it, partly because it also served the employer's ends to have the matter resolved in this way. So by agreeing to treat this patient, I was letting myself be used in a particular political way, and in a way that constituted a stand on the larger issues of racism and responsibility. He and I may talk about these things, but I have still agreed to treat him. It would seem naive to me to say that this is a politically neutral act.

Another patient came complaining bitterly about his wife. While he had thought of leaving his family, his attachment to his children and the guilt he felt when he thought about leaving them held him back. It seemed unlikely, in fact, that he would leave before the children had all left home, if even then. In the meantime he would mainly avoid his family and torture them with moments of paternal devotion. When I met him I had a number of choices, including recommending individual treatment, couples treatment, family treatment, or no treatment. Each of these choices would have had particular consequences that are not entirely beyond prediction, but I would like to comment here on some of the implications of the choice I made, which was to see him alone, in psychoanalysis. I should say that I think he would have accepted whichever recommendation I made— he was looking for guidance. It was likely that he would become quite attached to me, finding in me a new wife-confidant, and that with this need for a partner met he would withdraw even further from his wife. With this support (and, just to be clear about it, I am referring here to the kind of ordinary support that is intrinsic to any civilized analytic treatment) he might just put up with the marriage for the next decade, while the children grew up, and on termination leave both me and his wife. In the meantime, because of his feeling nurtured by his relationship with his analyst, he might be inclined to do less to try to actually improve the home situation than if he were not in treatment. His wife would probably avoid confronting him, at least for some time, in the hope that his analysis would bring him back to her. If he were not in treatment, she might find the courage to confront him. It was also possible that treatment might lead to the sort of personal growth that has positive consequences for family life, although I felt dubious about such a prospect in this case.

Psychoanalysis, because of its interpersonal intensity, generally tends to pull patients away from their spouses, at least for a time and too often for good. I've heard that an anthropologist who measured such things once pointed out that the average couple speaks together 24 minutes a week (including "You're blocking my view of the TV set" and "Have you seen the kids?"). That time length is eclipsed midway through the week's first analytic hour. And while treatment might open up a person to the benefits of talking with others, it often seems to have the opposite consequence of constituting enough communication to last for the week. Furthermore, the ending of psychoanalysis is often traumatic enough that patients choose to manage it by either dropping someone from, or adding someone to, their lives (or both)— a surprising number of analyses seem to end with either pregnancies or divorces. The point I am working toward here is that in choosing to begin an analysis we are making a decision that we know will likely have consequences not only for the patient but also for other people in his life, and that this is another political dimension of our work.

A typical way that therapists deal with this context is by deciding that we will practice our craft with whoever comes to see us—that the patient's arrival at the office sufficiently expresses the person's choice to try being in treatment and our only reasonable response is to give it a go, to do our work as best we can, and to set aside the kind of questions and consequences I am raising here. There is much to be said for this state of mind; without it we might all be as bound up as Hamlet. But I am arguing that not making a choice is actually a political position itself. Political neutrality is an oxymoron.

THIRD PARTIES

Increasingly, these days, we find someone peering over our shoulder. Insurance companies want to examine cases to see whether treatment, by their standards, is justified. The effort is to keep costs down and the criteria often seem arbitrary. These days all therapists have stories to tell. Here is one of mine:

> A year into treatment with a middle-aged architect, I received a request for information. I told the insurance company that he had come for help because he had been experiencing moments of intense anger that seemed uncalled for, had been feeling moderately depressed, had been having difficulty functioning sexually with his wife, and had been having trouble sleeping and eating. I reported that some of these difficulties had improved over the course of the year, thus justifying to

them that their dollars were being well spent, but added that the sexual
dysfunction continued and that he was still somewhat depressed. The
insurance company refused to continue supporting his treatment – to be
exact, they said that they would give us three months to finish up. I
called the company and spoke with the person who had reviewed the
case. He told me that lots of people were depressed and had difficulty
with sexual performance, that those were just the ups and downs of life.
I must say that I had the definite impression that he was talking to me
in a confessional voice, and that he was using his own functioning as a
standard for acceptable – that is, noncompensable – mental health.

In practice, we find ourselves tailoring our reports to indicate
enough illness to justify treatment, and to account for enough progress
to merit continuing support. We take care to frame the case in such a
way that the monitors don't decide that drugs, rather than talking
therapy, should be the appropriate, not to mention less costly, treatment, unless we happen to agree with that. It is generally, although
not always, my practice to give my patients copies of these reports, in
part so that they can have some say about what information gets
included. I do this because many of us have doubts these days about
the absolute confidentiality with which institutions handle our accounts. Another motive for sharing the report is to cut against the
impression of a collusion between doctor and insurance company in
which these parents will decide what is best for the child.

The disadvantage of the practice is that it sets the patient's
experience into a concrete form, treats states of mind as things that
can be labeled, establishes priorities among the patient's difficulties (I
choose to list some problems and not others), and alleges causalities
and asserts them with more certainty than could ever be justified. It is
intrinsic to our way of working that we try to keep the field of inquiry
as open as possible, allowing for expanses of uncertainty and doubt.
Any written statements, no matter how carefully we phrase them,
become authoritative and create closure. Making a diagnosis always
has this effect and it is traumatizing to the patient, in ways we might
not even imagine. I once agreed with a patient that we would diagnose
his condition as a depression. After leaving the hour he walked out

into the middle of traffic and almost got himself run over. I came to understand that he thought I had not appreciated the severity of his condition.

When my patients read the insurance report, what do they make of my effort to sell their condition to a third party, of my shaping the truth to make it most presentable? They might be led to believe that we are in a slight but definite collusion to defraud. What childhood conspiracies will we be reenacting? Will we find a way to talk about this? Halpert (1985) observes that "in regard to the question of diagnosis, there is often a conflict between the desire to protect the patient's right to confidentiality and the need to be honest. If, for example, the patient is in treatment for a perversion, most analysts would enter a diagnosis that validly expresses some part of the clinical picture, such as depression, but which evades the basic truth. In such an instance the analyst is to a certain degree participating in a collusion with the patient no matter how correct he may be in what he is doing" (p. 940). Rudominer (1984) points out that peer review creates countertransference problems for the analyst, stirring up, among other things, conflicts regarding exhibitionism, voyeurism, and perfectionism.

The subtle difficulty in working with this issue, as with all the issues I'm raising in this chapter, is that the patient's (and therapist's) response will always be based on an intricate mixup of reality and transference pressures. The therapist tries to find a way to explore the transference issues without denying the reality and the importance of the external situation. Rudominer (1984) offers one of the few detailed reports in the literature of work with a patient around a peer review issue. I found his essay quite engaging. At one point, as he is exploring the meaning to the patient of having submitted a statement, he quotes the patient as saying:

It is frightening to think one is writing an institution about one's mental state without any say in the matter. . . . I'm afraid to ask you about the report because I could lose you if you say no and I'll get angry. I will feel you're wrong. I don't know what I would think if I read that you felt it was going to be a short or long analysis. It would mean some kind of frame of reference I would have to reach up to. If my prognosis was good and I could finish up in a year, then I would feel I wasn't reaching up. If my prognosis was poor, then I'd be in despair. Also if I read it, then I would have stronger feelings toward you. It would be another area of interacting with you. . . . I want to see your willingness to protect me. [p. 787]

This is a very interesting statement. The patient expresses transference feelings as she speaks of her fear of losing the therapist (it's not clear actually who would leave whom in her reckoning) and of her wanting to experience him as willing to protect her. The latter could imply, however, that she felt unprotected by the way he had actually handled the report originally. As reported by Rudominer, he had felt awkward about that himself; he thought that he had written a much too detailed statement. After the session excerpted above, he asked the insurance company to return the report, which they did (they had already decided to support the treatment). He considered this request on his part also to be countertransferential acting out. I experience the author as too quick to make judgments against himself. How could any of us know for certain what would make a sufficient document? Is retrieving it so clearly an error? After the session in which he told the patient about his call to get the report back, she recalled her mother's drunken unpredictability.

Rudominer comments that he thought that the call was "a powerful transference gratification" (p. 788) satisfying the patient's need to be special. As I followed his chain of narration, I thought that perhaps she was unnerved by his anxiety and found him erratic, and was communicating this by her comment about her mother. There is certainly a great deal of tension in the air between patient and analyst, focused on the peer review issue. Perhaps they were reenacting something from her experience with her mother—miscarriages of assistance.

In the same regard, I don't agree with Halpert's view that "every time an analyst does anything other than make interventions in the pursuit of insight, any analysis is made more difficult" (1985, p. 947). Analysis is always extremely difficult, the field is very complex, and we can either acknowledge that and grapple with it or hide from it. At times it is precisely in sorting out the kind of interchange that Rudominer was having with his patient that we can discover something crucial we've been missing out on all along. Patients typically pick as their battlefield a place where they have a stake in reality. On the one hand, this serves defensively to conceal the neurotic aspect. But it also makes the conflict most palpably alive.

Before leaving this example, I'd like to comment on the issue of prognosis. The woman was quite concerned about whether her analyst thought she would need a short or long course of treatment. He had, I presume, probably expressed some sort of opinion about this in the report. A guiding principle in treatment is that we cannot predict the future. The kind of knowing that is involved in prognosticating is a state of mind antithetical to the state of uncertainty and openness to surprise in which we like to work. And I believe that our patients appreciate our being in this state of mind. It might be that narrowing this openness was what was troubling the patient—not that he had specifically predicted one way or the other, but that he had entered a position where he felt he could predict at all. Put in Winnicottian language, she might have experienced this as his abandonment of their shared "intermediate experience." I could be failing to understand adequately this particular case in this regard, but I believe that this is an inherent problem in offering prognoses, and one that would need interpretive attention should predicting be a requirement for the continuation of a treatment.

Another third party to consider, in our currently litigious culture, is our patient's family. Perhaps our greatest concern along these lines is that a patient will commit suicide and the spouse or parents or children will file suit. If the patient had not been receiving antidepressants we will certainly be at great risk. In a dark essay on what the future might hold for our profession, Eissler (1979) points out that even Freud himself can be used against us—in his last comprehensive work he speculated that "chemical substances" might exert "a direct influence" on disordered functioning (Freud 1940, p. 182)! Therapists are not immune from the temptation to practice defensive medicine, although the nature of our work is such that we feel considerable counterpressure to act courageously and resist such corruption. If the patient does not have the freedom to choose suicide, she cannot have the freedom to choose life. Knowing that, if the patient is not psychotic we try to keep her options open. (I should add that this position is not incompatible with seeing suicide as an absolute enemy. At times the protection of hospitalization is the unconditionally necessary alternative.) The corruption, when it occurs, is not likely to be blatant. It may take the form of being a bit too solicitous, a bit too anxious, a slight pulling back from the necessary edge. Our patients sense our hesitation and lose a bit of their confidence in us.

POLITICS PROPER

In yet another sense, the therapy hour is conspicuously apolitical. Patients rarely talk about the larger world they inhabit, their political sensibilities, the impact of the social world on their lives. It has been observed that Japanese patients rarely speak of Hiroshima and that the free associations of Germans tend not to include the Nazi epoch. When the radiation from Chernobyl was falling on Finland it reportedly did not penetrate the Finns' analytic hours. Although we have been living in a time when our species has threatened to eliminate itself with thermonuclear weapons, nuclear war themes have rarely surfaced in our adult patients' hours, except as an occasional metaphor, perhaps in a dream, for a feared personal destruction. There are a variety of reasons for this avoidance, certainly including the intense priority of immediate interpersonal conflict as the pressing business in our patients' lives, but I think that the avoidance also speaks to our patients' wishes to make treatment an enclave, a special place to which they can retreat, preserving a phantasy of the treatment space as a sacred monastery, and to keep us idealized as invulnerable parents.

Nothing unsettles our patients more than their seeing us as scared, and in the face of these external threats we are as vulnerable as they are. To be more precise about it, patients can bear our being anxious better than they can bear our being afraid.

The question has been raised whether we are colluding with our patients in avoiding these issues—does therapy covertly support self-aggrandizement and set aside concerns about altruism (Jacobs 1988)? If the therapist is not concerned about his patients' capacity for altruism, is he contributing to the encroaching comprehensive narcissism of our culture? Raising these questions is another way of reminding us that therapy is not silent in the area of values. The original conceit that therapy could actually exist outside values was replaced by the establishment of a set of values around treatment. Adaptation, reduction of intrapsychic conflict, and developmental progression (growing up) constitute a field of values consistent with the analytic conception. But a great deal falls between the cracks of the edifice supported by those pillars. As we listen to our patients we are continually deciding what falls into the realm of psychopathology and what does not, and our own value systems guide our listening far more than we acknowledge. One critique of our work has been that we excessively encourage individualism at the price of communality—a quality which, at one level, is a legacy of Freud's own personality.

NEUTRALITY

The concern that we practice from a position of neutrality reflects our sense that we are toiling in a dense pasture, rife with opportunities for going astray. Our choice of the word *neutrality* implicates our recognition that we work in a political minefield as well. We are told that we must stand equidistant between the demands of id, ego, superego, and external reality. It would be more to the point to say that we must recognize the legitimate claims of each. We are also told that we must receive our patients without memory or desire. We realize that this is impossible, even nonsensical, but we might take this caution to mean that we should respect the workings of memory and desire upon ourselves, and listen to the voices and urgings in our own heads as we listen to our patients.

One definition of neutrality that has made sense to me is that we work to extricate ourselves from repeated countertransference enactments with our patients. That the enactments take place is at the heart of our work; it is the way we come to know our patients. Just to be clear about the range of activities that I bring in under this umbrella, at certain points in a treatment, my listening attentively to my patient's free associations and making relevant interpretations, rather than staying silent and letting tension develop, will constitute not bad technique but rather a mutual enactment of anxiety-avoiding operations in the patient's life. Defining neutrality as our effort to work ourselves clear means that we need to be as aware as possible of all the things we need to get clear of.

In the greatest misunderstanding of the concept, neutrality is equated with anonymity. There is nothing anonymous about our enterprise, and intelligent practice is that which is entered into in a spirit of full discovery and disclosure. The goal of this chapter has been to outline some of the dimensions we need to attend to in our investigation. We do not expect that treatment rids anyone of his conflicts, but rather that we give our patients additional leverage in dealing with them, thereby doing what Freud referred to as replacing neurotic suffering with ordinary misery. The same applies to the process of treatment. The objective is not to have a stainless technical procedure free of parameters and imperfections, not to aim for control and mastery (the analyst as surfer waiting to ride the perfect interpretation all the way to shore), but to work toward awareness of all the nuances that make our ride inevitably a rough and perilous journey. Jesus' urging of Peter that he come with him and be a fisher of men catches for me the spirit of the enterprise.

12

Supervision

This chapter is offered as a cautionary tale about supervision. I've worked with nine supervisors since completing my residency training in psychiatry, for an average of about 4 years each. The range was from 1 to 10 years, and some were seen simultaneously. They have all been useful to me, no one remarkably more so than the others. Each had a particular point of view about the treatment process that was implicit, and in a few cases explicit, in their teaching. Like most supervisees, I've always felt torn between wishes for education and for validation. These wishes are at odds with each other, because the latter requires that the supervisor simply listen to me in awe. One supervisor helped me shut up more. Addressing my excessive busyness, he once told me that a supervisor had cautioned him, "Just at *that* point it would have been *best* if you'd been thinking about balancing your checkbook," which might have given the patient some room to breathe. (He also helped teach me tact.) Another taught me to be less vague and more rigorous in my thinking. There are moments that stand out with each of them. I offer this recollection as a balance against the problematic considerations that follow.

The psychoanalytic literature on supervision tends not to focus on what I consider to be the very unusual dynamics of the patient–analyst–supervisor situation. To a surprising degree it essentially considers supervision simply another form of education in which the teacher has an understanding to impart. While attention has been paid to particular psychological problems that may impede the work from both the analyst's and supervisor's sides (e.g., Anderson and McLaughlin 1963, DeBell 1963, Grinberg 1970), rather little consideration has been given to the process of the three-person setup. There is some recognition that the patient will evoke feelings in the analyst that may then be transmitted into the supervisory situation (Gediman and Wolkenfeld 1980, Blomfield 1985), although the vast majority of writers do not examine this interactive field. Among the paradoxical aspects of supervision that I explore here, I will be arguing that it imposes a three-person dimension on a dyadic situation, and that some of the difficulties that ensue can be understood as defensive reactions to this shift.

How one conducts supervision ultimately must be determined by what one thinks will help the supervisee to develop as a therapist. Faced with the student's helplessness and anxiety, the supervisor is tempted to offer rules of practice: establish the boundaries; attend to surface before depth; interpret defense before impulse; when in doubt, wait; no transference interpretations in the beginning (or *only* transference interpretations in the beginning), and so on. The application of these rules to the student's various cases will be demonstrated, and thus armored the student will feel less scared. Unfortunately, the student has been made less anxious by being offered tools with which he can distance himself from his patient. I say this in the context of remembering the early training experiences of my own peer group. To that extent the student is no longer treating a person; he is executing a procedure and excommunicating the patient, who, in all his novelty, vanishes, to be replaced by a concatenation of functions, structures, and internal objects. The patient as person has been replaced by patient as thing, although we soon hear therapists talking about themselves in the same estranged ways, the self as a carpetbag of good and bad parts that need tending. I don't think that we should stop giving our students rules and aphorisms; I'm just suggesting that we should dread doing it, painfully recognizing that we are at least temporarily reinforcing their schizoid defenses by this process.

After the rules have been established, the supervisor may settle down into straightforward competition with the student for superior understanding of the patient. This has been referred to as supervision by conduit, the student serving as the vessel for the supervisor's insights, which will be dutifully borne forward to the patient. As supervisors we feel irritated when our students repeat our interpretations, word for word, to their patients, but we don't seriously question their perception that this is what we expect of them because we are not prepared to hear their answer. As a therapist, when a patient tells me a story about her spouse, I don't believe that I have a privileged insight into her partner, or that I know the spouse as an independent being. I assume that the picture I'm forming in my mind is made from both the patient's projections and external realities. I understand that I'm getting the patient's view of some aspects of her marriage—a portrait, from one standpoint, of a relationship. And yet as a supervisor I find myself acting as though I actually could know my student's patient, independently as it were. Sometimes this illusion is supported by the use of audiotapes, or even videotapes. At best, as a supervisor, I am getting only a view of a relationship, again from a particular vantage point, and it is this perception of the relationship that I may be in a position to discuss. When I'm being conscientious I will recognize that any observations that go beyond this are speculations, and should be treated as such by the student.

I would like to shift now and talk about hate in the supervisory relationship. The stress for the supervisor is that he is the outsider, the voyeur, in the supervisory triangle. The attempt to claim privileged insight may be, at one level, an effort to deny that position. This resembles the situation of being the parent of a dating adolescent— suddenly the oedipal tables are turned and the parent is peering in on the primal scene. The parent may manage this by asserting his sexual authority and offering his child guidance, or by overidentifying with the child and treating his child's experience as his own. Both of these maneuvers are attempts to challenge his exclusion.

Twice in my career, supervisors have become infatuated with female patients I was treating. Both supervisors assured me that these patients were indeed rare finds, that I might never again come across another patient with such capacity for psychoanalytic work. They marveled at my patients' dreams and intuitions, as in time did I, and I felt in competition with my supervisors for my patients' affections, even something of an outsider during the supervisory hours, a remarkable position to be in for the person who is actually treating the patient. Both patients, it would turn out, were more troubled than any of us had imagined. Now this is quite a complicated setup. I think that each of us—patient, therapist, and supervisor—had needs to idealize one party and denigrate the other, although the denigration was generally concealed, and that we all contributed to the enactments. One patient discarded her husband when the treatment began, in some sense feeling that I was all she needed, and the other excluded me from her bedroom, as it were, by virtually never discussing her marriage during the treatment. Both treatments came at inaugural points in my career, one when I started private practice and the other when I began psychoanalytic training. My idealizations of the treatments were ways of managing my own anxieties in those situations.

Supervision gives an oedipal twist to a dyadic structure. While the instances I just cited were unusual, the shift is inescapable and accounts for much of the hate in the supervisory relationship. Supervision, however tactful, is always an intrusion, and always brings in elements of rivalry, jealousy, and envy, however well these may be concealed and defended against. Not infrequently, a parallel develops between the treatment and supervisory situations. The therapist treats his supervisor in the same way that his patient is treating him. I want to propose here that this parallel process may not only reflect the therapist's unconscious effort to more evocatively bring the treatment into the supervision, by enacting what cannot be remembered and told, but also serves to defend against the oedipalization of the treatment. I will illustrate this by discussing one of the classic examples of parallel process, brought to my attention by Gediman and Wolkenfeld (1980).

Jacob Arlow (1963) described a supervisory session with a therapist who was treating a young male homosexual. The patient tended to ingratiate himself with strong men he admired, whose strength he wished to possess, by engaging in fellatio. In this supervisory hour the therapist reported a dream the patient had related:

> In the dream the patient saw himself lying on the couch, turning around to face the analyst and then offering him a cigarette. "At this point in the supervisory session," Arlow writes, "the therapist reached for a pack of cigarettes, took one for himself, and although he knew very well that I do not smoke, extended the pack to me and asked, 'Do you want a cigarette?' " [p. 580]

Arlow understood this as the therapist's identification with his patient, probably prompted by shared pathology, which Arlow reports was subsequently confirmed. It seems possible to me that the therapist felt that to manage the threat the supervision posed to his relationship with his patient, which at that time was engaged with homosexual dynamics in the transference and countertransference, he had to curb his impulse to destroy Arlow by defensively submitting and offering him a cigarette, symbolizing his penis. It might puzzle us that Arlow needed to include in his report that the therapist's homosexuality was actually confirmed, since that actuality was not central to his argument and could only make the therapist feel ill if he discovered this paper. But Arlow had mentioned in his exposition that the therapist's patient was the sort of man who in phantasy castrates a more powerful man while sucking on him. Had the supervisor felt threatened by his student, and was he gratuitously putting him in his place? Was the patient's dream a parallel evocation of problems that had actually originated in the supervision? These are conjectures, but if they seem compelling they would support the thought that the parallel process, an enacted symbiosis, was a defense for managing oedipal rivalry in the supervision.

Supervision attempts to cure the supervisee without treating him. The poignancy of supervision is that it always yearns to be treatment, like a sculpture that longs to be human. I will observe in a later chapter that in any treatment that is truly useful the therapist must work through a personal crisis in himself, and that the working through of that crisis is the keystone of the treatment. The therapist's conflict will of course be intimately related to his patient's conflicts. That will be true not only because of our plasticity and the power of projective identification, but also because we tend to select as patients those people who touch us in a sensitive place — those are the patients our friends who know us well refer to us, the people we take on for more intensive work, the ones we work harder with and most deeply believe we can help.

I suspect that we choose supervisors along similar lines, and that the treatments we elect to present to them will be those in which we are most deeply engaged, this being most likely true when the supervision is freely chosen. What then evolves will be an intricate network of psychological conflict linking supervisor, therapist, and patient. In this situation, the supervisee is always treating himself as he treats his patient. The insights he gains about the treatment will resonate with his self-analysis — to the extent that he is open to self-learning at a given time — and supervision becomes crypto-therapy.

The supervisor's responsibility is not to interfere with this process. In ordinary supervision much does get in the way: the supervisor's need to be expert; the student's wish to (so to speak) believe in God; supervisory zeal; both parties' needs to master the supervisory situation in all its oedipal fullness; and the idea that there is a knowable right way or a best way, at least at a given moment. Much of this is packed into the etymology of supervision: the view from above. If the goal of supervision is to facilitate the sort of developmental progression I've been describing, how is it best conducted? It has been suggested that in psychoanalytic training, the student's personal analysis is the analysis of a psychoanalyst, while his supervision is the analysis of a psychoanalysis. This seems to me a step in the right direction, for it emphasizes the process rather than the patient.

I would like to continue this discussion by describing my own efforts to supervise a trainee. I had acquired a good impression of this man from our classes where I had taught him—he seemed bright, thoughtful, and eminently sensible, modestly experienced in psychoanalytically oriented work but eager to develop himself. It quickly became clear that he wanted supervision because he felt he was in over his head with a very difficult young woman whom he had been treating for a year, meeting for three double sessions a week. My supervisee had been seeing this patient for these lengthy sessions because he had felt it took him that long to get a useful hold of her.

The patient typically came in acting quite upset and rageful, talked in an intensely pressured way, shaking as she spoke, and eventually settled down a bit and became more coherent. The coherence, however, came at the price of detachment. The patient spoke mechanically, acknowledging that she was afraid of the therapist, at times expecting that the therapist would hit her. After leaving the session the patient would feel rejected and suicidal and spend the next few hours making many calls to the therapist's answering machine during which she would cry and relate sad memories of her childhood—memories she typically wouldn't share during the sessions. The therapist learned that if he waited a few hours to return the calls, the patient would by then have calmed down, and he wouldn't hear from her again until the next scheduled meeting. The patient had refused to discuss the phone calling during the sessions. She had made one of her numerous suicide attempts during this year of treatment, this one being on the occasion of the therapist's vacation. She had claimed to have drunk an entire bottle of vodka, although the therapist said that he was not actually certain that the patient in fact had done this.

The therapist was seeking supervision in part because he feared another suicide attempt during an upcoming interruption of the treatment.

The patient had previously been in a counseling relationship for many years with an older male pastor; the supervisee characterized the minister as a maternal presence who had taken the patient under his wing. I was told that this man had seen the patient daily, taken her to his church, regulated her contact with her family, and made her feel like a special child. Their relationship had been disrupted when the pastor was hospitalized after an automobile accident and returned in a weakened condition; he had said that he was cutting back his work and did cut back on his time with this most demanding patient. When, however, the patient discovered that the pastor had taken on new responsibilities in the church, she felt betrayed and terminated the relationship. The patient had made many suicide attempts during this therapy—we would imagine in response to the vicissitudes of the treatment relationship. She had also been hospitalized for six years, off and on, and on one occasion, in a halfway house, she'd had a lesbian relationship with another resident.

I will give you the briefest of outlines of the patient's childhood and background. She came from a wealthy freewheeling family, her father was a diplomat and they had lived all over the hemisphere. She claimed to have been regularly beaten by her tempestuous mother, who would then apologize in a seductive exciting fashion. Her father, she said, had been busy with embassy parties and had had little to do with her. She was the second oldest of many children, often given the responsibility of caring for them, which she had at times managed by hitting them. One sister was severely retarded and currently living in an institution. The patient had managed well enough to get admitted to law school, but this success had precipitated a collapse, further alcohol abuse and hospitalization.

In initially summing up his experience with the patient, my supervisee said: "At one level she's a treasure, a special delight; she has such tenderness and vitality. But she's tremendously depleting. It's like having a new baby on your hands. I do start and end my sessions on time, and I won't rearrange my schedule for her—her pastoral counselor dropped his other responsibilities to see her in emergencies." My supervisee was trying to contain the therapeutic situation, to the best of his ability, but the patient had recently been deeply in debt to him, the abusive phone calls had continued, and the therapist was following a practice begun by the pastor of hugging the patient at the end of each session. This last detail was told to me with understandable embarrassment.

This situation immediately impressed me as the sort of encounter in which offering interpretations would constitute adding insight to injury. The patient, in fact, had many interpretations of her own to make, both about her childhood and her treatment, but they seemed to be used not in the service of self-integration but as a way of maneuvering the therapy hours. She did not seem to have a clear sense of where her own thoughts and feelings left off and the therapist's began. The therapist seemed to be intimidated by the patient, afraid of her rages and unable to stop hugging her for fear of the patient's retaliation. And all this was in fact quite clear to the therapist. He felt that he was barely managing the situation.

Given the patient's determination to create provocative enactments in the treatment, and her history of having succeeded at that over the years, it seemed crucial to me that the supervisee work his way into a position of neutrality where he could then find a therapeutic voice. This would mean stopping the abusive phone calling, ending the hugging, and getting paid in a timely way. It would require, for a time, that the therapist endure a greater degree of his own anxiety—both anxiety generated by the patient's threats and anxiety about taking a stronger counteraggressive posture. Once a better treatment situation was established, I expected that the work for quite some time would center on trying to develop a subjective focus in the hours, an understanding of what the patient was thinking and feeling in the present time—especially, but not only, in the treatment. In this understanding, I hoped, the locus would shift from self-as-victim to self-as-perpetrator, in the broadest sense. It might, however, take a good deal of work before the patient could reliably make use of language, before words stopped being weapons disguised as ideas.

How, then, would I help my supervisee to work toward such developments? I doubted that I would get anywhere by simply directing him to stop the enactments, for he knew full well that what he was doing was destructive and already wished he could stop. I might have bullied him into modifying his behavior by threatening to stop supervising him. I felt, however, that at best I would be acting like the first therapist who took the patient to church and that at worst I would be setting a model of intimidation. Those would not be absolute reasons for not delivering an ultimatum, but at the moment, the situation did not seem precarious. I did need to consider the possibility that I was acting on the fear that if I forced the issue he would leave me, a parallel to his fear that his patient would quit. While I considered asking him why he was unable to stop hugging his patient, I decided this would have approached making the supervision into therapy. Instead, I tried to formulate my understanding of the enactments.

Beyond these objective considerations, however, I was stuck with my supervisee in a way that partially paralleled his position with his patient. The therapist was charming, but at the same time headstrong and determined. My overriding experience was that I was shut out, that I couldn't really engage with him about the treatment. Defeated, I became increasingly tentative and even passive, feeling rather like a witness to a curious spectacle. My supervisee seemed in the thrall of his patient, excited by the relationship, but also, beyond his recognition, I think *he* felt like an outsider. The exclusion was not obvious because in one sense the patient was quite obsessed with him. Nevertheless, the patient was dictating the terms of the encounter and not really letting the therapist in. In retrospect, had I been able to pay attention to my subjective experience, I might have articulated more clearly my own experience of being kept on the margins, and recognized my own defensive response to that (my surrender). In this position I might have had a better chance at opening up the supervision.

As it was, I continued in a rationalist mode. I pointed out that it seemed quite possible to me that the patient felt suicidal immediately after each session because the hugging had had the unforeseen consequence of turning the patient's rage back on herself. In this construction, the ensuing phone calls were following as retaliation disguised as pathos. These cycles of attack and reconciliation seemed to me to mirror what the patient had described as her relationship with her mother, alternate mauling and embracing, but with the patient now in the mother's position and my supervisee as the child. The patient told her therapist, again and again, that he just couldn't get it right. I also had the thought that my supervisee might be feeling that he was chronically damaging his patient, parallel to the patient's feeling that she had been responsible for her sister's mental retardation. My supervisee decided to take a firm position on the phone calling and, after he did so, the patient seemed to settle down a bit.

In the next supervisory hour, as he reported a dream the patient remembered, he ruefully told me that he had entirely missed the transference meaning. In the dream two women, both of whom had been the patient's lovers, were off together on vacation while she herself was in Seattle (the place that she knew her therapist would be going for a vacation). One of the women had "small breasts," which my supervisee declared was clearly a reference to him. The patient continued, "My mother thinks that having small breasts is the worst thing!" My supervisee (who prided himself on his maternal capacity) commented, not appreciating the irony, "She cuts me down so, I feel depleted." The patient seemed to experience the therapist's impending departure as a rejection, as though the therapist were leaving her for a better lover. Having prompted a depressive response in the therapist, a sharp feeling of inadequacy (at one level about his capacity for caring, at another level for missing the transference meaning), the patient now told another dream, an exciting one, making up for the first. "I was in bed with you. I massaged you with a pillow, rubbed it all over you, your face was all wet and slobbery from where I kissed you. It's safer for me to try to seduce you than to feel affectionate. This is more powerful, the other is more scary and vulnerable." Actually, I find the patient's analysis defensive, warding off the intense excitement.

It seemed to me that the telling of the two dreams, the first an attack and the second a seduction, enacted within the hour the mother–daughter relationship, with my supervisee first feeling depressed and then overstimulated. The hour then ended with the usual hug. My supervisee volunteered, "I'm preventing her from going through the grief of losing me as she wants me to be. She feels to me like a 3-year-old shaking girl." During the ensuing week the patient called her former counselor and screamed obscenities into the phone. The patient may have experienced the prohibition on calling, accompanied by the continuation of hugging, as a further provocation, which she was responding to in displacement by attacking the pastor.

While my supervisee wanted help from me on the case, it was clear that he also experienced me as threatening to disrupt the anxious attachment through which he and his patient were engaged. Our conflict crystallized around the issue of hugging—I was trying to break up their clinch. My involvement threatened their primary attachment. It was as though I were an intrusive father, imposing himself on the mother–infant dyad. This threat was represented in the patient's two dreams, a dream of exclusion by a couple being countered by another dream in which there was an intense bodily connection between two partners. The pillow may have represented the breast, implying a phantasy that the two would find a solution that didn't require the involvement of an actual man. Three-year-old girls are typically afraid to love their fathers as much as they want to for fear of disrupting their attachments to their mothers. By age 4, they begin to take that chance. We might conjecture that my supervisee was, at that juncture, wanting to participate with me but afraid of losing his primary connection; that might have mirrored his patient's position. Had I been able to help him cross that line, he might have had more success working it through with his patient. But I would have had to have believed that someone who was clearly a father had the right to be there, and I wasn't clear enough in my own mind about that. I was yielding to their truth about the situation. Not being clear enough about my own authority, I allowed myself to be replaced by a pillow.

In a curious footnote to the supervision, the therapist stopped working with me some months later directly after his father died. He had been estranged from him and ambivalent about this. I then wondered whether a dimension of our difficulty had been that he was trying to work out the conflict, in displacement, with me. Once his father died, the effort might have seemed futile to him. This is all conjecture, of course, but it would fit in with the ambivalence about allowing a paternal presence in the treatment.

The foregoing account is my attempt to work with this supervisee. My aim was to sort out the enactments in the treatment, insofar as I could get a hold on them, in an effort to make my supervisee's experience meaningful. As teachers we try to be clear about what we know. We have some idea about what is going on between us and our patients, from a limited vantage point, and we can at best make empathic speculations about processes outside that circle. The limitations of our supervisory wisdom parallel this understanding. We try to prevent foreclosure of knowledge.

Thomas Ogden (1986) has written about the protection of analytic space—the area of subjectivity within which analysis unfolds. "Analytic therapy," he reminds us, "is conducted in the realm of meanings, in the space between symbol and symbolized mediated by the self. . . . It is the task of the therapist . . . to provide conditions wherein the patient might dare to create personal meanings in a form that he can experience and play with" (pp. 240–241). Every assertion of truth we make about external or psychic reality collapses that space; possibility is replaced by inevitability. Ultimately we can only help the patient understand how he creates meaning. Similarly, in supervision, we can only help the supervisee understand how *she* creates meaning. In that sense, for me to tell her what things mean subverts her capacity in this regard. This may seem to be a relatively modest ambition for therapy and supervision, but it is one that understands their common purpose and acts without pretension.

PART 4

THE THERAPIST
AND CHANGE

13

The Turning Point

A crucial development in treatment involves the therapist's working through a countertransference problem that has been evoked in him by his patient. I will be arguing here that it is in the nature of the treatment process that the patient evokes the difficulty most central to his character pathology in his therapist's unconscious experience, and that the outcome of treatment hinges on the therapist's success in coming to terms with that conflict. The resolution of the counter-transference neurosis is thus the precondition for the patient's cure. Insight, for both patient and therapist, *follows* transformation and offers an explanation of what has transpired. Like all processes in therapy, this occurs in stages, although the therapist may single out a crucial moment to encapsulate the change—a "screen insight," we might call it.

Before I offer some examples of this phenomenon, I need to set my observation in context. Franklin (1990) comments: "The understanding that psychoanalysis exists at all times in the context of a two-person field of interaction, and that the analyst is always a participant in the psychoanalytic process, even if he engages in prolonged periods of silence, has become a generally accepted proposition in our field" (p. 212). As writers, especially in the past decade, have begun to struggle openly with the two-person dimension of treatment, the remarkable complexity of our venture has become more apparent. Therapist and patient bring to the treatment situation both their *capacities* for transference and their specific *needs* to use the other toward particular transferential ends. Sandler (1976a, b) proposes that we think of transference as the effort to impose a role relationship on the other—what is transferred in transference is not simply an image of another, but a form of relationship with the other. This is another way of expressing the idea that we are driven to enact our inner object lives with the figures in our contemporary worlds. The analyst, in Sandler's phrasing, is cast in a role *complementary* to that of the patient. He acknowledges that both parties work to impose roles on each other, and that the analyst may be able to recognize the process only after he has been caught in the enactment.

Both therapist and patient approach their conjunction with expectations, and these expectations organize their transferences. Schafer (1983) has observed that we encounter our patients with our best selves, which I take to mean that we treat our patients better than we treat our spouses, children, and friends. But it is hard to imagine that our motives are fundamentally different. My need to dominate the other intellectually, my need to submissively counterbalance my guilt-ridden patricidal impulses, my need to merge with the other to deny separation—these needs do not disappear because I have taken on the task of trying to be of use to my patient, although that interest, and the structured and circumscribed nature of treatment, will mute those needs and may even subordinate them, for a time and to a degree, to more adaptive aims. At some points my patients will have to come to terms with those aspects of my being, cope with my efforts to push them into complementary roles, and try to make use of me in spite of the difficulties I pose. I expect that those points are most likely to come not so much when I'm under the stress of other circumstances in my life, but rather at the times when I feel most provoked by them (which nonetheless does not deserve to be called poetic justice). My difficulties may become overtly manifest in the things I say to my patients, in my tone of voice, in my timing. But it is perhaps even more likely that I will make my transference demands through much subtler cues, cues that will certainly, at least for a time and perhaps for a long time, escape my own awareness.[1] If matters don't get too far out of hand, my patients may survive my transferences and find their own ways to manage me. Having had two analyses, I can compare my experiences with the two analysts and, after factoring out the enormous problems I caused for them, take some measure of the more subtle problems they posed for me. This comment, I fear, should be taken as both a bit competitive and patricidal—which does not, however, make it irrelevant.

It seems to me that this dimension of treatment, what we might call the analyst's characterological needs to make use of his patients in certain ways, has been underplayed in the literature. The prevailing sensibility seems to be that the reasonably well-analyzed practitioner will only get into difficulty at certain moments in a treatment or at certain junctures in his life. The rest is simply acknowledged as a manifestation of individuality. Peterfreund (1983), for example, comments that "we are never truly 'neutral' observers and interpreters. In every word and comment we implicitly convey something of our life experience, our standards and beliefs, something of what we feel about the patient as a human being (p. 108)" Along these lines Jacobs (1991, p. 44) says, "The way we analyze is as much a function of our personalities as it is of technique." This way of viewing it minimizes the pressure for role responsiveness exerted by the analyst—it's as though the analyst's personality is part of the room's decor, something to which the patient easily adjusts.

Perhaps we have been able to conceal our character pathology behind the defensive opportunities offered by our praxis. I notice the various ways I end sessions: "We have to interrupt now," (solicitous, denying aggression); "Let's continue tomorrow," (denying separation);

---

[1] Much of Jacobs's [1991] recent writing has been concerned with teasing out the nuances of such communication.

"We have to stop," (more forthright, but with the aggression still shaded behind circumstance, deflected by the mutual "we"); or even, no comment, just a rustling in my chair which cues the patient to leave (utter abrogation of responsibility!). To be sure, the way I end a given session will in part be a response to my patient's psychology and to the feel of the hour, and none of these responses, in and of themselves, need be particularly problematic for my patients. Yet this recognition does not undermine my point: that the structural aspects of treatment will also serve as vehicles for my own enactment needs, which will be manifest at infinitely more junctures than simply the endings of the hours. Jacobs offers illustrations of the ways in which empathic silence (the kind of silence we actually strive for), neutrality, attention to the transference, and technical correctness can all be exploited toward countertransferential ends. In Jacobs's examples, however, the analyst's enactment is always in response to the patient's. He does not take up the ways in which standard technique can be misused to serve the analyst's characterological ends.

A viewpoint that sits more comfortably in the analytic literature is that patients' conflicts will stir up corresponding issues in their analysts. Gardner (1983) traces out in fascinating detail one such intersection and comments, "Am I, then, so very like my patient? I suppose so. We are, it seems to me, very alike. And we are not. The confluences . . . the whole process of confluent image-making, I believe, reflect no more than the ordinary, extraordinary likenesses of one person and another, and a little more than the ordinary effort to get at it" (p. 66). Later he adds, "I find my patient always struggles with universal and never fully solved problems; there is always a lively counterpart in me" (p. 110). In listening to Gardner, I hear an acknowledgment of the ecumenical variety of forms of conflict, of our relentless plasticity. He reminds us: "In the mind of one man is the whole world" (p. 109). In reading other accounts of countertransference experiences, one senses that the analyst feels that on this particular occasion he stumbled into contact with someone whose conflicts chanced to be quite close to his own. Their implication seems to be that if they hadn't been caught up with a congruent issue themselves, the treatment bind would not have occurred. And so we have the universalists and the particularists.

None of us are comfortable with the idea that one person can evoke a state of mind of their own in another, unmodulated. Everything that happens between two people is a product of two psychologies. The Kleinian concept, projective identification, has been misunderstood by many outside the Kleinian orbit, however, to represent just such a proposition. The Kleinians are fond of countering this by recalling the story of Klein's response to a supervisee who had announced that her patient had put her state of confusion into her: "It's not the patient's confusion you're feeling, my dear. You're the one who's confused!" I take the telling and retelling of this bit of folklore to express the Kleinians' indignation about having their thinking misrepresented. *We're* confused, they want to tell us. We are sufficiently unnerved by the contagious nature of conflict, by our capacity to be wholly taken over by another's reality, that we feel compelled to insist upon our autonomy. Sandler (1976b), for example, in the midst of a well-argued paper, feels required to make this caveat: "Let me say emphatically that I am absolutely opposed to the idea that all countertransference responses of the analyst are due to what the patient has imposed on him" (p. 46). After recovering from Sandler's startling insistence that I sit up straight in my chair, I had the perverse suspicion that he was afraid I'd accuse him of being a projective identification sympathizer. Ogden (1982), who has offered the most articulate explication of the concept, comments:

> What has been said should not be mistaken as a proposal that all of the therapist's feelings should be treated as if they bore a one-to-one correspondence to an aspect of the patient's experience. This is clearly not the case. However, what the therapist is experiencing, even if it is a set of feelings recognized as having meanings determined by the therapist's internalized past experience, is at the same time a response to something that has occurred *in this hour with this patient*. Something that we have come to understand about our patients also holds true for

therapists: people do not project into a vacuum—there is always a kernel of reality onto which fantasies are hung. [p. 73]

This, then, is the reciprocal of Gill's argument, discussed earlier, that all of the patient's transferences are fastened onto at least a trace of the therapist's reality.

Overall, it seems fair to say that both parties bring to the relationship characterological as well as symptomatic demands that they will impose on the other, by which I mean that each will impose both habitual needs and needs borne of the moment on the therapy partner. The other will, in turn, process these demands in terms of the other's own defensive propensities. Complex reverberations of inter-action are thus set in motion. If a stable pathological solution is reached by the pair, the treatment will be immobilized. What makes the situation potentially workable is the set of joined understandings that underlie the treatment—the shared agreement to make the patient's difficulties understandable. In this context, the therapist organizes himself to monitor his own enactments, to make sense of them on his patient's behalf, and she in turn will attempt to take hold of his comprehensions. The therapist will miss much, for there is far too much to be grasped, but the hope is that he will catch enough to make for a useful treatment. Summing up the discussion of a case, McLaughlin (1991) confessed:

> While I have been able to go beyond some of the limiting aspects of the latter [the stereotypes of his earlier training], I ruefully rediscover the old truth in the former [his idiosyncratic regressive responses to his patient]: that the transference ghosts of the past are never entirely laid to rest. In the intensity of new work with qualities unique and not yet known, they return in fresh shape to revive shades of significance I had long forgotten I knew. Enactments are my expectable lot. [p. 613]

Having set my thoughts about countertransference in context, perhaps a long-winded way of doing what Sandler did in a sentence, I return now to the proposition I introduced at the beginning of the chapter. There are certain turning points in a treatment at which the therapist achieves what feels like a breakthrough. While on the surface the change may seem to have burst forth in the patient, that transformation will have been preceded by a decisive shift in the therapist. The most dramatic instances of this development occur when the patient's core characterological issues are at stake.

Mitchell (1988) brings to my attention Balint's (1968) description of his work with a flirtatious young woman who felt unable to achieve anything.

> Gradually it emerged that her inability to respond was linked with a crippling fear of uncertainty whenever she had to take any risk, that is, a decision. She had a very close tie to her forceful, rather obsessional, but most reliable father; they understood and appreciated each other; while her relationship to her somewhat intimidated mother, whom she felt to be unreliable, was openly ambivalent.
>
> It took us about two years before these connections made sense to her. At about this time, she was given the interpretation that apparently the most important thing for her was to keep her head safely up, with both feet firmly planted on the ground. In response she mentioned that ever since her earliest childhood she could never do a somersault; although at various periods she tried desperately to do one. I then said: "What about it now?"—whereupon she got up from the couch and, to her great amazement, did a perfect somersault without any difficulty. [pp. 128–129]

This interaction turned out to be a decisive moment in the treatment, for substantial growth in many areas followed. As Mitchell (1988) points out in retelling this story (and I am thankful to his writing for bringing it to my attention), Balint characterized the change as an emergence of a new behavior in the treatment, and yet clearly the action hadn't simply emerged; it had been invited. I imagine that something more was at stake, that Balint had been identified with his patient's cautiousness, treating her as she treated herself, perhaps experiencing forthrightness on his own part as a seduction. It was when he had worked that through (out of awareness, I assume, in line with his telling) that he could experience making such an invitation as not primarily a seduction—or at least not *only* a seduction—and thus could make a freer response. I am imagining that Balint had to work out a dimension of her oedipal conflict that she had drawn him into. As he came to discover the possibility of a less inhibited form of fatherhood with her, he was able to help liberate her from her oedipal paralysis. The somersault marked the change for him, but I imagine that it was an epiphenomenon—the crucial change had already occurred, first in him. From the very substantial progress that followed, I assume that her central conflict had been at stake in their transference–countertransference impasse.

Surely it is dicey to make too much of another person's case report, to build one's own theory on a foundation of such imaginative con-jectures, and I will shortly advance my argument by taking up material of my own. But I would first like to note that the sort of observation I am making here has in certain measures been made by others. Sy-mington (1983) noticed that there were moments in the analyses he conducted when he suddenly felt free to act in an unaccustomed way, each time resulting in the break-up of a stalemated situation. He was rather at a loss to account for this, and referred to it initially as the "x-phenomenon," later as the analyst's "act of freedom."

My contention is that the inner act of freedom in the analyst causes a therapeutic shift in the patient and new insight, learning and development in the analyst. The interpretation is essential in that it gives *expression* to the shift that has already occurred and makes it available to consciousness. The point though is that the essential agent of change is the *inner* act of the analyst and that this inner act is perceived by the patient and causes change. [p.260]

Symington does not take up how he believes he arrives at the moment in which he can act in a freer way, although the reader can make his own inferences. One treatment he described went this way. An obsessional man habitually hesitated in the middle of telling Symington something of importance, out of the fear that he would be considered pathetic. Symington found himself time and again tacitly reassuring his patient that he did not find him pathetic, each time to only temporary avail. Upon reading an account by Bion of *his* sense that a patient was trying to limit his freedom to think, in particular his freedom to think that she might be a whore, Symington had "a moment of illumination" and reached a decision. "The next time he expressed his apprehension that I would think him pathetic I said to him quietly, 'But I am quite free to think that.' " (p. 255). He realized that, in particular, his patient was afraid that Symington, if left to think on his own, might feel free to want to be rid of him. His patient now was able to tell him how he'd always felt that no one wanted to be with him, going back to the parents who had farmed him out to be raised by child-minders. Symington concludes: "Again the source of all this interpretive work and insight started from the moment of my own inner act of freedom" (p. 256).

The proprietary quality of that last statement catches my attention: *my, own, inner act.* I might think that Symington was reclaiming his mind from his patient, which might be one way we could describe the act of extricating ourselves from any countertransference position. Symington apparently had surrendered his mind to his patient, in resonance with his patient's sense that should Symington be allowed a mind of his own the results would be catastrophic—separation, abandonment, perhaps death. Speculatively, I wonder whether Symington in turn had feared that he would be discarded by his patient, recognized as a whore who took in clients by the hour? Did Symington need to be able to bear that his patient might be free to think that? Working his own way out to the clearing, his patient was able to follow.

While the therapist may, in Sandler's terms, unconsciously take on the role in which the patient has cast him, matters will not end there. The therapist will have his own defensive and adaptive responses to what he has taken in, which may combine identifications with his patient's defenses with favored defenses of his own. Feldman (1993) formulates the problem and solution this way: "I believe that the analyst's tendency toward enactment is a response to the anxiety and discomfort associated with a particular phantasy of himself in relation to the patient that has been induced in him . . . the unconscious response to this is to function in a way that will redress the situation, so that a less anxiety-provoking version becomes central, thus restoring the analyst's equilibrium" (p. 281).

For the sake of advancing this argument, I can imagine that Balint might have been repudiating a view of himself as a wanton incestuous rapist, substituting a self-presentation as obsessional, reliable parent (thus identifying with his patient's defensive—although not necessarily inaccurate—presentation of her father). And Symington might have been disavowing an image of himself as a hardened, indifferent mother in his solicitous efforts to reassure his patient that he found him worth listening to. The analyst needs to be able to allow these different versions of himself to engage in commerce with one another. The alternative, Feldman points out, is that the analyst becomes addicted to an exclusive and defensive view of his own motivations, which is supported by splitting and denial. This reduces his anxiety at the expense of his own psychic integration and, therefore, his functioning as an analyst. In these particular cases, it might have been that Balint needed to come to terms with his own unconscious rapist tendencies, Symington with his fantasy of being a whore. In the immediacy of the treatment situation it doesn't help much to comment from the sidelines that we are all, as therapists, both rapists and whores, although also much more.

ILLUSTRATIONS

I would like to pursue this further now by taking up again a number of the treatments I discussed in earlier chapters.

The Patient Who Turned Her Back on Me

During our first 3 years together this patient managed to turn far enough away from me that I couldn't see her face. She typically spoke for perhaps a total of a minute during the hour, making simple declarative statements about her life, which she then refused to amplify. My position, as I recall it now, was one of helpless pleading, trying as hard as I could to draw a response from her. I felt hopelessly pathetic and ashamed of myself. That feeling might have been a clue to understanding her position—looking back on it, she was quite imperious—but I was cowering too deep in her shadow to be able to recognize that.

I finally turned to a supervisor for help. We'd been discussing a more ordinarily treatable case, and he didn't seem very eager to get involved in this one, but he made two suggestions to me: read Melanie Klein (this being, I believe, his way of saying that treating my patient was beyond his ken, and of referring me to a higher authority) and interpret the grandiosity behind her self-abnegation. He speculated that she imagined she was Christ. I couldn't see the grandiosity at first—I imagine that after three years of submission to her will I was not exactly open to acknowledging what had gone on. And I was, in my own version, masochistically trudging to Golgotha. At first I felt taken aback by my supervisor's suggestion that I challenge her. I felt far too intimidated to consider that. On second thought, however, I felt intrigued; with the useful parental support provided by my mentor, I did indeed go after her, and over the next several months I gradually drew her into contact with me. During the following eight years a great deal unfolded.

In retrospect, I would say that seeing my patient as massively disabled was a way of my denying her devastating power. I felt squashed under her thumb. My abjectly solicitous efforts to draw her out defended against my narcissistic rage (she was one of my first private patients, and I was finding myself an utter failure) and my retaliatory impulses (I think I rarely let a silence go longer than ten or fifteen minutes). My efforts also had been a way of enacting my experience of being with an extremely judgmental parent whom I urgently needed to appease.

In one sense the countertransference enactment of being my patient's woeful, bullied child served to capture an essence of her relationship with her mother. She had moved to Washington in an effort to separate from this apparently tyrannical woman, and felt constantly guilty about having left her, all the more so after her mother developed metastatic cancer. While at a surface level she had been able to give as good as she'd gotten in their fights through her childhood and adolescence, in a deeper sense she felt unentitled to a life of her own. Her unquestioning belief that I would sabotage any positive development in her life spoke to this prior conviction.

In retrospect, once I was free to challenge her the therapy had turned a corner. Many corners were yet to follow, but I was no longer trapped in a blind alley. In my countertransference position I had been viewing myself as a mother's abused child. I needed to escape from my defensive position of experiencing myself as a victim who was entitled to mercy. I had to face the ways in which, in the course of our encounters, both in the transference and in reality, I was the abuser. And I also needed to recognize that I wasn't bound by her insistence that confrontation was a form of assault. My passivity had been far more destructive.

The Patient Who Paid the Low Fee

The turning point in this treatment was dramatic and hinged on my recognition that I had been infantilizing Anthony by charging him an unnecessarily low fee. Once we had made the shift he was able to move forward in the important areas in his life. My treating him like a child had been a way of avoiding more direct competition between us; I was acting like Anthony's father, who apparently had been afraid to take him on. Anthony's fee had been of little direct consequence to me, because clinic fees were averaged and I was thus paid at a pooled rate. With Anthony's parents mainly paying his expenses, the fee hadn't mattered much to him either. We were both neophytes, willingly impotent, feeling a bit devalued but avoiding conflict.

I could focus on a similarity in our developmental experiences. Like Anthony, I had had a father who was inhibited about challenging me, and I had felt anxious about asserting myself. An important screen memory for me is pressing my father to bring home a carton of bubblegum on the weekend, when he could have bought it at discount in a couple of days. I had thought that he couldn't refuse me because he couldn't bear disappointing me. The guilt and shame with which I recall the incident cover over my disappointment in him. Anthony's story of his father finding a pound of marijuana in the trunk of the car and threatening to punish him only if he was caught a second time captured the same themes: shame, guilt, and disillusionment. But focusing on parallel aspects of our development would obscure the transference enactment reality that he needed to put me in exactly the position in which I found myself; my parallel conflict may at best have brought me there a bit faster. In my position as Anthony's financial benefactor (ultimately, I think, a shared passive homosexual defense), I was ducking the experiences both of being father and son in oedipal combat. To be sure, there were other important transference–countertransference issues in the treatment, as there were in all the cases I am describing, but it was the working through of this particular conflict, most importantly working it through in myself, that opened up the treatment.

The Patient Who Watered My Flowers

The critical turn arrived unexpectedly in this treatment. One day it simply occurred to me that not only did I believe that at some point this woman would succeed in seducing me, but also that in fact this would never happen. Until then, it had been impossible to renounce a phantasy of which I had been unaware. The change was not as dramatic in this instance as the one just described, but over the course of the next half year the work shifted from what, in retrospect, had been an unceasing enactment into a useful treatment. Prior to the discovery I had been in what I would now consider to have been a primitive merger with my patient; my conscious experience, however, was that I was in the position of continually fending her off. Unconsciously, by my not, for example, telling her to stop watering my flowers, I was encouraging the continuation of that sort of behavior, by which I then felt beleaguered. It was hardly possible to explore the meanings of activities that I was unconsciously promoting.

My victimized stance served to defend against my awareness of my incestuous motives, and the incestuous motives in turn defended against separation. I recognized early on that my patient's nightly incest with her brother had served to provide a connection for her in a childhood remarkably devoid of parenting. Her experience with him had been intimate and meaningful, and she had felt terribly abandoned when, as he began to enter preadolescence, he turned away. It was for this turning away that she never forgave him. I believe that the incestuous subtext had a similar meaning in our relationship, and I think that this was unfortunately confirmed in the traumatic experience of our ending, which I described in Chapter 5. I hope that the useful work we did in the three years in between has stayed with her, but it is in the nature of things that I cannot know that.

The Family with the Dying Child

The family, which had been attempting to cope with its extraordinary crisis by finding scapegoats, managed to pull together in the manic remarriage ceremony. The therapist was left feeling helpless and destructive. His was now the defective heart. As supervisor, I felt inwardly furious with the parents for their inability to be of better support to their dying daughter and for the ways in which they were exploiting their older children to deflect their own guilt. Looking back on it, I imagine that I was feeling my supervisee's denied anger. The therapist was protecting the overwhelmed parents from his passion by depressively turning his anger against himself. Further, I imagine that he would have been fending off a degree of narcissistic rage over his forced helplessness that paralleled the family's own rage.

Such rage seems inescapable in these situations. What matters is whether we can survive bearing it or need to turn on each other for relief. The therapist's depressive turn was a response to the family's manic shift. I remember sitting with him and feeling that I was comforting a bereaved spouse. Had I been better able to sort out the anger I was feeling, I might have been of more help to him in dealing with his own anger and rage and helplessness, and this might have freed him to take on the family in a more constructive way. The supervisory term came to a close and we parted ways. I don't know how matters ultimately turned out.

The Surgeon Who Bypassed His Heart

In this treatment I was unable to find my way out of the woods, for three years into the analysis; after several months of struggling, my patient chose to quit. I think I can describe, however, the countertransference position I wound up in, and conjecture about what I needed to work out. As I reported earlier, I had begun to lose confidence in myself. I wondered whether indeed it was my own capacity for being remote, a quality I'm all too aware of, which led my patient to experience me as a stone wall. I certainly couldn't disagree with his complaint that I wasn't real and immediate for him. Although I worked hard to the bitter end to try to make sense out of his and our experience, I developed a fatalistic sense that it would ultimately be to no avail. I felt superannuated, as if I had outlived whatever usefulness I had been to him, and I thought that he was coming to treatment only out of conscientiousness, a sense of duty. He made matters more difficult by insisting that it was his problem, that he was incapable of making use of analysis, that he was too self-contained and self-controlled. Had he been able to attack me, we might have struggled better with the impasse. I had little doubt that he would feel it a great relief to be free of me; I felt life would be easier for both of us if I just disappeared.

Although I have run through hosts of theories to make sense out of what happened between us, and while I realize that I can have only a limited conviction about any explanation I arrive at, especially because my hypotheses cannot be tested, I do have an idea about the place we wound up in. I believe that I was identified with his internal experience of his father: a bit pathetic, pretty useless, past my prime, better off out of the picture (to be polite about it). When I was with this patient I was particularly conscious of his vitality, which I envied, and my own creakiness, which depressed me. I tried to act a bit more robust, defensively I fear; I imagined my kids thinking I was over the hill.

At the time, however, I was not paying much attention to this aspect of my experience. I was more intent on pursuing issues in the maternal transference that I thought were at stake—what I thought was my patient's growing attachment to me and his discomfort about that dependency, heightened by my long summer absence. Even now, I can't say that I was wrong about focusing in that direction, but I do think that what was more accessible at the end in the countertransference were issues related to his experience of his father. As I noted earlier, he had managed his oedipal rivalry by dismissing his father as *father*; by midadolescence he had seemed to consider his father his ward. In his work, older men were mainly in his way and needed to be pushed past. He didn't make much use of mentors. Half-successfully denying that I was in that countertransference slot was a way of avoiding my own anxieties about aging. And, at another level, being in that position was a defense against competing with him! I have no doubt that my own parricidal guilt was in my way, but I also believe that he would have posed this countertransference dilemma for any analyst. In my defense, I must add that I did challenge this patient quite forthrightly and from many angles about his leaving. But, perhaps because of my own need to hold onto him, I couldn't get away from feeling like a dispossessed King Lear.

Two Vignettes

I would like to take an intermission from this case reporting to briefly mention two episodes in which I was brought up short by the unmasking of countertransference positions.

A young woman had had a particularly intense relationship with her drug-addicted depressed father, full of sadomasochistic enactments, and both she and I wondered whether she'd had incestuous involvement with him. We became a bit obsessed with the idea that if we worked hard enough in the analysis, we might eventually get to incestuous experience in the transference, and we awaited this clarification in a tensely vigilant state of mind. I eventually came to realize, to my chagrin, that *this* had actually been the nature of her experience with her father: the two of them had been caught up in overwrought posturing, anxiously wondering whether one or the other would cross that barrier. I still don't know whether there were explicitly incestuous moments between them, but I feel pretty convinced that this state of excited tension, with the question hanging in the balance, characterized their relationship.

The second episode I want to describe involves a middle-aged man, who, during a lengthy termination phase, became increasingly depressed—he lost his appetite and couldn't work. Eventually his mood lifted, but paralysis of the treatment set in. Our hours together went nowhere; this ordinarily voluble patient had little to offer, and I was unable to move the analysis forward. After six weeks of feeling increasingly useless, I found myself ruminating hopelessly: maybe I hadn't helped him at all, he should start again with someone else, it was crazy to think of stopping. In the midst of this I remembered an earlier dream of his about civil rights activists, and connected it with a story of a protest fast recently in the news. Animated now, he said it was *amazing* to see the lengths to which people would go to embarrass their government! After I recovered from being nonplused, I appreciated the reproach in his stubborn helplessness—he intended to lie on the couch until I either expired or threw him out on the street. This clarified, the work opened up again and we worked our way to a termination.

The Patient Who Had Been Sexually Abused

I believe that this treatment was a substantially useful piece of work, but I also believe that I never found my way out of a countertransference position that was an undercurrent in our sessions. I earlier framed this as the patient's determination that she would not submit to my power. From my own side, I felt that I was always a child trying to please a mother. She set the terms of the analysis. Partway through, she decided that she could only manage to come three times a week. I would not agree to change the frequency, and so she simply decided to miss a session each week, the missed hours being rationalized as necessary for the conduct of the rest of her life. Efforts to make sense of this behavior on other grounds were to no avail. She prepared for her sessions in advance, keeping track of her dreams and considering in advance where exploration of them might lead. This was to be an analysis without surprises.

I felt it necessary to make a substantial interpretation of the material in every hour. Try as I might, I was unable to let an hour end without intervening. It wasn't that she insisted I speak—she didn't accuse me of being uninvolved—but if I had not had something to say by the time the end of the session was approaching I suddenly felt like a child who had to perform for his mother, and I hastened to collect some ideas together. This actually wasn't difficult because the hours were quite rich and I usually had lots of ideas, but I did not feel free to stay silent and just let the plot thicken. In one sense this simply mirrored my patient's own dogged conscientiousness. I think the hours were always a bit of an ordeal for both of us, even though I think we genuinely liked and respected each other. And I should make clear that I did not find her, in an ordinary sense, intimidating, for the intimidation was entirely unconscious. On the contrary, I experienced her as a bit fragile. I didn't feel the need to be extremely careful in the ways that I put things to her, although in retrospect I think I did consider certain territory off-limits. Rather, it felt as if she was always holding herself together with rope and baling wire. Then again, in an objective sense I didn't think that she was at risk; in the crunch, she seemed like a survivor.

I think that my tenseness reflected her internal sense of danger. She seemed trapped between an id she couldn't trust and a controlling superego she wanted to bribe. I use these technical terms here to convey something of the alien quality of my patient's experience of her desires and her conscience. It seemed she had to work overtime to keep all her ducks in a row, and I think that I was identified with that mission. Making interpretations was my way of making sure that meaning was always kept in order. The burden I felt in the work reflected her burdened compliance to her internal demands. When she was a child, she told me, her father at times made her sit perfectly motionless in a chair, and he hit her if she flinched. When she rejected him sexually in adolescence, he forbade her from taking showers in the house; I imagine that the thought of her naked drove him wild, and that he feared he wouldn't be able to control himself. This intense, controlled relatedness was internalized and reenacted by us in the analysis. I think that it would have been helpful if I had been able to relax more with her, let my own guard down, but at the time that would have made me too anxious. We were never able to make the world quite safe enough for her.

Finally, a last word about Elizabeth, the patient whom I earlier presented through the device of four separate narratives.

Elizabeth

I described earlier in some detail my central countertransference experience with Elizabeth of feeling unbearably controlled and rendered meaningless, and I developed my thoughts about this in relation to her experience with her parents. Much of the time I felt that I was only an internal object for Elizabeth, a construct that she could manipulate, without an independent existence of my own. She negotiated life with a series of props, all of which seemed to fall within her omnipotent control: the writings of medieval mystics, the icon of Jesus, her relationship with her spiritual advisor, the stack of books by her bedside (I imagine that she feared that if she were reading only one author, he might have a chance to capture her soul), her weekly outing with her parents, the details of her work, aspects of her children's lives, sex with her husband, alcohol (having two drinks put her in a predictably self-punitive frame of mind), and her analysis. She knew exactly what experience she could extract from each of us, and used us as selfobjects to regulate her states of mind. While it's impossible to have perfect control over an analyst you see five times a week—she had *moments*, at least, when she was caught by surprise—I actually found awesome the degree of control she achieved over the analysis.

Because ordinary analytic efforts proved so regularly futile, and because her transference moves were so coercive, I tended to protect myself by distancing a bit. This seemed preferable to evenly hovering submission. Which is not to say that I didn't, at times, have other experiences with Elizabeth—I felt moments of tenderness and moments of fury—but the status quo was so relentlessly reinstated that those moments lost their poignancy and became more like artifacts. There were times along the way when she succeeded in getting me to seriously doubt the decency of my motives in seeing her. Sometimes I could find refuge in recalling her abysmal experience with her first analyst. The most important task for me, however, seemed to be to find a way of regaining possession of my mind from Elizabeth's internal domain while staying connected to her. Certainly no simple rejoinder like Symington's assertion that he was free to think as he chose was about to dislodge me. Whether I will find a way to succeed at that remains to be seen—she is still in treatment with me—but I think that this is where the success of the treatment is hinged.

Therapy is a dialectical encounter. Patient and therapist are continually shaping one another, evoking meanings in each other, both consciously and unconsciously, through words and through preverbal influence. Each is changed, at least ever so slightly, by every moment of their confrontation. The understandings that emerge will be an unfolding product of two minds—two minds mainly set in opposition—which will struggle toward clearings of hard-won consensus, each clearing then being the departure point for the next struggle. Traditionally it is said that the therapist works to overcome through interpretation the patient's resistances, and yet we also recognize that the process works as much in the opposite direction, as our patients struggle to get through to us. Both of us resist changing, even as we are both committed to change, and in a useful treatment we will both be altered by the encounter. I have been arguing that in profoundly successful treatment the crux of the process is the patient's cure of the therapist, by which I mean that the patient helps the therapist to reach a new discovery about himself, a discovery that contains the heart of the patient's conflict, the reaching of which frees the therapist to cure the patient.

By framing therapy as a dialectical encounter I am offering a model of therapeutic action that is interpersonal without being tilted. The therapist does not stand in a higher position than the patient, as quasi-parent, which is not to deny that the therapist brings experience and expertise to his work. But if, as therapist, one accepts this dialectical view, then one must pay attention to the ways in which one is *at all moments* being shaped by the patient. Countertransference is no longer an occasional interference or help; it is an ongoing aspect of treatment, one side of the coin. This is a radically different contextual view of the treatment process than the surgical model, which I fear is still, in much subtler form and all protestations notwithstanding, the prevalent view. To move beyond this self-protective stance, we will need to become less fearful of the power of our own unconscious minds, more trusting of our innate capacities for mastery.

14

Psychotherapy and the Midlife Crisis

Our professional development as therapists depends on self-cure, and the cure that is required of us is that we abandon hope. Leslie Farber brought this to my attention in his paper, "The Therapeutic Despair" (1958).

Farber argues that in work with schizophrenic patients the turning point may come when the therapist reaches a feeling of profound despair from which the patient attempts to retrieve him. Until that point the therapist has been denying his own need for confirmation in his determined effort to confirm his patient. His own unsettled need corrodes the treatment until he reaches the impossible place at which the table can finally be turned.

I've begun, in a way, by talking about a developmental end point, and I'd like to reconnoiter now and talk about beginnings.[1] What moves us to choose this vocation? Surely the seduction for us, when it begins, whether in our twenties or even earlier, as adolescents, must be, at some level, the opportunity to take control of another's life. Becoming a psychotherapist is a sublimation of darker motives along these lines. The wish to take control of the other may be an effort at vicarious repair of an object we feel we have damaged; it may express our wish to use the other as a trash pile or as a victim; it may offer the prospect of a love cure for ourselves; or it may be the chance to settle

---

[1]The developmental sequence I outline in this chapter is built on the paradigm offered by Jaques (1965) in his seminal paper, "Death and the Mid-Life Crisis." In this essay, Jaques explores the individual's negotiation of the midlife crisis by framing this developmental crisis in terms of movement between Klein's (1946) paranoid-schizoid and depressive positions. For Klein, this movement is the crucial developmental step. This shift is given weight comparable with the emphasis Freud gives to the resolution of the Oedipus complex; within these two theories, these are, respectively, the crucial steps in personal growth.

In the paranoid-schizoid position, experience is fractured: good and bad experience are kept separate through splitting, introjection, and projection to protect the good object from being annihilated by the person's destructiveness. In the infancy prototype of this process, destructiveness is projected into the mother's breast, which then becomes the "bad breast," and the baby fears the breast's retaliatory persecution. Existence in the paranoid-schizoid position lacks subjectivity and the capacities for symbolization and for holding a historical perspective. Things simply are what they are; good is good and evil is evil, now and forever; that which oppresses should be destroyed; matters have always been the way they are now; nothing can ever change; and there are no alternative perspectives (in particular, there is no tragedy and no irony). For Klein, the first three months of life are lived in the paranoid-schizoid position because this is the only way that the infant can organize experience. The position continues, however, as a mode of being in the world throughout life; for Ogden (1986) the paranoid-schizoid and depressive positions are in an ongoing dialectical relationship with each other.

In the depressive position, the individual recognizes that he feels both hatred and love for the same person, that he has acted destructively toward the persons he cares about. When in this state of mind, the individual cannot take refuge in split experience to avoid responsibility and guilt. With this new capacity for bearing ambivalence, it becomes possible both to have mature relationships with others and to feel a personal sense of integration. In the depressive position one does not transcend hateful feelings, one realizes that these feelings must be reckoned with. Thus, in the depressive position, reparation and atonement become processes of reconciliation.

old scores or to make amends. These are the transference motives that bring us to this career – the potential world of patients appears to be an unusually plastic field, as careers go, for the enactment of our internal object motives. Unusually plastic, that is, until we encounter the obsidian of *their* internal object worlds, but this goes unnoticed for a time. In saying that we are longing to seize control of the other, I'm actually not making a radical observation, because that is what transference is always about – the shaping of the other to meet our needs. Transference relating always denies the separateness of the other person, always treats the other as within the reach of our omnipotent control. This is the lure of conjoined oneness. We are vampires and we are wizards.

Our transference motives are our wishes to rework the past, our effort to unpack history; our transferences confess who we are, who we have become. But we have other motives too: our wishes to create a future, to make something of ourselves that is more than we already are. In choosing a vocation we also hope to discover something in ourselves, a potential not already known. As we impress ourselves upon the world, we define it with our transferences. As we let ourselves be shaped by our encounter with the world, we let in the future. Farber thinks of this as our need for confirmation. In an ironic use of the term, I might call this desire our longing for countertransference.

The ways in which we come to terms with our wish to take control of the other will determine our vocational fate. Psychotherapy is an extraordinary profession. We burst through the shell of our specialty training and, like Athena sprung from the head of Zeus, arrive full-blown at the community's door. Unlike most other professionals and laborers, we don't have prolonged apprenticeships, and yet we work in a field where there are no easy cases. A lawyer might cut her teeth on an uncontested divorce, a carpenter might start on simple kitchen renovations, a teacher might work with the motivated children of the well-educated class, and a surgeon could begin with hernia repairs. Yet for those of us who intend to be insight therapists there are no uncomplicated patients to practice on – each patient brings us the full complexity of her conflicted self. And it is a further circumstance unique to our branch of the healing arts that novices are given the most difficult cases. If we refuse to simplify matters by reducing the patient to a diagnosable psychopharmacological entity, or to a behavioral object for which we can prescribe prepackaged exercises, we are stuck with facing the patient as a whole human being whom we must encounter with the entirety of ourselves.

At the same time, the nature of our work is such that absolutely anything we say to the patient will, at least at some level, be true—we are all, after all, full of envy, passion, resentment, courage, and despair. So, like the horoscopes, anything we have to say can carry the illusion of helpfulness. Our patients, by and large, idealize us, allowing us certainly to feel indispensable and possibly even brilliant. And so, in our twenties, we can come to feel like omnipotent psychic brain surgeons. When I was 17 I read Freud and decided that I could now understand the secrets of men's lives (actually, it was women's lives at the time). I remember applying for residency training and having the gall to say to the interviewer that I thought I understood everything about what made people tick, I just needed the training so that I could find out how to tell them what I knew. After residency training I entered analysis and was impressed to find my own dynamics scattered all over my caseload. Each season, all my patients seemed to share the same pathology, which happened to correspond to whatever I was learning about myself at the time. (Which reminds me that when I was a candidate in psychoanalytic training, one of the senior faculty, trying hard to be tactful, said to a classmate who was busy that month finding the negative Oedipus complex everywhere, "It's great to have ideas, Sam, but it's especially helpful to have something to back them up with." It rang a bell for me.)

Alongside these two ironies I would add the recognition that nowadays none of the primary mental-health professional training programs provides a decent education in the practice of insight psychotherapy. And so, poorly equipped, the graduate sends out announcements, hangs up his shingle, and goes to work, doing the best he can. Energy, good will, and enthusiasm count for something, and so the therapist may be of some use to his patients, but the activity sails on a manic tide. At its best, we encounter this blithe spirit of a young practitioner in his or her late twenties, full of himself or herself, ready to conquer the psychiatric world. Barring some mishap, an unexpected psychosis or suicide, the secret is well concealed that this is an unmoored profession—a compliant patient confirms each interpretation, and a complainant is just resisting. If the patient can identify with the therapist's manic spirit we may have, of sorts, a cure. This is psychotherapy in a paranoid-schizoid and manic mode: the therapist is good and well-intentioned, loving and not aggressive, illness is out there waiting to be extirpated, and nothing will stand in our way.

If we are able to gloss over our failures, our omnipotence may be preserved unharmed. The paranoid-schizoid mode of defense seems an appropriate way of coping in a situation where one is truly inept and in over one's head, as every beginning therapist must be. Maintaining self-esteem is a precarious business for a neophyte in any field, but in our profession we are uniquely vulnerable because it is with our entire selves that we engage our patients. If a football player drops a pass, he might be said to have bad hands; if a patient falls through our hands, we have bad selves. Thus the temptation toward taking a defensively omnipotent stance and toward fostering a mutual idealization with the patient is enormous, because these maneuvers protect self-esteem. I have always been impressed by the lengths to which supervisees will go to keep patients from dropping out of treatment, and by their determination to conceal from themselves their motive for doing this. And so as therapists contort themselves to accommodate to their patients, to accept a collusion, perhaps joining a conspiracy to turn the blind eye, I become aware of the intensity of their fear of rejection. That rejection is felt to be the repudiation of the therapist's self by its symbiotic object, a catastrophe, the baby dropped by its mother. The stakes are simply much too high for the therapist to risk holding his ground, and so he accommodates to the patient.

On the other side, I have been similarly impressed by patients' efforts to maintain their idealizations of their therapists even in the face of unworldly incompetence (and I'm remembering some of my own incompetencies here). The patient's dependence on the therapist—not driven so much by threats to self-esteem as by fear of abandonment and annihilation—mobilizes the patient to endure any price for admission; at worst we see the battered child clinging to the abusive parent. While what I've been describing here is seen most dramatically in work done by troubled therapists with sicker patients, in subtle form it is inevitably present in all treatment. For at the heart of the therapeutic process, in those therapies where both parties are truly engaged, we find cycles of collusion and extrication, corruption and redemption.

Let me pause here to quickly catalogue the forms of therapist–patient collusion in the paranoid-schizoid mode. Probably most common is the shared projection of evil into the world outside the pair—onto the spouse, the children, the employer, the co-worker, the friend, or more intangibly, onto fate. This most efficiently protects the pair's mutual idealization. Therapist and patient then join in heroic efforts to remediate the outside world. Much advice-giving falls into this category. Alternatively, the evil may be located in the patient, while the therapist is saved. Interpretations generically tend to have this effect, especially interpretations of the patient's behavior, defenses, or state of mind—it's not by accident that interpretations are so often experienced as blame. As the third possibility, evil may be assigned to the therapist. Free association and the rule of abstinence serve this end, as the therapist acts as a silent sponge for the patient's projections. And, finally, evil may be shuttled between the two in sado-masochistic adventures, or shared by the two in mutual hopeless despair. All of these operations may be necessary aspects of any therapy, but for the beginning therapist they may constitute the entire repertoire.

As we get some experience working with patients, we gradually develop our own style and our own way of encountering patients; our helplessness and anxiety lessen. Any style involves compromise formations, being open in one way and closed off in another, but a usefully fashioned style provides a basis for developing confidence, and with that confidence it becomes possible to be more open to the nature of our task, able to acknowledge, paradoxically, its impossibility. And so, if the therapist has not packed up his or her tent and set off for Samoa but has been able to glean a bit of help from supervision, courses, personal analysis, and experience with patients, he or she will reach midlife intact and then have the opportunity for new growth.

Transformation at midlife is not inevitable, but a new potential exists. With the recognition of the inevitability of death comes an awareness of limitation, and for the therapist this involves a recognition of the limitation of his power to heal. The limitation rests not only in the patient, in the ultimate boundaries of psychic flexibility, but also in the therapist. We become more aware of the contrary forces in our natures, the wishes to bind that oppose the wishes to liberate, the needs to exploit that counter the need to receive our patients freely. We also become aware of our ignorance of the diverse complexities of life and relationship. This is our midlife encounter with the depressive position, and we may respond to it in various ways. One possibility is a continuation of the manic defense—the route, for example, of the charismatic therapist—but now if we listen closely that defense seems hollow, grandiose, fighting off life rather than embracing it. Another possibility is numbing, going through the motions, earning a living; and a third is resignation and despair, dead coals in the hearth.

The remaining choice, of course, is being open to the midlife encounter, opening up to oneself. The depressive position is worked and reworked throughout the life cycle, but its working through takes new meaning at midlife. We shift ambitions, from "Be All That You Can Be" to "be what you are." In denial of death we imagine that our patients can be perfected, projecting our wished-for consummation into them. With the acknowledgment of death, the sense of our mission radically changes. When I began practicing it was impossible for me to stop with a patient because I was never done. When patients decided to terminate I felt a bit depressed, defeated. With time I came to set more modest goals in my work, but they were still my goals, and so we continued to part uneasily. Eventually I came to notice that therapy had rhythms that were outside both my control and the will of my patient. At a point in our work the patient would begin to wrestle toward going it alone; as I suggested earlier, this movement toward departure often had an adolescent quality, and in fact I frequently began to hear tales from those years during this phase. I came to recognize that this was always the beginning of our ending. However long it might take to reach it, whatever backing and filling might occur along the way, our ending had become inevitable. Once I was able to accept this I had a new understanding of the therapeutic process. As partners we would be born together, spend our time as best we could, and die. While suicide and murder were always possibilities, our death would most likely be of natural causes. My job was to make the best possible use of our time together. As we mature our ambitions become modest—*lifesize*, you might say. We'll have some time to spend together, and we'll make of it what we can. I find this view of the therapy process greatly liberating, though I mourn my loss of omnipotence, even my loss of control.

Epilogue

Some authors, in prologues or acknowledgments, offer reminiscences of how they came to write their books. Consistent with my ironic disposition, I instead close this text with an accounting of how I might not have written it.

While preparing a presentation that would later be developed into two chapters of this book, I had the following dream:

> I was on a bridge, high over the city, at the midpoint of the span, where I found a text on psychoanalytic supervision written by an esteemed female analyst. The text was in a special metal enclosure, sort of an industrial shrine, a library with one book, there for the public's perusal.

In fact I had by my bedside a copy of a paper on supervision by this author and her colleague (Gediman and Wolkenfeld, 1980), which I had begun reading before going to sleep. The authors had been arguing that patient, therapist, and supervisor are linked in a "complex, multidirectional network" in which enactments in the therapy and supervision mirror each other, and in which the driving force of the enactment may at a given juncture issue from the supervisor, the therapist, or the patient. The most important force creating this parallelism, they had decided, was the fact that both therapy and supervision were "helping processes." I thought that this was a distinctly maternal intuition, this intersubjective linking of patient, therapist, and supervisor through mutual projective identifications, something akin to Winnicott's observation that there is no such thing as a mother (apart from her infant—the mother and infant are a unit).

A library with one book is like a dictionary with one word, a symbol for that which precedes meaning. The dictionary of one word precedes meaning because a word only takes on meaning as it confronts other words, words to which it can contrast itself (see Ogden 1986). Similarly, the library of one book precedes meaning because meaning can only be formed in the dialectic of opposing ideas. Thus the library with one book is, symbolically, the mother-child, the single entity before language and meaning. And so, I thought, this dream expresses *my* intuition that there is something at the heart of both therapy and learning that has to do with beginnings, the time of conjoined oneness.

At the same time, I could not help but realize (try not to realize it as I might!) that the bridge must represent the span of my life, with the single book, the Book of Life, situated at its midpoint, midlife, signaling the solitariness of both death and creation. The industrial enclosure loosely surrounding the book reminded me that this was about working, teaching, treating . . . and writing. The other paper by my bedside, a favorite essay that I planned to read again in the morning, was Elliott Jaques's "Death and the Mid-Life Crisis." In the space between these two papers, one on conjoined oneness and the other on solitude and the acceptance of limitation, I planned to write my own essay on the development of the therapist.

It is only at midlife, with a greater apprehension of death, that we fully become historical beings. The essence of our historicity is that we are able, working with each other, to create meaning. It is that which makes us human, and it is over this capacity that therapy and supervision stand guardian. And so I have traveled from the mother-child, which exists before meaning, to the life which is saturated only with meaning, with the meaning that develops through dialogue.

My dream continued:

I took the book from the bridge, although I knew this was not allowed, intending to borrow it for a few days while I wrote my essay. I next found myself in my former analyst's office—I was there for an appointment but the room was empty. I had arrived early. Later I discovered that the book was missing.

I was appropriating the mother lore for my own purposes and I experienced this as robbing both the mother and the public, usurping knowledge in defiance of her and of the social order for my own gain. I reassured myself that I would be returning the book shortly, but soon the book was nowhere to be found. I thought I might have surrendered the book to the analyst-father whose space I had tried to appropriate, but apparently such was not the case.

I was certainly struggling with parricidal feelings. I tried to console myself with Blake's aphorism from *The Marriage of Heaven and Hell*, "The cut worm forgives the plow" (1965, p. 35). In creating my own essay I would be standing on the shoulders of my progenitors: would their footing be quicksand? But the dream and my associations suggested that beyond the issues of plagiarism, triumph, hubris, and retaliation, the act of creativity would be accompanied by loss, loss without reason, loss not as punishment but as part of the natural order. The act of creation brings me into the natural order that is circumscribed by birth, midlife, and death. Until I create I live in the illusion that I am safely unborn, prehistoric. Writing, treating, and supervising at their best are all quickenings, breathing life, sowing seeds, discovering fire.

References

Abrams, S., and Shengold, L. (1978). Some reflexions on the topic of the 30th Congress: affects and the psychoanalytic situation. *International Journal of Psycho-Analysis* 59:395–407.

Adler, G., and Buie, D. H., Jr., (1973). The misuses of confrontation in the psychotherapy of borderline cases. In *Confrontation in Psychotherapy*, ed. G. Adler and P. Myerson, pp. 123–146. New York: Science House.

Adler, G., and Myerson, P. G. (1973). *Confrontation in Psychotherapy*. New York: Science House.

Alexander, F. (1954). Some quantitative aspects of psychoanalytic technique. *Journal of the American Psychoanalytic Association* 2: 685–701.

Anderson, A. R., and McLaughlin, F. (1963). Some observations on psychoanalytic supervision. *The Psychoanalytic Quarterly* 32:77–93.

Arlow, J. A. (1963). The supervisory situation. *Journal of the American Psychoanalytic Association* 11:576–594.

Balint, M. (1968). *The Basic Fault: Therapeutic Aspects of Regression*. London: Tavistock.

Beckett, S. (1981). *Ohio Impromptu*. In *Rockaby and Other Short Pieces*. New York: Grove.

Bion, W. R. (1959a). Attacks on linking. *International Journal of Psycho–Analysis* 40:308–315.

———— (1959b). *Experiences in Group and Other Papers*. New York: Basic Books.

Blake, W. (1965). The marriage of heaven and hell. In *The Poetry and Prose of William Blake*, ed. D. V. Erdman, pp. 33–44, 4th printing with revisions (1970). Garden City, NY: Doubleday.

Blomfield, O. H. D. (1985). Psychoanalytic supervision—an overview. *International Review of Psycho-Analysis* 12:401–409.

Blos, P. (1967). The second individuation process of adolescence. *Psychoanalytic Study of the Child* 22:162–186. New York: International Universities Press.

———— (1977). When and how does adolescence end? In *Adolescent Psychiatry*, vol. 5, ed. S. C. Feinstein and P. L. Giovacchini, pp. 5–17. New York: Jason Aronson.

Blum, H. P. (1974). The borderline childhood of the Wolf Man. *Journal of the American Psychoanalytic Association* 22: 721–742.

Bollas, C. (1987). *The Shadow of the Object: Psychoanalysis of the Unthought Known*. New York: Columbia University Press.

———— (1989). *Forces of Destiny: Psychoanalysis and Human Idiom*. London: Free Association.

Boris, H. (1973). Confrontation in the analysis of the transference resistance. In *Confrontation in Psychotherapy*, ed. G. Adler and P. G. Myerson, pp. 181–206. New York: Science House.

Brunswick, R. M. (1928). A supplement to Freud's "History of an Infantile Neurosis." In *The Wolf-Man by the Wolf-Man*, ed. M. Gardiner, pp. 263–307. New York: Basic Books.

Buckley, P., Karasu T. B., and Charles, E. (1981). Psychotherapists view their personal therapy. *Psychotherapy: Theory, Research and Practice* 18:299–305.

Buie D. H., Jr., (1982–1983). The abandoned therapist. *International Journal of Psychoanalytic Psychotherapy* 9:227–231.

Cavell, S. (1981). *Pursuits of Happiness: The Hollywood Comedy of Remarriage*. Cambridge, MA: Harvard University Press.

Corwin, H. A. (1973). Therapeutic confrontation from routine to heroic. In *Confrontation in Psychotherapy*, ed. G. Adler, and P. Myerson, pp. 67–95. New York: Science House.

Culler, J. (1981). *The Pursuit of Signs: Semiotics, Literature, Deconstruction*. Ithaca, NY: Cornell University Press.

DeBell, D. E. (1963). A critical digest of the literature on psychoanalytic supervision. *Journal of the American Psychoanalytic Association* 11:546–575.

Dicks, H. V. (1967). *Marital Tensions: Clinical Studies Towards a Psycho-analytic Theory of Interaction*. London: Routledge and Kegan Paul.

Dostoevsky, F. (1991). *The Brothers Karamazov*. New York: Random House.

Edelson, M. (1963). *The Termination of Intensive Psychotherapy*. Springfield, IL: Charles C Thomas.

Eissler, K. R. (1953). The effect of the structure of the ego on psychoanalytic technique. *Journal of the American Psychoanalytic Association* 1:104–143.

_____ (1979). A possible endangerment of psychoanalysis in the United States. *International Review of Psycho-Analysis* 6:15–21.

Eliot, T. S. (1943). *Four Quartets*. New York: Harcourt, Brace.

Erikson, E. H. (1968). *Identity: Youth and Crisis*. New York: W. W. Norton.

Fairbairn, W. R. D. (1952). *An Object-Relations Theory of the Personality*. New York: Basic Books.

Farber, L. H. (1958). The therapeutic despair. *Psychiatry* 21:7–20.

Feldman, M. (1993). The dynamics of reassurance. *International Journal of Psycho-Analysis* 74:275–285.

Ferenczi, S. (1920). The further development of an active therapy in psycho-analysis. In *Further Contributions to the Theory and Technique of Psycho-Analysis*, vol. 2, ed. J. Rickman, pp. 198–217. New York: Basic Books, 1926.

_____ (1933). Confusion of tongues between adults and the child. In *Further Contributions to the Theory and Technique of Psycho-Analysis*, vol. 3 (1926), ed. M. Balint, pp. 156–167. New York: Basic Books.

Fish, S. (1980). *Is There a Text in This Class: The Authority of Interpretive Communities*. Cambridge, MA: Harvard University Press.

_____ (1986). Withholding the missing portion: power, meaning and persuasion in Freud's "The Wolf-Man." *Times Literary Supplement*, August 29, pp. 935–938.

Frank, J. A. (1989). Who are you and what have you done with my wife? In *Foundations of Object Relations Family Therapy*, ed. J. Scharff, pp. 175–184. Northvale, NJ: Jason Aronson.

Franklin, G. (1990). The multiple meanings of neutrality. *Journal of the American Psychoanalytic Association* 38:195–220.

Freud, A. (1954). The widening scope of indications for psychoanalysis: discussion. In *The Writings of Anna Freud* 4:356–376. New York: International Universities Press, 1968.

_____ (1958). Adolescence. *Psychoanalytic Study of the Child* 13:255–278. New York: International Universities Press.

Freud, S. (1905 [1901]). Three Essays on the Theory of Sexuality. *Standard Edition* 7:130–243.

_____ (1912). Recommendations to physicians practising psychoanalysis. *Standard Edition* 12:111–120.

_____ (1916–1917 [1915–1917]). Introductory lectures on psychoanalysis. *Standard Edition* 15, 16.

_____ (1917 [1915]). Mourning and melancholia. *Standard Edition* 14:243–258.

_____ (1918 [1914]). From the history of an infantile neurosis. *Standard Edition* 17:7–122.

_____ (1923). The ego and the id. *Standard Edition* 19:12–59.

_____ (1937). Analysis terminable and interminable. *Standard Edition* 23:216–253.

_____ (1940). An outline of psychoanalysis. *Standard Edition* 23:144–207.

Frosch, J. (1967). Severe regressive states during analysis. *Journal of the American Psychoanalytic Association* 15:491–507.

Gabbard, G. O. (1989). *Sexual Exploitation in Professional Relationships*. Washington, DC: American Psychiatric Press.

Gabbard, G. O., and Pope, K. S. (1989). Sexual intimacies after termination: clinical, ethical, and legal aspects. In *Sexual Exploitation in Professional Relationships*, ed. G. O. Gabbard, pp. 115–127. Washington, DC: American Psychiatric Press.

Gardiner, M. (1971). *The Wolf-Man by the Wolf-Man*. New York: Basic Books.

_____ (1983). The Wolf Man's last years. *Journal of the American Psychoanalytic Association* 31:867–897.

Gardiner, M. R. (1983). *Self Inquiry*. Hillsdale, NJ: Analytic Press.

Gartrell, N., Herman, J., Olarte, S., et al. (1989). Prevalence of psychiatrist–patient sexual contact. In *Sexual Exploitation in Professional Relationships*, ed. G. Gabbard, pp. 3–13. Washington, DC: American Psychiatric Press.

Gay, P. (1988). *Freud–A Life for Our Times*. New York: W. W. Norton.

Gediman, H. K., and Wolkenfeld, F. (1980). The parallelism phenomenon in psychoanalysis and supervision: its reconsideration as a triadic system. *Psychoanalytic Quarterly* 49:234–255.

Gedo, J. E., and Goldberg, A. (1973). *Models of the Mind: A Psychoanalytic Theory*. Chicago: University of Chicago Press.

Gill, M. M. (1979). Psychoanalysis and psychotherapy–1954–1979. Paper presented to the Washington Psychoanalytic Society, October.

_____ (1982). *Analysis of Transference*. Vol. 1. New York: International Universities Press.

_____ (1988). The interpersonal paradigm and the degree of the therapist's involvement. In *Essential Papers on Countertransference*, ed. B. Wolstein, pp. 304–338. New York: New York University Press.

Greenberg, J. R., and Mitchell, S. A. (1983). *Object Relations in Psychoanalytic Theory*. Cambridge, MA: Harvard University Press.

Greenson, R. R. (1967). *The Technique and Practice of Psychoanalysis*. Vol. 1. New York: International Universities Press.

Grinberg, L. (1970). The problems of supervision in psychoanalytic education. *International Journal of Psycho-Analysis* 51:371–383.

Grünbaum, A. (1990). "Meaning" connections and causal connections in the human sciences: the poverty of hermeneutic philosophy. *Journal of the American Psychoanalytic Association* 38:559–577.

Halpert, E. (1985). Insurance. *Journal of the American Psychoanalytic Association* 33:937–949.

Hanly, C. (1990). The concept of truth in psychoanalysis. *International Journal of Psycho-Analysis* 71:375–383.

_____ (1992). Inductive reasoning in clinical psychoanalysis. *International Journal of Psycho-Analysis* 73:293–301.

Havens, L. L. (1976). *Participant Observation.* New York: Jason Aronson.

Hillman, J. (1975). The fiction of case history: a round. In *Religion as Story*, ed. J. Wiggins, pp. 123–173. New York: Harper & Row.

Hughes, J. M. (1989). *Reshaping the Psychoanalytic Domain: The Work of Melanie Klein, W. R. D. Fairbairn, and D. W. Winnicott.* Berkeley, CA: University of California Press.

Jacobs, D. (1988). Love, work and survival—psychoanalysis in the nuclear age. In *Psychoanalysis and the Nuclear Threat: Clinical and Theoretical Studies*, ed. H. B. Levine, D. Jacobs, and L. Rubin, pp. 173–187. Hillsdale, NJ: Analytic Press.

Jacobs, T. J. (1991). *The Use of the Self: Countertransference and Communication in the Analytic Situation.* Madison, CT: International Universities Press.

Jaques, E. (1965). Death and the mid-life crisis. *International Journal of Psycho-Analysis* 46:502–514.

Jones, E. (1955). *The Life and Work of Sigmund Freud.* Vol. 2. New York: Basic Books.

_____ (1957). *The Life and Work of Sigmund Freud.* Vol. 3. New York: Basic Books.

Kernberg, O. F. (1975). *Borderline Conditions and Pathological Narcissism.* Northvale, NJ: Jason Aronson.

Khan, M. M. R. (1975). Introduction to D. W. Winnicott. In *Through Pediatrics to Psychoanalysis* by D. W. Winnicott, pp. xi–1. New York: Basic Books.

Klauber, J. (1981). Elements of the psychoanalytic relationship and their therapeutic implications. In *The British School of Psychoanalysis: The Independent Tradition*, ed. G. Kohon, pp. 200–213. London: Free Association, 1986.

Klein, M. (1935). A contribution to the psychogenesis of manic-depressive states. In *Contributions to Psychoanalysis, 1921–1945*, pp. 282–310. London: Hogarth, 1950.

_____ (1940). Mourning and its relation to manic-depressive states. In *Contributions to Psychoanalysis, 1921–1945*, pp. 311–338. London: Hogarth, 1950.

_____ (1946). Notes on some schizoid mechanisms. In *Envy and Gratitude and Other Works, 1946–1963*, pp. 1–24. New York: Delacorte, 1975.

_____ (1952). Some theoretical conclusions regarding the emotional life of the infant. In *Envy and Gratitude and Other Works, 1946–1963*, pp. 61–93. New York: Delacorte, 1975.

_____ (1959). Our adult world and its roots in infancy. In *Envy and Gratitude and Other Works, 1946–1963*, pp. 247–263. New York: Delacorte, 1975.

Kohut, H. (1971). *The Analysis of the Self*. New York: International Universities Press.

_____ (1977). *The Restoration of the Self*. New York: International Universities Press.

_____ (1979). The two analyses of Mr. Z. *International Journal of Psycho-Analysis* 60:3–27.

Lampl-de Groot, J. (1960). On adolescence. *Psychoanalytic Study of the Child* 15:95–103. New York: International Universities Press.

Langs, R. (1973–1974). *The Technique of Psychoanalytic Psychotherapy*. Vols. 1 and 2. New York: Jason Aronson.

_____ (1976). *The Bipersonal Field*. New York: Jason Aronson.

Leavy, S. A. (1980). *The Psychoanalytic Dialogue*. New Haven, CT: Yale University Press.

Loewald, H. W. (1960). On the therapeutic action of psycho-analysis. *International Journal of Psycho-Analysis* 41:16–33.

_____ (1962). Internalization, separation, mourning and the super-ego. In *Papers on Psychoanalysis*, pp. 257–276. New Haven, CT: Yale University Press, 1980.

_____ (1973). On internalization. In *Papers on Psychoanalysis*, pp. 69–86. New Haven, CT: Yale University Press, 1980.

_____ (1979). The waning of the Oedipus complex. In *Papers on Psychoanalysis*, pp. 384–404. New Haven, CT: Yale University Press, 1980.

_____ (1980). *Papers on Psychoanalysis*. New Haven, CT: Yale University Press.

Luber, M. P. (1991). A patient's transference to the analyst's supervisor: effect of the setting on the analytic process. *Journal of the American Psychoanalytic Association* 39:705–725.

Mahony, P. J. (1984). *Cries of the Wolf Man*. New York: International Universities Press.

Malcolm, J. (1987). Reflections: J'appelle un chat un chat. *The New Yorker*, April 20, pp. 84–102.

Mann, J. (1973). Confrontation as a mode of teaching. In *Confrontation in Psychotherapy*, ed. G. Adler and P. Myerson, pp. 39–48. New York: Science House.

McLaughlin, J. T. (1991). Clinical and theoretical aspects of enactment. *Journal of the American Psychoanalytic Association* 39:595–614.

Meissner, W. W. (1977). The Wolf Man and the paranoid process. *The Annual of Psychoanalysis* 5:23–74.

Miller J. P., Jr., and Post, S. L. (1990). How theory shapes technique: perspectives on a self-psychological clinical presentation. *Psychoanalytic Inquiry* 10:459–624.

Mitchell, S. A. (1988). *Relational Concepts in Psychoanalysis: An Integration*. Cambridge, MA: Harvard University Press.

Myerson, P. G. (1973). The meanings of confrontation. In *Confrontation in Pyschotherapy*, ed. G. Adler, and P. Myerson, pp. 21–38. New York: Science House.

—— (1991). *Childhood Dialogues and the Lifting of Repression: Character Structure and Psychoanalytic Technique*. New Haven, CT: Yale University Press.

Obholzer, K. (1982). *The Wolf-Man: Conversations with Freud's Patient—Sixty Years Later*. New York: Continuum.

Ogden, T. H. (1982). *Projective Identification and Psychotherapeutic Technique*. New York: Jason Aronson.

—— (1986). *The Matrix of the Mind*. Northvale, NJ: Jason Aronson.

Peterfreund, E. (1983). *The Process of Psychoanalytic Therapy: Models and Strategies*. Hillsdale, NJ: Analytic Press.

Phillips. A. (1988). *Winnicott*. Cambridge, MA: Harvard University Press.

Racker, H. (1968). *Transference and Countertransference*. New York: International Universities Press.

Roazen, P. (1975). *Freud and His Followers*. New York: Alfred A. Knopf.

Roth, P. (1969). *Portnoy's Complaint*. London: John Cape.

Rudominer, H. S. (1984). Peer review, third-party payment, and the analytic situation: a case report. *Journal of the American Psychoanalytic Association* 32:773–795.

Rutter, P. (1989). *Sex in the Forbidden Zone: When Men in Power—Therapists, Doctors, Clergy, Teachers and Others—Betray Women's Trust.* New York: Ballantine.

Salinger, J. D. (1953). A perfect day for bananafish. In *Nine Stories,* pp. 3–18. Boston: Little, Brown.

Sandler, J. (1976a). Actualization and object relations. *Journal of the Philadelphia Association for Psychoanalysis* 3:59–70.

———— (1976b). Countertransference and role responsiveness. *International Review of Psycho-Analysis* 3:43–47.

Sass, L. A., and Woolfolk, R. L. (1988). Psychoanalysis and the hermeneutic turn: a critique of *Narrative Truth and Historical Truth. Journal of the American Psychoanalytic Association* 36:429–454.

Schafer, R. (1970). The psychoanalytic vision of reality. *International Journal of Psycho-Analysis* 51:279–297.

———— (1976). *A New Language for Psychoanalysis.* New Haven, CT: Yale University Press.

———— (1982). The relevance of the "here and now" transference interpretation to the reconstruction of early development. *International Journal of Psycho-Analysis* 63:77–82.

———— (1983). *The Analytic Attitude.* New York: Basic Books.

———— (1992). Reading Freud's legacies. In *Telling Facts: History and Narration in Psychoanalysis,* ed. J. H. Smith and H. Morris, pp. 1–20. Baltimore, MD: Johns Hopkins University Press.

Scharff, J. S. (1989). *Foundations of Object Relations Family Therapy.* Northvale, NJ: Jason Aronson.

———— (1992). *Projective and Introjective Identification and the Use of the Therapist's Self.* Northvale, NJ: Jason Aronson.

Searles, H. (1965). *Collected Papers on Schizophrenia and Related Subjects.* New York: International Universities Press.

———— (1979). *Countertransference and Related Subjects.* New York: International Universities Press.

Segal, H. (1973 [1964]). *Introduction to the Work of Melanie Klein.* New York: Basic Books.

Shapiro, E., and Carr, A. W. (1991). *Lost in Familiar Places: Creating*

New Connections between the Individual and Society. New Haven, CT: Yale University Press.

Shapiro, R. (1989). Family dynamics and object relations theory: an analytic, group-interpretive approach to family therapy. In *Foundations of Object Relations Family Therapy*, ed. J. Scharff, pp. 225–245. Northvale, NJ: Jason Aronson.

Sharpe, R. A. (1987). Psychoanalysis and narrative: a structuralist approach. *International Review of Psycho-Analysis* 14:335–342.

Simon, B. (1992). "Incest—See Under Oedipus Complex": the history of an error in psychoanalysis. *Journal of the American Psychoanalytic Association,* 40:955–988.

Smith, J. H. (1971). Identificatory styles in depression and grief. *International Journal of Psycho-Analysis* 52:259–266.

——— (1991). *Arguing with Lacan: Ego Psychology and Language.* New Haven, CT: Yale University Press.

Spence, D. P. (1982). *Narrative Truth and Historical Truth: Meaning and Interpretation in Psychoanalysis.* New York: W. W. Norton.

——— (1987). *The Freudian Metaphor: Toward Paradigm Change in Psychoanalysis.* New York: W. W. Norton.

Steiner, J. (1985). Turning a blind eye: the cover up for Oedipus. *International Review of Psycho-Analysis* 12:161–172.

Stone, L. (1961). *The Psychoanalytic Situation.* New York: International Universities Press.

Sullivan, H. S. (1953). *The Interpersonal Theory of Psychiatry.* Ed. H. S. Perry and M. L. Gawel. New York: W. W. Norton.

Symington, N. (1983). The analyst's act of freedom as agent of therapeutic change. In *The British School of Psychoanalysis: The Independent Tradition*, ed. G. Kohon, pp. 253–270. London: Free Association, 1986.

Twemlow, S. W., and Gabbard, G. O. (1989). The lovesick therapist. In *Sexual Exploitation in Professional Relationships*, ed. G. O. Gabbard, pp. 71–87. Washington, DC: American Psychiatric Press.

Valenstein, A. F. (1989). Pre-oedipal reconstructions in psychoanalysis. *International Journal of Psycho-Analysis* 70:433–442.

Welpton, D. F. (1973). Confrontation in the therapeutic process. In *Confrontation in Psychotherapy*, ed. G. Adler, and P. Myerson, pp. 249–269. New York: Science House.

Wetzler, S. (1985). The historical truth of psychoanalytic reconstructions. *International Review of Psycho-Analysis* 12:187–197.

Whitehead, C. C. (1975). Additional aspects of the Freudian-Kleinian controversy: towards a "psychoanalysis" of psychoanalysis. *International Journal of Psycho-Analysis* 56:383–396.

Winer, R. (1989). The role of transitional experience in development in healthy and incestuous families. In *Foundations of Object Relations Family Therapy*, ed. J. Scharff, pp. 357–384. Northvale, NJ: Jason Aronson.

_____ (1991). The whole story. In *The World of Samuel Beckett*, ed. J. H. Smith, pp. 73–85. Baltimore, MD: Johns Hopkins University Press.

Winnicott, D. W. (1948). Reparation in respect of mother's organized defense against depression. In *Through Paediatrics to Psycho-Analysis*, pp. 91–96. New York: Basic Books, 1975.

_____ (1954). Metapsychological and clinical aspects of regression within the psycho-analytical set-up. In *Through Paediatrics to Psycho-Analysis*, pp. 278–294. New York: Basic Books, 1975.

_____ (1960a). The theory of the parent–infant relationship. In *The Maturational Processes and the Facilitating Environment*, pp. 37–55. London: Hogarth, 1965.

_____ (1960b). Ego distortion in terms of true and false self. In *The Maturational Processes and the Facilitating Environment*, pp. 140–152. London: Hogarth, 1965.

_____ (1965). *The Maturational Processes and the Facilitating Environment: Studies in the Theory of Emotional Development*. New York: International Universities Press.

_____ (1971). *Playing and Reality*. London: Tavistock.

Wolf Man (1971). The memoirs of the wolf-man. In *The Wolf-Man by the Wolf-Man*, ed. M. Gardiner, pp. 3–132. New York: Basic Books.

Zetzel, E. R. (1965). The theory of therapy in relation to a developmental model of the psychic apparatus. *International Journal of Psycho-Analysis* 46:39–52.

Index